Using Narrative
in Research

Christine Bold

Los Angeles | London | New Delhi
Singapore | Washington DC

First published 2012

SAGE Publications Ltd
1 Oliver's Yard
55 City Road
London EC1Y 1SP

SAGE Publications Inc.
2455 Teller Road
Thousand Oaks, California 91320

SAGE Publications India Pvt Ltd
B 1/I 1 Mohan Cooperative Industrial Area
Mathura Road
New Delhi 110 044

SAGE Publications Asia-Pacific Pte Ltd
33 Pekin Street #02-01
Far East Square
Singapore 048763

Library of Congress Control Number: 2010940963

British Library Cataloguing in Publication data

A catalogue record for this book is available from the British Library

ISBN 978-1-84860-718-7
ISBN 978-1-84860-719-4 (pbk)

Typeset by C&M Digitals (P) Ltd, Chennai, India
Printed in India at Replika Press Pvt Ltd
Printed on paper from sustainable resources

£22.99

Using Narrative
in Research

CONTENTS

ABOUT THE AUTHOR

Dr Christine Bold is a lecturer, writer and researcher who began her working life in mental health nursing, office work and occupational care before becoming a teacher in schools and eventually a principal lecturer at a university. She has most recently worked as a senior lecturer at Liverpool John Moores University teaching mainly on MA programmes, Leadership and Management, and Research modules. She has had a long-standing interest in communication in classrooms and her doctoral thesis focused on the use of mathematical language using dialogue analysis in an interpretive approach. Her methodological preference in researching educational contexts has always been qualitative, with a particular interest in exploring meaning making through dialogue. A sustained interest in narrative methods of research began when Professor Anne Campbell gave an inaugural lecture introducing the power of the narrative in exploring teachers' practice. Narrative as a learning, teaching and research tool became part of degree programmes for which Christine had responsibility, with a focus on action research methodologies. During the period 2003–2009 Christine actively researched the expansion of students' skills in developing reflective practice and in particular reflective writing, in which the use of narrative has been a part of the whole learning environment. Engagement with colleagues from a range of professions in groups such as the international Collaborative Action Research Network, or within the local academic community, has supported the development of Christine's understanding of the parallel research developments within the various professions involving social engagement. She believes that the different professions and their associated subject disciplines would benefit from greater collaboration in research to establish a stronger grounding for narrative's place as an essential part of the researcher's toolkit when researching social situations.

ACKNOWLEDGEMENTS

Thank you to each student who submitted their assignments and class activities to an electronic or hard copy archive of materials with permission for me to use them anonymously in academic research and publication. Their enthusiasm for their studies, and in particular for developing their expertise through action research, was a wonderful experience. They took brave steps with narrative, ventured into the unknown and emerged glowing with the success of better understanding their working lives.

Thank you to Philip Chambers, whose 2003 article 'Narrative and reflective practice: recording and understanding experience' stimulated much discussion and thought about the nature of narrative between students. It was inspirational, encouraging thoughts about issues that many had never considered before. It was a stepping-stone, crossing the divides between objectivity and subjectivity, conformity and non-conformity, academic writing and creative writing. It helped us view our work differently.

Finally, a thank you to everyone who has shaped my thinking in recent years, enabling me to follow my interests and be true to my own beliefs about research in social and educational settings, regardless of various pressures to conform to positivist expectations. What is academia about if it is not to pursue with some rigour, innovation and creativity an issue, a concern, a belief, a set of values … or even to have a sense of rebelliousness in following one's cause?

Christine Bold

1

NARRATIVE BEGINNINGS: AUTOBIOGRAPHY, BIOGRAPHY AND FICTION

CHAPTER OUTLINE

- Why should you read this book?
- An outline of the chapters
- Introducing my research story
- Why use narrative approaches to research?
- Introducing a narrative approach to research
- Narrative themes

  - Theme 1: autobiographical self-reflection
  - Theme 2: biographical data
  - Theme 3: representative constructions (or fictions)

- The narrative 'turn'
- Summary
- Suggested reading

Why Should You Read This Book?

This book provides an accessible text for anyone who is interested in the use of narrative in research. In particular, it is for those who are interested in the relationships between reflection, reflexivity and narrative approaches to research, in social settings of any kind. It tells the story of my experiences, and those of students I taught, in exploring narrative approaches to research that suited our professional situations. The book also discusses and highlights a range of suitable texts from which you can draw in supporting your own development in using narrative approaches to research. In this chapter, *narrative* generally means *spoken or written story*, but I also write about Barbara Czarniawaska's (2004) notion of a narrative approach, which has a flexible, broader meaning. For her, narrative in research is not just about stories or specific data collection and analytical methods; instead, narrative may be used in various ways and at different stages of research as and when appropriate. Later, in Chapter 2, I explore the nature of narrative and different perspectives in more depth with reference to a range of different academics experienced in narrative research.

In addition to providing an appropriately accessible text for students who are novice narrative researchers, and anyone interested in knowing what narrative research might involve, *Using Narrative in Research* also aims to support tutors and supervisors who are new to the use of narrative in research in supporting their students. The requirement for students to engage academically with professional and social issues, to prepare them for employment, is generally present in a range of subject areas, and it is important to continue developing appropriate methods for contextual research about human activity. Narrative research is a growing area of increasingly acknowledged and accepted international research practice, although there is a range of differing views and approaches to its use. The challenge for any researcher is to choose the most appropriate methodology for the social context of the research, that is, it should be *fit for purpose*.

Using Narrative in Research thus provides a specialist text focused on supporting anyone interested in narrative research practices, in developing a theoretical and practical understanding of possible uses of a narrative approach when researching professional or other social contexts. I agree with Molly Andrews, Corinne Squire and Maria Tamboukou (2008) and others who assert that there are no overall rules about narrative approaches to research, and I emphasise that the meaning of the word *narrative* is in dispute amongst different groups of researchers (as discussed further in Chapter 2). Sometimes academics try to label or apply different approaches too rigidly, sometimes creating a mystique about research that prevents novice researchers engaging effectively with the conceptual process. Arthur Bochner (2001) expresses similar views and notes that most academic journals (and in my experience most university courses) generally require writers to provide a strongly analytical paper in a distanced academic voice rather than a personal narrative. Such emphasis on depersonalising academic writing serves to discourage narrative approaches to research, which often seem more subjective and personal in nature.

I would like to assure you that using narrative does not mean losing rigour in your approach to research. A narrative approach requires rigorous collection, collation and synthesis of appropriate data followed by critical analysis and reflection. It requires the ability to communicate, orally and in writing, the research story from first conceptions of an area of interest to thoughtful and thought-provoking conclusions. A narrative approach opens doors to alternative ways of conducting and disseminating research that is illuminative, novel and accessible to readers. Narrative is also a means of developing and nurturing the skills of critical reflection and reflexivity that are essential for anyone conducting research into their own practice, and therefore very useful for action research projects. For the purpose of this text, I use the word 'reflection' in the ways that Donald Schön (1984) describes its different functions:

1   reflecting-in-action, while we work, thinking on our feet about how to react to situations and events – an automatic response in an experienced practitioner
2   reflecting-on-action, looking back at an event afterwards and considering how a response to it might have been different, how to modify and change it.

A third type of reflection based on this is the idea of reflecting-for-action, to think of the next steps that need to be taken. In general, reflection engages us in extended periods of thinking, seeking commonalities and differences and the relationships between actions. Critical reflection, as an extension of reflection, means that we challenge our underlying beliefs, values and assumptions when looking back at events. If we are critically reflective, we question actions and challenge accepted truths or claims and we consider various alternative ways of interpreting and analysing situations.

Reflexivity brings into the process a more personal dimension, a thoughtful self-awareness of the dynamics between you and the people you are researching (Linda Finlay and Brendan Gough, 2003). It means that you are aware of how others perceive you and how you perceive them, and involves all the attributes of critical reflection. Different researchers describe the skill of reflexivity differently in different contexts. Gergen and Gergen (1991) discuss one example of a researcher taking a stance towards a problem and gradually elaborating it through experience and the interactions with others. They link the approach they discuss to social constructionism but also emphasise the role of self-reflexivity. Mason's (1994) notion of researching from the inside is essentially the development of self-reflexivity. It is not just about knowing oneself but about knowing oneself through multiple ways of seeing the world. It is also about describing the world as seen through those reflexive eyes and according to Mason, creating a reaction in others, thus continuing the reflexive chain.

An Outline of the Chapters

This section outlines the contents of each chapter. The chapters are presented in an order that aims to support the development of a research project involving a narrative approach.

Chapter 2 'What Is Narrative?', with reference to a range of authors from across different disciplines, explores historical and contemporary influences on the use of narrative in professional development and research.

Chapter 3 'Designing Research Projects with a Narrative Approach' aims to encourage readers to position themselves within the research project and plan

3

to choose appropriately from a range of ways to use narrative, including drawing and other media as illustrated in other chapters. The final section provides an example of a draft research proposal.

Chapter 4 'Ethics and a Narrative Approach' emphasises that ethics is about balancing the principle of reducing harm with that of providing benefits to all involved. Roles and relationships are important and ethical consideration goes beyond the completion of a checklist for an institution or society.

Chapter 5 'Narrative Thinking: Provoking and Sustaining Reflective Thought' focuses on the relationship between narrating and reflecting, the development of critical reflection and reflexivity. The first section illustrates and discusses the use of drawing or other creative activity to provoke reflective thought. Examples from reflective diary entries demonstrate the diary's value as a vehicle for sustaining reflective thinking in narrative research.

Chapter 6 'Collecting Narrative Data' includes the use of interviews to elicit stories in addition to a range of alternative approaches such as asking participants for written narratives, constructing observational narratives and collecting various images as narrative. The internet is also a source of useful narrative materials.

Chapter 7 'Analysing Narrative Data' focuses on two broad analytical approaches. First, it provides an overview of the structuralist approach that focuses on seeking common elements within stories, examining their structure rather than their meaning. Second, it considers a thematic experiential approach that focuses on the meaning within the narratives. Examples from undergraduate students demonstrate ways of moving from personal analysis to the development of a more critical stance.

Chapter 8 'Representative Constructions in Narrative Analysis' aims to introduce readers to the innovative use of fictional writing as a means of collating and analysing a set of data into a coherent, valid, reliable and accessible piece that represents the whole data set and begins the analysis in a realistic and formative way.

Chapter 9 'Reporting Narrative Research' pays some attention to the normative expectations of dissertations and theses but then explores some alternative ways to present narrative research. It draws on a range of articles from recent academic journals.

The chapters contain materials from three themes that emerged during my work with students as important for the development of critical reflection through narrative approaches:

- theme 1: autobiographical self-reflection
- theme 2: biographical data
- theme 3: representative constructions (or fictions).

Each theme emerges in the different chapters but in different measures. For example, Chapter 5 focuses mainly on autobiographical self-reflection but the theme is not as strongly represented in Chapter 8. I describe the nature of the themes more fully later in this chapter. Each chapter contains an introduction sharing key ideas within the chapter and a summary that also outlines the connections between the themes throughout the text.

Most chapters contain extracts from students' research projects. To ensure that you can identify these clearly within the text they are numbered as figures and framed. I have placed them where I think they fit best as part of the discussion – indicating the points at which you ought to read the extract to understand more fully the ideas I present. References to other texts within the extracts are included within each frame rather than in my reference list at the end of the book. *Using Narrative in Research* thus provides empirical materials for discussion and debate in academic and professional contexts in addition to supporting a novice narrative researcher with some of the practicalities. Because it draws on literature from a range of experts in the field of narrative research and other useful sources, it will help you establish the links between critical analysis and reflection and narrative. The chapters take you through some possible approaches to identifying a project, establishing a sound methodology, becoming analytical and being able to communicate research in a rigorous yet interesting and unique way.

Introducing My Research Story

For parts of the book, I have chosen to write in autobiographical style because for much of it I am relating to you my own experiences through my own research and that of the students who have allowed me to include extracts of their work. For this purpose, the autobiographical style is important since I have no desire to depersonalise my own experience. For some of you, writing in a personal voice rather than a depersonalised voice might be contentious, or at least seem 'less academic'. Indeed, one of the major criticisms of using narrative in research is its subjective rather than objective stance. This is one of the criticisms that I wish to address within the book since I have a strong belief that a personalised approach to writing, where appropriate, is no less 'academic' than a depersonalised piece. For me the issue is one of criticality and the ability to present a critically reflective and analytical piece of writing in whichever genre is appropriate for the task. Critical thinking may be evident in any genre. You will therefore find that I do not maintain the autobiographical approach where it is not appropriate. I will begin with my story, which explains my reasons for wanting to write this book.

Using Narrative in Research has its roots in my experience of teaching undergraduate and postgraduate students, mainly education professionals, about narrative methods of research from 2004 onwards. Initially, influenced by Gillie Bolton's (2001) publication on using stories to aid reflection, I encouraged students to use oral storytelling to explore their practice and to make connections between personal experience and academic ideas. I promoted Bolton's (2006) idea of narrative, or storying, as a way of creating order and security out of a chaotic world. This notion appealed to a range of students from different cultural backgrounds who all worked in busy, ever-changing, demanding workplaces. They worked in unique professional contexts; for example, one was a bilingual support worker for children of several different cultures and languages, another was a learning mentor in a boys' secondary school. Their oral stories and subsequent discussion helped each member of the teaching group to interpret a range of professional contexts and experiences, thus enabling them to understand their personal story within a wider educational and societal context. Storytelling was also a way of developing student confidence in their writing skills, moving them from descriptive writing in telling story events, to reflective writing when reflecting upon their professional practice, to critical reflection and analysis of their own practice and others' scholarly works. Gradually the notion of telling stories became something that we used beyond the taught session, as a means of exploring practice in a systematic and rigorous manner – a valid research method, informed and influenced by Jean Clandinin and Michael Connelly (2000), Peter Clough (2002) and a thought-provoking article by Philip Chambers (2003).

Why Use Narrative Approaches to Research?

There is no simple answer to this question, but I must emphasise that you should choose narrative approaches when the purpose of the inquiry is best served by using them. Narrative is one research tool amongst a host of other methods and its use must be justified as fit for purpose, as any other method must be. In my work with students, the greatest challenge for me was to persuade students that narrative approaches were valid, reliable and just as rigorous as any other research when used well.

While working with both undergraduate and postgraduate students, in the field of education or training, over a number of years, I identified two recurring issues that seemed to prevent students from accepting qualitative research methods, including narrative methods, as valid and reliable, and usually more appropriate for the nature of their research projects. First, the overwhelming majority of students assumed that all research was about establishing facts and truths and many assumed that numerical data within a scientific 'fair test' environment were the normative expectation. Where they formed these assumptions was unclear, but for some it involved experiences of science at school level and observations of the nature of much reported research in the media, which often cites numerical data. Most students claimed that previous tutoring strongly encouraged these assumptions and so they rarely questioned the reliability, validity and truthfulness of numerical data. Students needed convincing that numerical data are just as easily manipulated to support a particular interpretation and to sway people's opinion as qualitative data might be. Second, the students had generally experienced a limited number of research methods in previous learning activities, usually questionnaires, interviews and observations of various kinds.

A significant number of students mentioned the need for objectivity, before I had discussed such concepts with them, and they thought there was no room for subjective responses or anything that allowed subjectivity in research. These thoughts persisted, despite the fact that many of them were interested in researching issues that were necessarily subjective, for example, their own practice, other people's opinions, or children's responses to situations. Students with previous research or inquiry-based learning experience had often chosen a method without consideration of its fitness for purpose and with little real justification for its choice. None claimed to have been encouraged to explore research methods beyond those previously stated; for example, none of the students I have taught over the years had experienced ethnographic methods. Few, even at master's level, had explored the qualitative/quantitative debate and most assumed that analysis of results required graphical representations of data regardless of the research question and the need to use methods appropriate to the question and the context of the research.

While I recognise that a deliberate reduction in the range of student experience and choice introduces them to specific research methods, this approach could result in a weak understanding of research as an inquiry process designed to be fit for purpose. If the methods are not suited to the specific research contexts that students are engaging with, then the outcomes of their research projects are unlikely to be valid and reliable. At all levels, students can be introduced to the idea of 'fitness for purpose' in choosing and learning how to justify the choice of methods they consider most appropriate for their projects. In social and educational contexts involving research into people's lives, a narrative approach may be most appropriate, and therefore learning how narrative may be used as a valid and reliable research method is an important part of becoming a researcher in such contexts.

I have thus encountered students who had not become aware of, or been encouraged to explore, methods such as narrative that would have been more effective for the purpose of their chosen research questions. This might be due to previous tutors not having enough research experience or knowledge and understanding of a full range of methods. Tutors may also prefer to support students who are using familiar research methods, that is working within their zone of research experience, which is quite understandable and generally desirable. In some cases, students have reported that they had requests to alter their research questions to suit a tutor's preferred methodology and this resulted in a complete change of focus in the students' research. In such circumstances, a student has to be very confident and competent in their preferred research question and methodological choice to provide clear justification. Of course, a tutor might advise a student to change a research question for a variety of valid reasons, and in general I advise students to heed their tutors' suggestions.

Where students have two supervisors, it is possible that students feel pulled in different directions – with each supervisor professing that their approach to the research is the best. For example, a recent doctoral level student felt torn between a supervisor who supported a narrative approach to the research and one who was rather sceptical and questioned the validity and reliability of such an approach. When I observe such events, I sometimes begin to wonder who owns the research, the student or the tutors. Of course, it is the student's research, and having two supervisors with different perspectives should enable the student to develop strong powers of critique and justification of the chosen methodology.

At all levels, students ought to be encouraged to demonstrate the ability to choose and adapt methods to suit a research question, or the area of interest and the specific context. Ideally, a tutor *should* supervise students working with methods within their own experience; if one is mostly used to qualitative methods it can be challenging to supervise someone using advanced quantitative techniques. However, a flexible approach and a willingness to learn new methods, such as narrative, when students justifiably apply them to appropriate questions and contexts, are essential. Although my experience is mainly within the field of education, with a student body mainly involved in school teaching and learning, it easily translates into other academic disciplines and professional practices, such as social work or nursing, where the emphasis is on researching social activity of any kind.

In summary, over the past few years I have increasingly engaged with narrative approaches to learning, professional development and research. I have done so because such approaches have enabled the development of critically reflective practitioners. I chose narrative initially as a vehicle for learning about practice and for developing skills of critical reflection, and subsequently as a valid, reliable and most appropriate research method for students in professional educational and other social contexts to use. Narrative offered the students new ways of exploring their professional worlds in a rigorous and critically reflective approach to their practice.

Early introduction to appropriate methods of research, for example a narrative approach, within the students' research contexts is essential in order to develop rigour in clearly justifiable and relevant academic projects at undergraduate level and beyond. Barbara Czarniawaska (2004) summarises the narrative approach in social science research as an ample bag of tricks, making use of any relevant approaches such as deconstruction (the active interpretation of meaning, raising questions and problematising), without rigidly applying a set procedure in the mistaken belief that it will provide 'testable' results. According to Czarniawaska, a narrative approach is a set of devices that should lead to more inspired reading and writing about social contexts including a range of caring, educational and other organisational settings. I agree with this description of a narrative approach and embrace its adaptability as a useful quality for researchers devising research projects within unique social contexts. I also acknowledge that some researchers have devised specific methodological approaches to collecting and analysing narrative data that are appropriate choices in a range of projects.

The challenge for anyone new to using narrative in research is one of finding, justifying and using a method, possibly adapting a method, or even devising one's own. The range of practice emerging across different disciplines and professions is varied and potentially confusing to the novice narrative researcher. However, I believe that students ought to engage with the broad range of available literature and be prepared to explore approaches used in unfamiliar contexts. For example, education students may learn much about approaches to narrative research from academic papers in nursing or social care. Education as topic of academic study draws from other disciplines, and educational practice has parallels with many other professional practices in the medical profession or business world. This book aims to bring together ideas developed in different research communities in support of the novice narrative researcher in any field of study trying to make sense of the differing perspectives on narrative in research.

The next section introduces the narrative themes around which the book is developed.

Narrative Themes

Theme 1: autobiographical self-reflection

Autobiographical self-reflection is one of the most important forms of narrative for developing skills of critique about one's professional practice. It forms the basis of analytical thought about the relationship between the researcher and the context of the research. Acknowledging and understanding the researcher/context relationship is essential in any research, but particularly in action research.

Chapter 5 includes discussion of a range of different authors' perspectives on the use of narrative in supporting autobiographical self-reflection. Too often a novice researcher, and even those more experienced, will rely entirely on discussing the written thoughts of others in their field of interest without extending and expressing their own knowledge and understandings of the explored context. John Mason (1994) discussed the importance of 'researching from the inside' – the importance of the researcher's 'self' within the research process. He identified the need to develop one's sense of 'attending to' or 'noticing' those practice incidents and theoretical insights when they occur and to keep them available for re-questioning in the future. Researchers may also fail to acknowledge their own beliefs, values and assumptions in conducting and presenting their research, and in many higher education programmes the exploration of the self as part of the research process is lacking.

If you are developing new research skills and techniques then I believe that you should formulate your own reflective thoughts about your developing research so that you may compare these with others in developing your analysis and powers of critique. You need to identify your place in the process, develop reflexivity and be open to changing your perspectives as you gather more data and identify emerging patterns. Having self-knowledge and belief helps you defend your research position to others.

Autobiographical self-reflection supports research in different ways, briefly outlined as follows.

Identifying or clarifying a focus for enquiry

This is especially useful if you are involved in researching your own practice as in action research or in autoethnography, developing a personal narrative focusing on your subjective experience. If you are studying for a professional higher degree you will most likely have an aspect of your practice that you wish to explore when you enter your programme of study. However, if you are an undergraduate, maybe within a professional or work-based degree programme and possibly with significant life experience, you might require some university-based activity to encourage a deeper reflective focus. In either case, identifying a clear focus may involve creative approaches such as drawing, poetry and humorous tales of observed events, which all support self-reflection. For example, John White (2006) used painting and drawing to identify a focus for an MA dissertation researching educational management. John's supervisor introduced him to the idea of using creative activity, creating a picture that told a story, to stimulate reflection. I followed John White's example and introduced drawings to undergraduates to support their initial reflections, with some interesting outcomes and varied levels of success; some students found the process of drawing less helpful than did others (Bold, 2008c).

Drawing can make you feel vulnerable in some way; you might have experienced limited success with art at school, or it might not be your preferred way of thinking through your ideas. I found that drawings, completed in class, were most effective when students followed up the drawing activity by working in pairs to interpret the story behind each other's drawings. Thus you might find working with a reflective partner very helpful to encourage joint reflection on professional issues and support the identification of areas of interest for research. I discuss in more detail the use of imagery and drawing in conjunction with narrative writing in Chapter 5.

Autobiographical data consist of accounts about the communicant's own life. Collection of such data is not limited to the researcher producing autobiographical accounts. The participants in the research might each provide an autobiographical account from their own perspective. Their reflective accounts or stories might form the main data of the project. For example, patients with life changing illnesses may provide stories in which they describe and reflect upon the changes to their lives. Different professionals working collaboratively in the same setting may each keep a reflective diary in which they record and reflect upon events in their work situation. Children may keep a record of their responses to lessons, or patients their responses to treatment. Some examples of different kinds of autobiographical data collected by students in their research are presented in later chapters. However, one type, the oral history, which will undoubtedly include some self-reflective elements, is not evident. In my students' projects the collection of oral histories, or life stories, has not been appropriate, yet such histories are a valuable data set in some types of historical, political and social research.

Oral histories might be very relevant in your own research projects, especially if you are interested in other people's experiences over time.

Deeper analysis of initial reflections

In reflecting on one's performance, or another person's social situation, several sources of information – observations, conversations, artefacts – might support the creation of a personal reflective narrative about that performance or situation. A research diary usually contains some information such as logs of events, immediate thoughts about those events and other notes. In keeping a diary you may later reflect on individual entries and develop deeper thoughts about the event in retrospect. Alternatively, you might explore a set of diary entries by writing an additional reflective piece from a personal point of view, and with brief reference to other sources of information, enabling deeper reflection on a set of original thoughts. In addition, the 'living theory' approach to action research, promoted by Jack Whitehead and Jean McNiff (2006), often results in an autobiographical style of research reporting (including photo and video) which is becoming more widely accepted in professional research communities such as nursing and teaching. Examples of such living theory doctoral theses are accessible by a link on the ActionResearch.net website (www.actionresearch.net).

Theme 2: biographical data

Biographical data are collected and constructed by the researcher with the intention that they be as realistic as possible within the context. Collection of biographical data is common in social research. For example, Peter Clough (2002) uses a conversational approach to interviewing, and Czarniawaska (2004) discusses the processes of collecting stories and producing stories from interviews. Jane Elliott (2005), another influential writer about narrative research in social science through interviews, includes researching through focus groups, while ethnographic replication of the scene was Paul Atkinson's (1990) discussion focus. Paul Atkinson has written extensively on the subject of narrative research over the past 20 years. Ethnography, which is a way of recording biographical data as lived events, has been a research method for a significant period, such as the studies of adolescent behaviour in a Polynesian society by the anthropologist Margaret Mead (1928). Mike Crang and Ian Crook (2007) bring ethnography into the modern world with their consideration of filmic approaches to data collection. Young children or other vulnerable people with oral communication difficulties might use photography or drawing to support the telling of their stories about their experiences.

You might be interested in biographical data as a way to try to create a record of the experiences of others that is as true to life as it can be at a particular point in time. In later chapters I will highlight some of the challenges faced in attempting to remain impartial either when recording events or in the interpretation of interview transcripts.

Theme 3: representative constructions (or fictions)

Representative constructions or fictions may provide a stimulus for research, support reflexivity or enable initial analysis of a range of different data. Fiction as a stimulus to inquiry can be very useful, enabling you to establish a clear focus. It may be your own fiction, about your working life for example, or one chosen from another source. Bolton (2006) used fiction to encourage medical practitioners to become reflexive about their practice. For example, doctors created stories that helped young patients understand the doctor's role. This placed them in a position of needing to understand what it would be like to be a child and what that child needs to know. This type of activity can become a highly relevant part of a data set for an action research project where the purpose is to review and change practices. Representative constructions are also beginning to emerge as a means of capturing and collating a range of data from different sources, enabling the researcher to analyse and make choices about the materials that create the narrative of the context and people in the research project. I have explored them in my own research (Bold, 2005; 2006b; 2008b) and in Chapter 8 I draw on other examples.

The Narrative 'Turn'

Using Narrative in Research challenges the boundaries to the *acceptability* of a broad base of narrative approaches within the broader research community and seeks to establish clear justification for using them with students at all levels, in appropriate situations. The relationship between narrative and other methodological approaches such as ethnography will emerge across the chapters as appropriate. Because of its purpose and length, the book will not include comprehensive discussion of the qualitative versus quantitative debate except within the context of the materials covered and the examples provided.

Interest in narrative research across several professions and disciplines is gaining momentum as researchers break through the traditional, generally positivist, boundaries that appear to constrain them. The use of narrative has clear links with postmodern thought since narrative creation usually encourages reflexivity and acknowledges that truth and certainty are unstable. Alan Bleakley (2004), a professor of medical education, emphasises the postmodernist requirement that researchers scrutinise the conditions under which they validate their knowledge claims. Although use of narrative cannot ensure that such scrutiny occurs, it usually does because narrative researchers require a strong awareness of their position within the process. Pat Sikes and Ken Gale (2006) suggest that there has been a narrative 'turn' within the social sciences that is associated with postmodernism, thus opening up possibilities to research social contexts by using a most appropriate and purposeful communication – the narrative. My research interest is in constructivism and constructive interpretivism; I am interested in how people construct meaning of the world around them, and how researchers make sense of what they see. I believe that narratives of various kinds help people to construct and understand their social world. Ethnographic researchers also tend to work within an interpretivist paradigm; they wish to capture, describe and understand the world around them (Robert Gephart, 1999). Narratives therefore have a place in several different research paradigms. I am sure you will have your own particular interests and theoretical bases, possibly from experts in the field not cited in this text, underlying your own professional practice and research. A common factor among many who use narrative in research is a belief in the importance of subjective meaning and emotion in making sense of social events and settings, together with the need for reflexivity in that sense making.

Summary

Using Narrative in Research is grounded in my work with students and my own research experiences. The emphasis is on using research methods that are appropriate and justified, that is fit for purpose, with transferability across different disciplines and fields of inquiry. Each chapter has a distinct purpose in helping readers understand and make use of narrative within their research as appropriate to the situation and people involved. The chapters support the development of three core themes: autobiographical self-reflection, biographical data and representative constructions. Examples from either student unpublished or academic published research exist throughout the text, with the aim of demonstrating particular uses of narrative drawn from my own experience and a comprehensive range of other texts. My aim is to provide materials that are relevant to any discipline or field of study.

Suggested Reading

Chambers, P. (2003) 'Narrative and reflective practice: recording and understanding experience', *Educational Action Research*, 11 (3): 403–14. A thought-provoking article that discusses different types of narrative writing from different professional contexts, with a focus on using story as a medium for facilitating understanding and generating new knowledge.

2

WHAT IS NARRATIVE?

Introduction

The previous chapter identified some of the key proponents of narrative research, together with additional references to people who would not necessarily think of themselves as narrative researchers, but whose ideas contribute to the debates about the nature of reflection and reflexivity and the links with narrative approaches. In this chapter, you will find discussion of some key ideas about the nature of narrative. For example, we structure narratives around a set of events over time. Many writers use the term 'event' when describing features of narratives. An event is something that has happened to a person or thing, at a particular time or in a particular situation. Narratives necessarily tell the events of human lives, reflect human interest and support our sense-making processes. They have the ability to transform our lives and the contexts in which we live. If you are interested in narrative you will probably accept its importance in society, but not necessarily agree that narrative's sole description is 'story' since it can take many forms.

This chapter provides you with some of the historical thinking within and development of narrative research, and the diversity of approaches. It draws on the work of people renowned for their work in this field, such as Catherine Reissman (1993) and Jean Clandinin and Michael Connelly (2000). Through reading the chapter, you will find that narrative research usually sets out to explore an interesting phenomenon and sometimes its aim is to instigate change. Narrative research does not usually set out to test a hypothesis, which is more typical of scientific research. You might wonder whether a distinction is made between narrative as data (the content narrative) and the meta-narrative told by the researcher (e.g. the research story or report about the research that brings together all the component parts). Later in the chapter are some examples, but you should recognise that some qualities of both content narratives and meta-narratives are the same: for example, you may find critical reflection or self-evaluation in either. You will find that the three themes introduced in Chapter 1 – autobiographical self-reflection, biographical data and representative constructions (or fictions) – are not discussed explicitly until the summary, where the links will be made clear.

The Narrative Influence

Some of the most enlightening texts about social events do not present a researcher's interpretation of events but tell the stories of perceptive human beings about the social and educational situations in which they have found themselves. I recommend reading Booker T. Washington's *Up from Slavery: an Autobiography* written in 1901 (2009 e-book), which provides a clear, personal account and some critical insights into what it was like to be born into slavery, to strive for and gain freedom. It captured my interest as a story of significant social injustice, and the author's powerful strength of character made this captivating and emotive reading. This was not research and it clearly holds some very personal, subjective views. However, anyone reading the account gains a clear sense of meaning in the narrative. You can identify with and explore the issues raised by the text. A modern-day autoethnography is similar – a narrative of the researcher's lived experiences, analysed and reflected upon with reference to the broader social context. Booker T. Washington's story cannot claim to represent 'all slaves', but other slaves in that historical period and context will have told similar stories. The many overlapping stories generate a convincing set of evidence to support understanding of the impact of freedom on a previously enslaved culture.

A text that influenced my early thoughts about education during my teacher training in the 1970s was John Holt's *How Children Fail* (1964). This was not a research text but a deeply reflective account of late 1950s and early 1960s classroom events by a person who was prepared to challenge his state education system and identify possible ways in which it caused children to fail. The impact of this text when published was phenomenal since it encouraged many educators across the world to begin questioning the school education system in relation to the ways that children learn. Subsequently, Holt wrote a further text about how children learn. Anyone reading Holt's (1964) book will recognise similar events and issues arising in many contemporary social and educational situations, regardless of historical and cultural context. One might claim that it is not only meaningful but also reliable and valid in terms of professional knowledge about the development of many young learners today, especially those within education systems similar to those in the United States. Being able to transcend temporal and in some cases cultural boundaries is an important quality of some narrative accounts.

It is important to recognise the strength of the narrative, the way that human existence relies on synthesis and analysis of narratives, if one is to accept its place in the repertoire of research methodologies. However, one must also recognise the dangers associated with the levels of interpretation at the level of creation and re-creation in both the creator's and the recipient's minds. The creator interprets events as the narrative develops, and each individual recipient re-creates the narrative based on his/her previous knowledge and understanding. As Webster and Mertova note, 'Narrative is not an objective reconstruction of life – it is a rendition of how life is perceived' (2007: 3).

How Do We Define Narrative in Research?

In the research context, narrative may take different forms depending on its medium and its purpose. One of the aims of this text is to encourage readers to develop and justify their own conceptual understanding of narrative in relation to their own research. Historically, researchers have used narrative in a variety of different ways. For example, Donald Polkinghorne (1988), a psychologist, viewed narrative as a story, and considered that the researcher was interested in both the storying process and the final product. He suggested that narrative is always tentative and cannot provide certainties. It also involves both practical and theoretical elements. He explained that before the 1950s psychologists were interested in individual storying, particularly in relation to perception and memory, that is the cognitive structures. Since then psychologists' interests have broadened, with the recognition that stories are embedded in a social context. Historians and theologians also use narrative to describe, understand and explain human activity. Narrative is central to human experience and existence, providing opportunity to share the nature and order of events at particular times in history. It helps to define self and personal identity. Naturally, different approaches to analysing narratives as research data over time have supported the identification of different features and definitions of narrative.

Original oral versions of personal experience, rather than constructed written narratives, are necessary to examine the formal properties of narrative in relation to their functions, according to William Labov and Joshua Waletzky (1997). A reprint of their original work from the 1960s, this article outlines their approach to narrative analysis, which was to focus on what they called the basic units of narrative, leading to a very specific conception of a narrative. They describe narrative as units that construct a temporal sequence of events and as having two functions which provide meaning: the referential function of personal interest and the evaluative function related to social context. Labov and Waletzky suggest that the fundamental question of narrative analysis is about relating the sequence of clauses (parts of sentences) to the sequence of events (happenings in the story). Thus their analysis is not one of interpreting the meaning or the content of the stories, but a formalised approach to examining linguistic structures. Such an approach is relevant to their research, in which they are examining and comparing narrative structures across different communities and cultures. However, it also appears somewhat decontextualised, with a fixed narrative structure applied to all cases, partly to identify whether speakers fit the structure or not. Those who tell narratives that do not fit Labov and Waletzky's 'normal form' are considered to have less verbal ability than others who duplicate it.

Catherine Reissman (1993) also worked on developing a systematic method for analysing narratives in response to her students requesting support for using the narratives collected in their interviews during research. She notes that definitions of narrative may be too broad and fail to focus on systematic methods of analysis. Alternatively they become restricted to one model, such as Labov's assumption that all narratives are stories about a past event and all have common properties (Reissman, 1993). Reissman notes the importance of paying attention to the multilayered meanings within the narrative and the context in which the narrative is set; for example, in researching divorce, she found that the respondents' narratives contained assumptions about the expectations of late-twentieth-century America in marital interactions. Most important is the notion that a personal narrative is not an exact record of what happened and nor does it mirror the wider world, although it might have common points with other similar stories across space and time. Each person witnessing the same event will tell a slightly different story, depending on what captures their attention and how they make sense of the event in relation to their own experience. Wendy Patterson (2008) seems to agree with Reissman's criticism of Labov and critiques the Labovian approach, in particular citing its limitations. For example, a Labovian narrative has to be complete; the method of analysis does not allow for partial constructions. For some kinds of narrative research data, the Labovian approach will cause information to be lost. The approach is inflexible and unsuited to narrative approaches that require exploration of meaning, partial constructions, and dialogic features such as talk.

In contrast to the work of linguists such as Labov and Waletzky, researchers interested in social contexts and the meaning of narratives focus on sets of different features, such as those identified by Clandinin and Connelly (2000) during their research into teachers' lives: temporality, people, action, certainty and context.

Temporality

In agreement with Cortazzi (1993), Clandinin and Connelly (2000) state that events have a past, a present and a potential future which narrative inquiry accepts, while other approaches to research want things to 'be' without time being relevant. Martin Cortazzi (1993), whose focus was educational linguistics, notes that literary theorists suggest three criteria for identifying a narrative, which combine to form a plot structure:

- temporality – a sequence of events in time
- causation – one event causes another, inferred by readers or hearers
- human interest – without this there is no narrative.

These features form the basis of structuralist models of narrative by which we may identify common elements, even within non-literary media such as a conversation or a television broadcast.

I agree that temporality is an important feature of research into social situations of any kind since change is inevitable. In my experience, some educational research becomes out of date before publication because it does not accept the temporal nature of events such as the implementation of a new initiative. Instead, it embraces a positivist paradigm that seeks the truth through results and educational outcomes. Quite often, educational practice has changed before the research becomes publicly available and therefore it has no impact except to record a historical moment in time. Narrative research of the same events would embrace the change process, recording and analysing the impact as events unfold over time.

People

We are always at a point of personal change, so it is important to narrate in terms of process. For example, a child in a learning situation has a history of learned information and approaches to learning that have an impact on how that child responds to any new learning initiative. If research processes ignore the history then the potential future development of the child is at jeopardy. This occurred with the introduction of the National Numeracy Strategy in England during 1999 before the pilot project was complete. Government had taken the improved test results during the pilot as evidence that the *strategy was working* when the reality was that the change in test results was because of children's improved mental agility – not necessarily proof that the strategy as a whole was effective. As predicted by many in academia, the improvements in test results levelled off very quickly because mathematics teaching overall did not change as teachers focused on getting through the curriculum schemes instead of on how children learned mathematics.

A narrative approach in researching the impact, through analysing the impact on children, teachers and schools over a period, might have demonstrated where the real needs were in terms of improving mathematics capability. I suspect that such research would have shown that real improvements occur in mathematical learning where teachers also improve their understanding of the connections between mathematical concepts and how to teach these most effectively to children. The future narrative might have been much different if the government had taken notice of research by Mike Askew, Margaret Brown, Judith Rhodes, Dylan Wiliam and David Johnson (1997) that demonstrated this through qualitative analyses, rather than leading teachers into following a prescribed curriculum without altering their perceptions of mathematical learning. I am sure that similar claims of changes being implemented, without sound research and reasoning to support them, are evident in other professions and social contexts.

Action

Narrative meaning has to be applied in order to understand; for example, a child's level of achievement in a test is understood by knowing the learning history. This is an interpretive mapping between the action (the child's test and its outcome) and the history (previous test results and learning activities) and not just an acceptance of the level achieved. We must view the level within the context of the child's whole situation to know how much progress a child has made, not just their level of achievement. We understand particular actions (in this case test results) with reference to past actions and future potential actions (target setting and future learning) in a temporal relationship. Imagine how you might apply this relationship between historical and current action in health care or in a business environment.

Certainty

There is no certainty in narrative research. It seeks not to establish certainty but to apply tentativeness due to the different interpretations that are possible. For example, a child achieving a certain level on a test could be due to several influences: cognitive ability, parental involvement, cramming, the ability to memorise and apply without real understanding, cheating, extra tuition, strong interest in and aptitude for the subject, or chance. A simple relationship between cognitive ability and performance does not exist and outcomes are not a clear indicator of quality teaching, yet governments believe they are. A narrative approach to analysing performance in school would highlight the range of different influences on a child, bring into discussion the range of potential causes and accept that sometimes we cannot provide a clear correlation between two events. It is not always possible to establish clear cause and effect relationships. I believe that the acceptance of no certainty makes narrative approaches vulnerable to criticism by those who want definitive answers to difficult questions about human behaviour. In any social context the lack of certainty about outcomes is evident, and perhaps seeking for definitive answers is a rather utopian ideal.

Context

I agree with Clandinin and Connelly (2000) who believe that understanding the context is necessary for making sense of the person's narrative. For example, a child's achievements have to be set into the contexts of the school, the home and relationships with peers, that is the contextual influences on their performance. Each child is an individual, influenced by different contextual settings and situations in different ways over time. A child is not a universal case that can fit into any context and perform in an expected way, so it must be unrealistic for some individual children if generic targets are set across the year group for all children to achieve. Understanding how individuals are affected by different contextual influences, through a narrative approach, is more likely to help teachers provide the most appropriate support for the child's learning. Cultural contexts are particularly important, as highlighted by Roshan Ahmed (2011) in small-scale research into the family backgrounds and experiences of bilingual children in her class. In many situations the generic solutions to problems, for example the provision of standard medical treatments for particular conditions, will result in a range of responses. The outcomes are not always the same for everyone despite them having the same experiences. Narrative captures the contextual influences in a way that other research methods may not.

Other key features

Other researchers focus on features different from those identified by Clandinin and Connelly. Like Reissman (1993), Czarniawaska (2004) highlights emplotment as an important feature in a story and she provides a sound argument that sense making is a retrospective feature, that is one can only make sense of the story *after* its telling. However, for many narrative approaches within social contexts the structural features such as emplotment are less important than the meanings that narratives generate and share. Sikes and Gale (2006) prefer a broad definition of narrative – *an account of something* – but they acknowledge that in research the use of narrative is a contested, complex field in which there are no fixed definitions, meanings and practices. For example, Bolton (2006) justifies stories as a way of making sense of and organising our lives and views them as an automatic function of our minds, which play and replay stories so that characters alter and perspectives change. Like Clough (2002), Bolton does not try to define narrative as having a particular structure but focuses on the *meaning* that stories hold for us individually and collectively. A story generally involves characters passing through a series of events over a period. It may tell of real events or be fictional. It may belong to a particular literary genre. My students and I developed the view, which others promote, that narrative may involve or consist of other communication media that we would not usually define as a story, such as drawings, photographs, poetry, plays, video recordings, interview scripts, *ad hoc* conversations and sequential observations. Narrative is not limited to word-based communication but includes gesture, body language, visual images and different media effects (Clandinin and Connelly, 2000; Whitehead and McNiff, 2006; Hedy Bach, 2007; Reissman, 2008; Paul McIntosh, 2008). A focus on meaning rather than language structure allows us to include these different elements.

Sikes and Gale (2006) identify several qualities of a good story that are useful to note since writers such as Clough (2002) have made use of some of these qualities in their research publications. These qualities also exist in the different types of communication listed above. Visual data will often have stronger evidence of these qualities. In brief they are:

- liminality – providing spaces in which the reader can open their thoughts to something new
- transgression – moving beyond the actual to the emotional responses to experiences and future dreams about the world
- evocation – being emotionally moved by the communication
- complexity – interweaving of ideas, repositioning of the creator to explore layers of ideas
- creativity – creating concepts, representing fluid and multiple views
- audience engagement – capturing attention by communicating in a particular way.

These qualities will not necessarily exist within all narratives collected as data, but may exist in the representations created by the researcher in retelling the story. They are the qualities that cause concern to the positivist, scientific researcher who seeks truth and verification in the research process.

As Andrews et al. (2008) describe, an experience-centred approach to narrative focuses on internal representations of phenomena, thoughts and feelings to which narrative gives external expression. They also emphasise the variability of approach, including the notion of co-constructed narratives between researchers and researched. Andrews et al. propose that the audience shapes narratives and they are multilevel; each person brings to the narrative a different interpretation. They discuss a controversial belief, held by some, that narrative is linked to human agency (the capacity to make choices and act on them). The experience-centred approach discussed further by Squire (2008) accepts that all talk is significant and that the relationship between storyteller and listener encourages a co-coordination of story development. There is an assumption that experience can become part of one's consciousness through stories. No sequential and meaningful structure is excluded from Squire's definition of narrative, which includes, for example, description, theorising about future experiences, dialogic exchange, documentary and imaginary happenings. Squire expands the definition of stories to focus on non-oral methods of telling, and identifies some key features of narratives of experience, namely that they:

- support human sense making
- re-present experience rather than providing the reality
- promote transformation of those involved.

Much depends on the nature and purpose of the research, but in sensitive topics such as illness researchers might identify a transformation of the storyteller, such as an acceptance of the inevitable consequences of a terminal illness. The notion of transformation links with that of human agency or the capacity to make choices. Storytelling may increase the storyteller's capacity to make important life changing choices through re-presenting a past event and speculating about future developments. If the storytelling process has an impact on the teller, then it seems safe to assume that there will be an impact on the listener, albeit a different one. All participants may have their lives changed in some way by the shared experience. For example, if you read *Bereavement Narratives: Continuing Bonds in the Twenty-First Century* by Christine Valentine (2008) you will empathise with the stories told, regardless of your previous experience of bereavement. They provoke thought by providing insights that may lead to transformation of the ways we deal with death, dying and the provision of professional services.

Narrative is another source of data that Bochner (2001) claims social scientists use to advance social theory and social criticism. Bochner, who researched narratives of ageing, explores conflicting views about the use of narrative in research and discusses the dilemmas faced in accepting the multiplicity of meanings in narratives. He takes a pluralist view that promotes multiple forms of representation, focusing on meanings from local stories rather than the seeking of facts by categorising and abstracting. Bochner presents a radically different view of narrative in social science research; he suggests that the growing interest in this field correlates positively with a desire to reform social practices, and thus he merges the boundaries between research and practice. However, he accepts and promotes the idea that there is no single correct or preferred way of using narrative.

You will find an example of narrative used to further a social cause and address misconceptions about particular communities in Amani Hamdan's (2009) PhD research. Hamdan uses narratives from Arab Muslim women to counter the perceptions of those who view them as passive victims of their faith. She claims that her research demonstrates that the women participants were very active agents of change in their families and communities. However, some readers of her work may be critical of the potential bias due to her status as an Arab Muslim woman and due to her position at the start of the research being one of promoting a cause, that of demonstrating that Arab Muslim women are not passive victims. Despite this apparent potential for bias, the extracts of participants' narratives help the reader develop a stronger understanding of the particular circumstances and life choices of each participant.

Atkinson and Delamont (2006) also state that there is no single way that social researchers of various kinds might analyse narrative in any of its forms. They emphasise that narratives are social phenomena created within social situations and expressing skills, knowledge and understanding. According to Atkinson and Delamont, the use of narratives has increased over the past 20 years across social science disciplines including psychology, health, education and organisational research, where understanding people's lived experiences is important. Their introduction to *Narrative Methods*, a comprehensive four-volume collection of papers, provides an overview of different approaches to narrative analysis over recent years. Narrative is part of a repertoire of methods that inform a range of empirical research contexts and therefore requires analysis in different ways to suit the purpose of the inquiry. As the previous chapter outlines, *Using Narrative in Research* does not focus solely on the use of narrative as data for analysis, but considers it as a means to engage researchers and participants in reflective and reflexive processes and to present outcomes of research through representative constructions. In some research, blurred lines between these different uses exist since each project requires a unique approach.

Describing Some Typical Narrative Types in Research

Narratives in research are not a new idea, and since the 1850s different disciplines in the social sciences – sociology, psychology, anthropology, economics, political science and history – have used them in different ways. They are now gaining stronger acceptability in other fields where there is an interest in human matters such as the caring and health professions, theology, education, business and management studies. Cortazzi (1993) provides a useful overview of narrative methods from sociological, sociolinguistic, psychological, literary and anthropological models of narrative in relation to the study of teaching that can easily relate to any professional or business context. Current social science research tends to focus on using interviews, ethnographic observation and conversations as narrative methods to collect data and analyse specific social contexts.

Different researchers identify different qualities and characteristics of the stories they gather as data, usually through interviews. Reissman (1993) focused on the collection of first-person accounts of interviewees' experiences. She analysed the structure of stories to examine the linguistic and cultural resources they drew on, and she considered how they persuaded the listener of their authenticity. Such an approach necessarily involves interpretation including decisions about what is included or excluded from the narrative. Human agency and imagination play a part in making these decisions. Reissman suggests that many people when interviewed will tell a story of their experience, especially if there has been conflict; for example, she experienced women telling long stories about their marriages to explain their divorces. She focused on the stories that emerged naturally by allowing interviewees to take responsibility for what they wanted to tell. Reissman (1993) defines personal narrative as talk organised around consequential events and states that researchers should keep the narrative whole in their analysis rather than splitting it up into different parts. For Reissman, the wholeness defines the meaning.

Elliot (2005) describes narratives as having three facets: temporal, meaningful and social. Each of these facets means that a story will have a different meaning at a different time and in a different social context. Thus there are dangers in attempting to elicit stories in interview since they will be different from stories that arise naturally in other contexts. Wolfson (1976, cited by Cortazzi, 1993) asserted that such stories are a form of summary, short and to the point. Wolfson characterised them as answers (to a question) rather than as a performance (as in naturally occurring stories); the stories give detailed accounts of a chosen event in an appropriate way for the audience. However, Cortazzi (1993) found that teachers' stories in interviews had many features of performance, possibly because the teachers interviewed were used to performing and telling stories as part of their professional role. Hence researchers cannot assume that any story told by a particular person will be told in the same way in any situation; for example, the same story about a work issue told by a nurse to a colleague in the staff room will be different in nature to that told in a formal staff meeting. The different contexts determine how the story unfolds, yet it is essentially the same story.

Cortazzi also explores evaluation models of analysis in which researchers such as Labov and Waletzky in the 1960s sought to elicit a more natural response to questions demonstrating the narrator evaluating his/her story in explaining it to the audience. Labov and Waletzky's interview technique supported the elicitation of evaluative narrative in the interview situation by engaging speakers cognitively and emotionally. Evaluation is a natural part of storytelling that may not emerge in a formal interview situation. Cortazzi (1993) also believed that eliciting evaluative responses is relevant for teachers, and I would extend this to other professional and business personnel. When people talk or write about workplace situations, they also tend to provide the contextual information for their audience, along with cultural and particular performance features of groups in different settings, thus evaluating the process.

A life history is a particular type of story that focuses mainly on past events in a person's life but aims to provide an overall picture of an individual's life. Jaber Gubrium and James Holstein (2009), with an interest in analysing spoken narrative in preference to analysis of the written transcripts of narrative, present a brief summary of Henry Mayhew's social research from the 1850s, which consisted of collecting stories from London's 'humbler classes'. Mayhew provided knowledge about the existence of poorer people (generally ignored by society) through gathering their stories.

In summary, stories elicited in interviews are usually organised round a set of consequential events and may be evaluative in nature. Some might be summaries, rather than more detailed stories that occur naturally. The context in which the story is told affects the narrator's decisions about what to include. The same story told in a different interview at a different time will have a different meaning.

Characteristics of ethnographic accounts

Ethnography is an exploration of a social or cultural setting, for example a workplace, most often through participant observation, with the researcher already part of the setting or immersing themselves as a new person within the setting. According to Kees van der Waal (2009) much of the fieldwork is usually participant observation, conversational interviewing and analysis of relevant materials pertaining to the setting, such as documents or artefacts. Van der Waal explains the challenges faced by researchers in organisational ethnography; much relies on developing contacts and relationships with people, even within one's own organisation. These differing relationships, including differential balance of power, must influence the nature of the final account. The following paragraphs describe some characteristics of different types of ethnographic accounts.

Atkinson (1990) stated that researchers rarely construct ethnographic accounts entirely in narrative form. He described narrative in ethnography as the representation of events rather than the description of settings. Ethnographic accounts always have an interpretive element. Authors tend to weave in their interpretive observations when creating an extended account based on data gathered in a variety of ways. They are creating a meta-narrative, which is a story *about* a story, encompassing and explaining the stories gathered as data within the whole account. In an ethnographic account the events are often categorised into themes, so the account is not necessarily a chronology of events but may be a set of relationships decided upon by the researcher.

For example, a piece of ethnographic research about relationships in a particular workplace, such as a car dealership, may be collected as a chronological field diary, but the final report may include themes focusing on the relationships between colleagues within each sector – the mechanics workshop, sales and reception – followed by themes focusing on the relationships between each sector and management. It will not be a chronological narrative of the daily workings of the organisation but an in-depth exploration of specific relational elements, with the purpose of documenting and improving practice in and between sectors and management.

Reissman (1993) described a different type of traditional ethnographic account, one that is a realistic description of people, events and situations, not the stories created around them. Some ethnographers try to distance themselves and claim to take an objective rather than a subjective stance in writing their accounts. I believe that pressure to conform to scientific expectations of objectivity leads researchers to apply the concept where it may not be easily applied. Thus ethnographic accounts can have different characteristics: they might be chronological and realistic accounts or they might be thematic and interpretive accounts. Despite a claim to realism in some accounts, usually some level of interpretation by the researcher is evident. Ethnographic accounts can be described as meta-narratives which bring together a set of smaller narratives to create a whole account.

Conversation and dialogue as narratives

Narrative in conversation is the ongoing sequence of talk, created dynamically by teller and audience (Cortazzi, 1993). Sociolinguists may be interested in the role of turn-taking in the development of the conversation and may identify specific sequences of types of utterances that tend to work together in pairs. Such features may be useful in analysing conversations between groups of professionals in the workplace to examine how they reach decisions and develop shared meaning in the resolution of issues, for example. This will provide strong evidence of the perceptions, ideas and values held by the participants.

Educationalists may be interested in analysing conversation and dialogue for the ways in which participants understand each other and develop shared meaning. I adopted this approach in my doctoral research into the ways children developed their understanding of mathematical language in a primary classroom. Figure 2.1 contains a very small extract of the dialogue from a mathematics lesson on 'even chance' with part of my accompanying analysis. Even without my analysis the extract tells the story of how the teacher elicits the answer he wants from the children. The dialogue can tell its own story. Clough (2002) uses the dialogue from conversational interviews to tell parts of the stories he presents. The dialogue is real and tells part of the story without any explanation.

27

Figure 2.1 Extract from mathematics lesson

Liam:	We got ten red and ten blue.
Teacher:	Ten red … What can you say about that then Liam? … mathematically.
Liam:	Even chance.
Teacher:	Even chance … what else could you say? Jake.
Jake:	Fair test.
Teacher:	Yeah, I was thinking of something else. Sophie?
Sophie:	Fifty-fifty.
Teacher:	Fifty-fifty, I was thinking [small rocking gesture with one hand] … you got what you expected didn't you?

Discussion

The teacher elicited the terms he wanted from the children: 'even chance' and 'fifty-fifty'. A small, balanced rocking gesture exemplified 'fifty-fifty', which was different from the previous side-to-side balanced gesture for 'even chance'. This difference is interesting because it suggests that fifty-fifty is like a rocker balance, while even chance is like a smooth, flat beam. However, the two different phrases have the same mathematical meaning. If the gestures are an important part of sharing the meaning, then the difference might cause children to consider the two phrases as having a different meaning. The teacher's aim was to link the language 'even chance' with an equal numerical outcome. However, Jake introduced 'fair test' and the teacher *agreed*, thus causing another opportunity for confusion.

(adapted from Bold, 2001)

The Impact of Memory

Psychologists have explored the impact of memory on people's ability to tell stories, and Cortazzi (1993) provides a clear overview of a range of studies involving memory. In all cases, the focus is on the telling of narratives and on exploring the links that people make in establishing understanding. Robyn Fivush (2008) researched how family narratives shape individual identities from the moment we are born. Fivush states that psychologists consider autobiographical narratives as essential in the study of individual and cultural analysis. Emphasis is given to autobiographical memories, which are distinguished from other memories because they focus on the self and they try to explain and evaluate the recalled experiences. Thus they are not simply recounted as a remembered set of events but are evaluated and interpreted, leading to developmental changes in understanding through the act of reminiscing. Fivush found that different family members encourage reminiscing in different ways as soon as young children can begin to talk about the past, and in particular the mother (more specifically the white middle-class mother) uses a style of questioning to aid reminiscing about and reinterpretation of past events. For example, on a visit to the zoo the mother might ask the children if they remember a specific event from their previous visit: 'Do you remember the chimpanzee hiding under the sack last time we came?' In fact, sometimes it might be difficult to distinguish whether a young child is really reminiscing about the actual event or is remembering what parents have said about that event.

The issue of memory is one that concerns those who seek facts about a situation, for example a road traffic incident in which identification of fault is necessary for insurance claims and prosecution processes. In professional workplace research, the identification of facts may be less important since the narrative data collected will most likely contribute to a collection of different perceptions and actions within the context. Each narrative adds to the others, creating a patchwork of information on the whole situation from which similarities and differences are identifiable. In research that supports the development of practice in the workplace, exploring the ways that participants understand each other's narratives is highly relevant since relationships between people rely on developing common understandings of events and situations. In addition, the impact of memory and previous experience on the telling or the understanding of a narrative serves to remind us that any narrative is a representation of actuality. Many researchers keep a research diary or an *aide-mémoire*, which is a fluid narrative of their research process, maintaining chronological records and sustaining reflective thought. As they continue to reread and reflect further, the meaning they attach to the content will alter.

The Meta-Narrative

The researcher produces a meta-narrative as a research story or report about the research that brings together all the component parts. Ethnographic accounts are meta-narratives, as are living theory theses as described by Whitehead and McNiff (2006). You may use any type of data within the meta-narrative, not just narrative data. Clandinin and Connelly (2000) provide an excellent discussion of the various data they used including teacher stories, autobiographical writing, journal writing, field notes, letters, conversation, interviews, family stories, documents, photographs, family/social artefacts (perhaps in memory boxes) and life experiences. No single data collection method is exclusive and each one adds to the interpretation of events because of the complexity of relationships within and external to a particular social environment.

You might wonder how the researcher brings together all the data into the meta-narrative. Clandinin and Connelly noted that both practitioners and researchers committed themselves to reflection and deliberation when constructing narratives of their own and others' experiences. They also make an important point that all the participants within a narrative inquiry are involved simultaneously in living, telling, retelling and reliving stories. Their research with teachers in schools involved jointly living out two people's narratives, that of the practitioner and that of the researcher. Clandinin and Connelly believe that a discursive relationship between researcher and practitioner, to develop a collaborative and reflective retelling of the story, is an important part of understanding the change processes in the setting.

Thus the meta-narrative is not always solely the responsibility of the researcher but is a joint construction between the researcher and the researched. The researcher's goal of developing a theoretical construct about the work will be different from the practitioner's goal, which might be about improving practice. Involving both in constructing the meta-narrative ensures that the story is rigorous in terms of research method and analysis but also plausible in terms of practice development. One key aim of the final report is to foster readers' reflection on their own or others' practices and to encourage comparison with their own stories and restorying within their own setting.

You will read more about the nature of reporting research in Chapter 9.

Summary

In answer to the question 'What is narrative?' the chapter has identified several characteristics that apply to narratives in any context. If we are interested in their structure then is it useful to know that we structure them around sets of events over time, usually to develop a plot in which one event causes another that affects people and/or their social contexts. Narratives may be about real or fictional events and they can belong to any literary genre. We can expand our perspectives of narrative beyond the spoken or written story. Narrative may involve or consist of other communication media such as drawings, photographs, poetry, plays, video recordings, interview scripts, *ad hoc* conversations and sequential observations. It includes gesture, body language, visual images and different media effects.

If we are interested in meaning then it is useful to know that narratives reflect human interests and support our sense-making processes. They have the ability to transform our lives and the social contexts in which we exist. Human existence relies on narratives, the ability to analyse and synthesise them, the way they help us evaluate situations. Narratives help us understand ourselves and others by describing and explaining, by defining self and personal identity. However, a personal narrative is not an exact record of what happened, and nor does it mirror the wider world. It is always tentative and cannot provide certainties because of its multilayered meanings. Narratives have the power to evoke emotional responses, providing spaces in which people open their thoughts to new ideas and possibilities for the future and forging links with human agency. They are complex, creative and engage the audience. Each person brings to the narrative a different interpretation. The narrative re-presents experience rather than providing the reality.

If you wish to use narratives in research then you must be aware of the dangers associated with interpretation at the levels of creation and re-creation in both the creator's and the recipient's minds. Narratives that form the content of the research may be collected during observational ethnographic research, in interviews and life histories. The point in time and the context in which the narrative is collected serve to make it unique, so that if the same person told the story a week later it would have variation. One reason for that variation is memory. Our memory affects our interpretation of events over time. Narratives that form the meta-narrative, the narrative that you as researcher will construct, are also subject to the same influences; our interpretation changes over time. This can be a useful, formative phenomenon, enabling revisiting, reviewing and rethinking our ideas about the data, thus adding rigour to the research process.

How do these ideas fit with the three themes introduced in Chapter 1? Much of Chapter 2 appears to be about biographical data – stories collected for analysis rather than representative constructions. Yet, I believe that the characteristics of narratives identified within the chapter hold true for the latter. In representing others' lives through our reconstructions of their data we must pay attention to both structure and meaning, and be aware of the inherent dangers of interpretation. Autobiographical self-reflection will be evident in some collected data, in which participants naturally reflect on and evaluate their situations. It will also be evident in the meta-narrative of researchers who believe strongly in identifying their own values and who reflect on the whole process of the research, not just the outcomes.

Suggested Reading

Andrews, M., Squire, C. and Tamboukou, M. (2008) 'What is narrative research?', in M. Andrews, C. Squire and M. Tamboukou (eds), *Doing Narrative Research*. London: Sage.

Bochner, A.P. (2001) 'Narrative's virtues', *Qualitative Inquiry*, 7 (2): 131–57.

Clandinin, D. and Connelly, M. (2000) *Narrative Inquiry: Experience and Story in Qualitative Research*. San Francisco: Jossey-Bass.

Elliot, J. (2005) *Using Narrative in Social Research: Qualitative and Quantitative Approaches*. London: Sage.

3

DESIGNING RESEARCH PROJECTS WITH
A NARRATIVE APPROACH

CHAPTER OUTLINE

- Introduction
- What do I put in the research proposal?
    - ○ Title
    - ○ Introduction and research question or area of interest
    - ○ Literature sources
    - ○ Methodology
    - ○ Analysis
    - ○ Ethical implications
    - ○ Schedule

- Where do my ideas come from?
    - ○ Where do I start?
    - ○ What is my position in the project?
    - ○ Why am I doing the project?

- Using narrative to stimulate enquiry
- An example research proposal: first draft
- Summary
- Suggested reading

Introduction

The chapter begins with an outline of a typical generic research proposal structure. Each institution is different, but this example contains the elements you need to think about before you start. Usually a strong proposal will lead to a quality research project. Weak proposals often lead to aborted projects or projects fraught with difficulties along the way. The most difficult question for many novice researchers is, 'What do I really want to explore?' You know your interests but might have difficulty framing these into a viable project, resulting in a proposal that includes too much and lacks focus, or possibly a project that is not feasible because of access issues or timescale.

The chapter discusses a series of questions that you might ask yourself about putting a proposal together, getting ideas for research projects and identifying your position in the whole scheme of things. Many researchers fail to acknowledge adequately the values and beliefs they bring to the research project. In narrative research, acknowledging these is almost a prerequisite since the ways in which you collect and analyse narrative data will reflect these. Another common omission in research proposals is consideration of access to situations and people for the purpose of research. Even in your own familiar workplace or home situation you should not assume rights of access; these should be negotiated at the earliest stage. Of course, access issues relate strongly to ethical concerns and, although you might not be required to complete a 'statement of ethics' for ethics committee approval at the proposal stage, you should certainly give ethics some serious thought. The whole project relies on the researcher having strong ethical justification for the people and situations involved and the methodology used. In Chapter 4, you will find full discussion about access and other ethical concerns.

Later in this chapter are some brief examples of how to use narrative to support the development of research ideas, not as a data collection method but as a reflective tool to stimulate your research project development. Narrative as data, within the analysis, and narrative report writing are not included in this chapter but are discussed in depth in Chapters 6–9. In developing a proposal including narrative methods you should refer to each of these chapters, as appropriate, to inform your methodology and your proposed approach to analysis and to start considering the best approach to writing up the final report.

What Do I Put in the Research Proposal?

First, I will present a brief overview of common features found in research proposals, not specifically for narrative methods of research but typical of many higher education institutional formats. Common features in research proposals are as follows, but not necessarily with the same headings or in the same order:

- title
- introduction and research question or area of interest
- literature sources
- methodology
- analysis
- ethical implications
- schedule.

Title

At the stage of the research proposal you might not have a firm title, but you should broadly focus on your area of interest and in some cases you might include reference to the proposed methodology (e.g. action research) or specific methods (e.g. interview, observation). By the time you submit the final research report, the title will most likely change as the focus of the project becomes refined. The title should give a clear indication of the nature and focus of the research.

Introduction and research question or area of interest

Your introduction should answer the following questions to provide the reader of your proposal with some understanding of the purpose of the research:

- What is the context of your research? Where will it take place and who will be involved?
- What is the broad area of interest you are researching? Is it about professional practice; social issues and dilemmas; political agendas and policy?
- What are your current assumptions, beliefs and understandings about this area?
- What is your interest in this topic? Why do you want to do this research, and what values do you bring to it?
- What have others said about this subject that has stimulated your interest in it?
- What is your main research question or specific area of focus?

Literature sources

Before engaging in practical research activity, even in a context which is very familiar, you ought to have some knowledge and understanding of the literature that concerns itself with the broad area of interest. This is how you will develop your conceptual framework for the focus of the research. The literature base at the proposal stage should include some key texts that have influenced your thinking about the area of interest. It should include materials that provide different perspectives on the issues you are interested in. Depending on the focus of your research, the literature base may include:

- policy documentation (that has an impact on practice)
- popular media (news stories, television productions, web discussion boards) that have taken a political or social stance on an issue related to the context
- practice-based academic literature that informs practice
- research-based academic literature that informs theoretical and practical understandings.

I believe that research in all social contexts where the focus is on people and their situations, and particularly research involving narrative data, should draw on a broad literature base that seeks to explore, examine and inform real-life perspectives on social situations. The literature base thus complements your practical experiential knowledge and understanding of such contexts. However, the balance of the type of literature will change according to the level of study and the nature of your research project. For example at doctorate level you will usually be expected to have a very strong academic literature base, often grounded in the seminal works of key researchers in the field.

Methodology

Sometimes confusion exists about the difference between methodology and methods. A simple way of relating the two is to consider the methodology as the overall approach, for example an action research methodology in which the researcher's purpose is to research practice with the aim of making changes in practice. An ethnographic methodology will make use of a range of research methods such as observation, interview and documents. We might similarly describe a narrative methodology as one that uses a range of narrative data collection methods and/or a form of narrative analysis.

To develop your research methodology, you choose a range of methods of data collection to suit the purpose of your research. Any methods may be relevant, such as participant observation, the collection of life histories and keeping a reflective diary. You should choose methods that will help you answer the research question or support inquiry into the specific area of interest. Your chosen methods require justification through reference to relevant research methods literature, published research papers and your previous experience. Just as you need to develop a conceptual framework for the focus of your research, you need to develop a conceptual framework for the methodology. Having such a conceptual framework will enable you to understand the strengths and weaknesses of your chosen methods and establish a clear justification for them in relation to your context.

Analysis

A common fault in research proposals is that their writers give little thought to the analytical process. Sometimes this occurs because of the inexperience of the writer of the proposal, but sometimes it occurs because the contextual setting of the research is complex and the analytical process may require a flexible, developmental approach. You must give some thought to analytical procedures when deciding on the methods and data collection. There is little benefit in collecting narratives, for example, if you do not have any suggestions for their analysis. The analytical procedure may evolve as the project develops and the exact content and nature of the narrative data become clear.

The development of a conceptual framework for your research also occurs here. In addition to understanding the issues and areas of interest in your research and understanding the development of a methodology for your research, you also need to show that you have considered alternative approaches to analysing your data with reference to relevant academic literature about research methods.

Ethical implications

You should give the ethical concerns full consideration at the point of preparing your proposal. Narrative methods of data collection such as life histories can be intrusive to individuals, causing sometimes unpredictable and far-reaching emotional responses. Despite the difficulty in determining how people may react, you must consider all consequences of the research, however unlikely they may seem. The two main questions you should ask are:

- What are the benefits of this research to the participating people or organisations, and the wider social or political context?
- What harm may the research cause?

Ethical consideration is about weighing up the benefits and balancing these against the potential harm. Researchers cannot eliminate the potential for harm of any kind, but must seek to reduce it by ensuring that participants have awareness of both the benefits and the potential harm. Vulnerable people will need the involvement of their carers.

Ethical concerns are much deeper than the practicalities of seeking access and asking permissions. However, access is an important concern at the proposal stage too, and you should seek access and broad permissions to conduct the research. Chapter 4 contains fuller discussion and practical suggestions about ethical issues and access.

Schedule

Every research project requires a proposed timetable of events although, this may require alteration as the project progresses. If you produce an outline schedule at the proposal stage, it helps with organisation and management of the whole project.

Where Do My Ideas Come From?

You might have a very clear idea of your research interests, and how to develop a proposal for them, but you might also struggle to develop an idea of the research direction. Sometimes people have difficulty deciding what aspect of their work or their experience interests them. Sometimes your tutors will present you with a set of suggested titles or areas of research from which you choose. This section of the chapter explores some different ways to start thinking about your research interests and encourages you to consider the attributes, values and beliefs that you bring to the project.

Clandinin and Connelly (2000) state that narrative inquiry involves studying phenomena, engaging in searching, re-searching, and searching again in a process of continual reformulation of one's ideas about the chosen phenomena. The researcher does not need a problem to solve, or a question to answer, but instead focuses on an experience that is of interest. The narrative inquirer draws on elements of phenomenology (imaging events), ethnography (understanding the context) and grounded theory (identifying themes and categories in data). Thus, in Clandinin and Connelly's view, the narrative inquirer begins with experience rather than theory and explores the phenomena rather than a comparative analysis of theoretical frameworks.

Unfortunately, an emphasis on beginning from experience is one of the criticisms levelled at practitioner or work-based research by those researching within a positivist framework. There is some foundation in the criticisms since practitioners are not necessarily experts in their field and they often require development of a theoretical framework in which to situate their practice to enable them to explore it effectively. This might be a theoretical framework grounded in practice. The essential ingredient is that of critical reflection; if you can engage in critical reflection about practice you are well on your way to developing a theoretical framework for it.

There are no fixed rules about when you should analyse critically some relevant literature, but many undergraduate and postgraduate students require development of some academic knowledge and understanding about the phenomena they have an interest in before engaging actively in the field. They are not all experts in their chosen fields, even those with many years of practice. The balance between starting from experiential and theoretical frameworks remains a decision for individual student researchers and their tutors. Thus there is no fixed way to design a narrative research project, but there is a set of potential uses of narrative in a 'fit for purpose' approach to research design. Only you, in discussion with your supervisor, can make the final decision about the starting point for your research, the place of practice and theory, and the choice of narrative data collection and analytical methods.

Novice narrative researchers at all levels often have difficulty in reconciling the different perspectives on how to plan and conduct research, especially when they have been required to develop a theoretical framework before entering the field in previous projects. A theoretical mindset has a tendency to lead them towards positivist frameworks for exploring practice, perhaps focusing on collecting facts and figures from large and diverse groups of people instead of in-depth analysis of narrative collected from a few key participants. There is also a danger that starting with a specific theoretical framework can lead you to ignore the relevance and importance of critical exploration of practice. However, starting with experience, as advocated by Clandinin and Connelly (2000), can lead you to a lack of criticality in the research, for example by failing to make comparisons with other relevant research findings. For well-established knowledgeable and reflective practitioners in any work context, narrative research often starts with experience-based exploration and analysis *alongside* critical appraisal of its emerging ideas through other recent and relevant literature. Thus a critical theoretical framework develops in parallel to the practical exploration of experience. Practical theory develops; that is, theory grounded in practice. It becomes part of the search, re-search and search again in the continual reformulation of ideas.

I have tried to visualise the continual reformulation of ideas, to provide a diagrammatic model, but the process is neither linear, nor circular, nor spiral in nature. For each project the process diagram would look different and rather amorphous in nature as the researcher researches, reformulates, influences and is influenced by the situation. You should take strength from this ambiguity since it allows a certain freedom from constraints by others, providing the opportunity to develop and justify new research approaches. It enables your development as a researcher, a critically reflective thinker about experiential phenomena.

What is my position in the project?

A consideration of ethics requires you to be transparent about your position in relation to your research, ensuring that everyone involved understands your role, and clarifying the underlying attitudes and reasons for the research.

Kim Etherington (2004), a university professor who has researched narrative and reflexive practices for several years with a focus on counselling and therapy, discusses researcher reflexivity as the capacity of the researcher to acknowledge how their own experiences and contexts (which might be fluid and changing) inform the process and outcomes of inquiry. Each of us has particular experiences and traits that enable us to become who we are at a given moment in time. Any researcher enters the research process for particular reasons and with a set of beliefs and assumptions about the people, the context and the issue of their research. Sometimes, researchers perceive themselves as the knowledgeable ones, the advocates for a cause or the change agents.

In all research, you must be mindful of the relationships between participants, the levels of consultancy and collaboration, the agency and power relationships. Participants must be confident that your voice can represent their voices in ways that they would choose. Further discussion of the ethical issues is given in Chapter 4, but here you are encouraged to consider how you will acknowledge your role in the research and develop your skills of reflexivity.

This is particularly important if you are a practitioner researcher because you will have dual, potentially conflicting roles.

Why am I doing the project?

If you are an undergraduate or a postgraduate researcher, be prepared for your supervisor to ask your reasons for wanting to conduct your research, what knowledge you bring to the research and what you consider your role to be.

Most of the students I supervise complete their research in a social context: the workplace, their home or another social setting. Many are involved in education or training, but some are more interested in the organisation, management, performance, health care or social care aspects of their work. Most of their research is broadly described as practitioner research (in which practice of some kind is explored) and some of it more specifically as action research (in which they explore their own practice). When I ask them for their reasons behind their research, I aim to determine a joint understanding of the values, beliefs and assumptions they are bringing to the project. If you read published research papers and then try to determine the values, beliefs and assumptions of the author you will find they are not always explicit. They are usually more explicit within qualitative reports and in particular those that have a narrative quality such as ethnographic accounts, living theory or action research. Many qualitative researchers believe that such open admission of the qualities brought to the research arena demonstrates that they are not hiding anything; they are embracing those qualities as an unavoidable and often useful or essential part of the whole process.

In Figures 3.1, 3.2 and 3.3 are some examples of reactions to the question, 'Why are you interested in conducting this piece of research?', re-created from various incidents in my experience specifically for the points they raise for discussion within this text. They are fictional in the sense that I created them; they represent certain types of response and therefore they are not typical of all students' responses. The discussion following each one is not intended to be a definitive response to their communication. You may have a different but equally valid response to the scenarios presented.

Example 1

The representative student in Figure 3.1 has an interest in a valid and relevant area of study: provision for children with special needs in a specific context. The interest in this experience has emerged from a change of teacher (and therefore a change in classroom provision) and has the potential to be a useful piece of research that can enhance practice. However, the student's reasoning is judgemental, stating that the teacher does not use her effectively and does not know how to cater for special needs. This leads to an assumption that the research can change the teacher's practice. A stronger consideration of ethics

Figure 3.1   Example 1: second-year undergraduate part-time student, full-time Teaching Assistant Grade 2

> I am interested in studying the way we plan for children with special needs because the teacher is new and does not use me effectively. I have more knowledge of the children than she does and think that she feels threatened by my greater experience at the school. She has only been teaching a couple of years and really does not know how to cater for the special needs. I will use the research to help her learn to work more effectively with me so that I can support the special needs children in a better way.

is needed here since the student, as a researcher, ought to be aware of the potentially damaging nature of the judgements made about the teacher's capabilities. In addition the student's position, that of teaching assistant, places her in a less powerful position than the teacher. This leaves her with the dilemma of how to approach this research for the benefit of all: herself, the teacher, the children with special needs, and the broader contexts of the classroom and school. Using narrative methods in this situation might be most effective because they will allow the collection of everyone's perspective and could engender a collaborative approach to altering practice.

Example 2

The student in Figure 3.2 clearly blames the employers for placements that do not work without providing alternative reasons for the failure, for example, her own methods for matching clients and work placements. Ethically, the student can argue that the research will benefit her clients, but in doing so there is potential harm to employers and their other employees if the student enters the research with the stated beliefs. The student's interest in the dilemmas posed by work placements *is* worthy of systematic inquiry, but the reasons for failure require clear identification. The student has an important placement role that may also contribute to the failure. It is a sensitive phenomenon which may leave the employers, their employees, the clients and the student researcher feeling under threat of criticism through the research experience.

Figure 3.2   Example 2: postgraduate student, MA in guidance and counselling

> My area of work is providing employment opportunities for people who have learning difficulties. Sometimes I find a placement for a client and it does not work out despite the fact that I have spent a significant amount of time matching the work placement to the particular client. This has been my job for many years now and I think that the fault lies in the way the employers, and their employees, react to the new employee in the first few days. The clients cannot always tell me what has happened but some have indicated dissatisfaction with events that have occurred. It is their word against the employer. I would like the opportunity to go into the workplaces with the client and research their experience to find out what is happening.

Such research will require a sensitive approach for the benefit of all concerned, in particular the clients, with the student researcher acknowledging the possibility of her own or at least her organisation's practice requiring some change. Narrative methods of data collection might be useful here, including the use of drawing perhaps, for those who have difficulty remembering and communicating their ideas in words. Observing the client's first few days in a placement could be useful but the student researcher will need to understand the danger of entering these situations with a biased perspective. The ethical issues raised by this particular project might result in the student not gaining access to the placements. This student's organisation, the clients and the different workplaces will all need to be involved in designing a project that will benefit them all, and such a project might be beyond the remit of the master's degree. If this is the case, the student might instead conduct action research, keeping a reflective diary of practice and seeking ways of gathering narrative data from clients and possibly others involved in the work placements; the focus will be on the student's professional approach rather than the situation.

Example 3

It is good that access is already negotiated, but in Figure 3.3 the student appears rather naive in thinking that dropping in unannounced will reduce reactivity, that is changes in meeting agendas or approaches to dealing with issues on the agendas. Whenever someone enters a management meeting as an observer an element of reactivity exists, and in this situation the observer is someone of lesser rank from another setting who may be perceived as a 'spy in the camp'. The student does seem to have a question implicit in the purpose of the study, for example, 'How does the role of senior manager vary in different workplace environments?' However, the student claims to want to leave the direction of the research open.

The interest in the senior management of schools is suited to an ethnographic methodology, but this would require observation of more than just the senior management meetings. I also wonder whether the student's ideology about management and leadership could lead to different ways of interpreting

Figure 3.3 Example 3: PhD education management student

I just want to go in and find out what happens in other schools' senior management meetings. I don't really have a question, I just have an interest in finding out the exact processes of being on the senior management team. I thought I would compare three different schools that I know have different approaches to organising the departments and their approaches to learning. I want to drop in unannounced so that no-one can change their meeting agendas just because I am there. I have a background in secondary school middle management so I am familiar with the context. I have access to other settings through my work and I have already negotiated with the head teachers how the research will progress.

practice in three different settings; this is not clear. The main methodological focus appears to be observation, but there may be better methods to gather relevant information from the senior managers, including the elicitation of narratives about their experiences. Overall, the project seems limited in scope for a PhD, and the student must give much more thought to the implications of researching in other settings.

What can you learn from these examples?
The examples highlight the challenges that you face in formulating an initial idea for a research project. They demonstrate how your position emerges from the assumptions, values and beliefs that are explicit or implicit within your explanation of the reasoning behind your research. Course demands and expectations, and limited time, may lead you to skimp on this stage or omit it altogether, with the danger of rushing into collecting data before establishing your real purpose and giving deeper consideration to the issues, the literature pertaining to those issues, the research methods and the ethics related to the context of the research.

Using Narrative to Stimulate Enquiry

In Chapter 1 I outlined the importance of autobiographical self-reflection. The following examples from my practice with students aim to provide activities that can support development of your critical reflection and reflexivity from the start of a project, with the purpose of ensuring that you consider all possible dilemmas in the context of the research.

Sometimes students have difficulty identifying a suitable project, possibly because of the biased perspectives they hold about a particular situation, as in the three examples previously discussed. Alternatively they cannot identify anything that stands out as worthy of further research, especially when they are focusing on their own practice. Examining oneself can be very challenging and throws one into the realms of self-critique that can, if not controlled, become self-destructive.

First, I focus on the use of narrative to engage students in reflection on practice dilemmas in search of a suitable practice-based research project. This is a useful technique for experienced researchers too. I asked one group of second-year undergraduate students to write a reflective piece about a day at work to bring to the next taught session. Julie, a teaching assistant student, created a story 'Sore feet' to support the development of her ideas for an action research project. Part of the story is reproduced in Figure 3.4.

This piece of writing identifies the tensions of a new working relationship between an established teaching assistant and a new teacher in the classroom. It is a common situation, but for Julie it has the potential to lead into an interesting

Figure 3.4 Sore feet

Today is the day I get no relief from my sore feet. They are being trodden on all the time, not by the children though. Perhaps Timothy ought to review where he places his size elevens. Getting to know new colleagues is not easy and there are adjustments to be made but by whom? My feet are suffering … while Timothy fails to receive an award for treading lightly. Is it me? Should I move my feet out of the way? At the moment, I am not prepared to adjust and he needs to learn to manoeuvre his way around the room and relationships with more finesse.

(Julie, unpublished reflection, 2005)

project about the development of this relationship, although there are many ethical issues to consider before embarking on such a project. This student responded well to the suggestion of using creative writing to support the development of her ideas, and in a later research project she used poetry to explain her thoughts about classroom practice. She had been aware that something was missing from the classroom despite its positive and busy atmosphere. She used poetry to gather her thoughts together as a vehicle for making the issue explicit and alive, as you will see in Figure 3.5. Julie embraced the opportunity to use creative approaches, possibly because she found them motivating in an academic situation where writing can become very 'dry' and presented in depersonalised terms. Not all students embrace such opportunities to use their creativity and others will write in a more factual style.

All the students valued the opportunity that writing a story about their work offered in relation to developing ideas for research projects. The act of writing a series of events as narrative, sometimes including thoughts and feelings about them, seems to promote deeper reflection about everyday workplace occurrences. It makes the small but critical events stand out in our minds, stimulating and prompting ideas for opportunities to change, to find alternative strategies to resolve problems.

Working with Julie reminded me of the value of creativity, of being able to think beyond the obvious and to express oneself in any way one chooses rather than to follow the expected mode. The idea of using creative approaches to stimulating reflection on practice developed further after White's (2006) conference presentation; this engaged my interest in drawing and imagery as part of the reflective process, and I began to use this idea with my students too. I began to recognise that I viewed reflective processes and reflexivity as essential prerequisites to becoming and being a narrative researcher in whatever context. In addition, Swaroop Rawal introduced me to the concept of reflecting-for-action (based on Schön, 1984) during a role-play activity in the ETEN 2006 Thematic Interest Group (Bold and Chambers, 2009). This seemed to fit perfectly with the direction of my thoughts. I wanted my students to reflect-for-action, to use their reflections as a stimulus for future research action.

DESIGNING PROJECTS

Figure 3.5 What's missing?

The classroom is busy
There's a teacher, children and their noise!
The classroom is colourful
Lots of pictures, posters, books and toys
But something is missing, what is it?
What is it?

The classroom is happy
Lots of laughs, chatters and smiles
The classroom is messy
Glitter, glue and shiny paper going for miles
But something is missing, what is it?
What is it?

The classroom is quiet
No blowing, banging or rattling sounds
The classroom is empty
No triangles, tambourines or drums around
So something is missing, what is it?
What is it?

I know now, I know!
The classroom needs music
Loud music, soft music, classical or rock
The classroom needs instruments
Chimes and recorders and wooden blocks

The classroom needs sounds
We'll talk about the music and what it can say
The classroom needs change
I'll provide what is missing and I'll find the way

The classroom needs sounds
We'll listen to different music and get the beat
The classroom needs change
We'll start to dance and use our feet

(Julie, unpublished work, 2006)

My experiences with students have increased my understanding of the impact of creative approaches. Their responses vary according to their attitudes, perceptions and capability to respond to materials in a creative way. Students who do not have the same interest as Julie did not embrace such approaches with as much vigour. Although such creative approaches to exploring practice may not seem appropriate for everyone, I believe their use may be crucial to the development of reflection and reflexivity. Too many of us are inhibited by our self-belief that we are not artists, poets or writers; to lose some of those inhibitions can only be beneficial in the longer term.

For people who are uncomfortable with creating their own narratives, drawing or role-playing in exercises to stimulate ideas for research into practice, an alternative is to take an article that is already published, or to create a narrative that replicates what you want people to think about. This idea is particularly useful if you want to stimulate group discussion about an issue that is affecting the whole group, with a view to setting up some collaborative research.

One of my MA education students, a deputy head teacher, was having a difficult time with some more experienced members of staff being unpleasant to the less experienced. She could not address the issues directly with the staff concerned, and she thought that she could not engage them in creating their own narratives about their practice. Instead, she wrote a story that mirrored events that were happening in her school and shared it with the staff at a meeting. The story created some common ground for discussion without anyone feeling threatened. It raised much discussion and debate, prompted identification of issues within the school and led the staff into a collaborative research project in which they all decided to keep a reflective diary for one week to help them think in more depth about their practice.

Another alternative you might be interested in is to use a published article that lends itself to stimulating thoughts about practice. I found Dennis Beach's (2005) allegorical tale of a child torn between two tribes, who both wanted to shape the child, very thought provoking. It made me think of the issues I find in my own practice where different tutors want to work with students in different ways. People have different philosophies and practices that affect student progress and development. And, of course, we all think we are right! Beach's tale is fictional but it mirrors contrasting ideologies that exist in many professional and social contexts. It could lead to some very interesting comparative research.

This section has provided you with some ideas about the ways that narrative in its broadest sense can help you think about your practices, your social situation, your understanding of relationships. It can help you start to design a research proposal that is grounded in your own experiences of the world. Further examples appear in Chapter 5 which focuses on autobiographical self-reflection.

The next section provides an example of the first draft of a research proposal in the early stages of development. It focuses on my role as a carer for an elderly person. I have not yet explored the literature in depth, and at this stage I have some experiential knowledge of the local services for those with dementia. I am therefore starting from experience and expect to use and explore the relevant literature before firming up my proposal.

An Example Research Proposal: First Draft

Title

Who cares? A narrative case study of support services involved in the care of a person with dementia

45

Introduction and research question or area of interest

My research focuses on the care of an elderly person and the relationship we have with the various support services. My interest in the research stems from concerns about the number of different people involved in diagnosis and care and the apparent lack of coordination of such services. As the main carer, I aim to seek an improvement in the communication between the different support services and between the support services and ourselves, ultimately to improve the quality of care for people with dementia in the local community. I currently have no funding for this research. However, with recent government concern about the cost of caring for the growing number of people with dementia, I am sure that some funding will be available if I seek it. I plan to extend the project over two years since change takes time to establish and the services are currently in a process of change due to increased national funding.

Literature sources

My main literature sources to date have been the local authority website, government websites and specialist organisation websites dedicated to explaining the rights of people with dementia and the rights of carers. They place much emphasis on ensuring procedures and regulations are followed. For example, from 2007 to 2010 specific dementia medication was only supplied to a person who demonstrated a particular score on a mental assessment, regardless of the fact that by the time this score is reached the person's quality of life was such that they were reliant on other people to help them manage their daily lives. The law on this issue has recently been changed so that medication may begin in the early stages of dementia. Some research has been completed on the nature and progress of dementia conditions, for example by the Alzheimer's Society, and on the rights and needs of carers, for example by the Centre for International Research on Care, Labour and Equalities (CIRCLE) at the University of Leeds (www.sociology.leeds.ac.uk/circle/about/). However, I have found little evidence of research into the nature of support provided, yet the government is clearly keen to develop better coordinated services and has provided funding for mental health care services.

Methodology

I will describe the methodology broadly as practitioner research since I am a carer within the contextual situation I wish to explore. The main data collection methods I propose are as follows:

1   I will construct a personal account of my experiences with the support services over the past two years. This provides essential background information that explains the concerns I have and provides a baseline for the project. The person I care for has dementia and cannot recall events over the last two years.

2   I will keep a reflective diary in which I will log all communications with the services and my thoughts and feelings about those communications. A diary is particularly suited to this research since it supports self-reflection on experiences and encourages me to consider my own role in the communications with services.
3   At each meeting, I will ask the services to summarise their meetings with us to date, and either make notes or ask if I may copy their records. I will also ask for a proposed plan of action or treatment so that we have a clear record of the next part of the process. I will ask if I may tape record the conversations.

Analysis

A significant part of the analysis will be representative constructions of each set of service communications over a period of two years, with the aim of identifying the changes that take place and providing critical evaluation of those changes. The narratives will be created from each of the three data sets outlined previously. The personal account sets the scene for each service, and the story will develop through reference to the reflective diary and the meeting notes. Once a narrative is created for each scene, further analysis will draw together similarities and differences across the different service narratives with the purpose of identifying common concerns and developments. Because this is a small-scale project with local implications, the narrative approach provides the most easily disseminated medium across a diverse audience.

Ethical implications

Potentially the beneficiaries will be first the person with dementia, and second the carer (myself) and members of the person's family. I have avoided including specific details about the person I care for, so there is little chance of identification and potential embarrassments for that person or members of the family. The research could potentially harm the services and the people who work in them, since it might highlight some weaknesses (which they may already have knowledge of) in addition to their strengths. Alternatively, the identification of issues by a client could be a benefit, raising the concerns to a higher level where people might take notice and fund more effectively the opportunity to change.

Schedule

For example:

- March 2011 to June 2011: negotiate access and permissions to conduct research, carry out literature searches.
- June 2011 to June 2013: over two years, attend meetings and clinic appointments, keep a reflective diary, and gather information from the service providers.
- June 2013 to October 2013: analyse data and draft report to share with service providers.

The draft research proposal is the first attempt to make sense of the research I would like to conduct in the near future. I present it here to provide an opportunity for you to raise questions and discuss alternative ways to develop such a piece of narrative research. For example, you might reflect on my position in the research, my close proximity to the other participants, and the potential for a biased perspective to emerge from my findings. You might also discuss my weak literature base, and the lack of a developing conceptual framework as an academic basis for this proposal.

Summary

In Chapter 3 you have been introduced to some common requirements for developing a research proposal together with some indication of the opportunities to use narrative methods as appropriate. In developing a research proposal including narrative methods you are encouraged to fine-tune your ability to reflect on your experiences and to examine your own values, beliefs and other attributes that you bring to the research. Whether starting from experience or from theoretical constructs, or from a mixture of both, you are encouraged to develop your ability to make informed choices and justify your methodology.

Of the three themes introduced in Chapter 1, autobiographical self-reflection emerges as being important in developing your research proposal – thinking through why you want to do a particular research project and establishing the qualities that you bring to it. Biographical data will be collected through the methods you adopt for a project, fully discussed later in the book. I use representative constructions to illustrate some points I wish to make, thus modelling the potential for such approaches to writing and the initial analysis of situations.

If you are stuck for ideas, the chapter provides some ways to help you begin to develop your reflective skills, to identify an issue worth exploring. You will find more ideas in Chapter 5. The last section of the chapter gives an example of a draft research proposal intended to open up discussion and debate. You will need to read further chapters for detailed discussion of methods, analyses and report writing. Chapter 4 follows with in-depth consideration of ethics, including access, which builds on the initial points raised here in Chapter 3.

Suggested Reading

Beach, D. (2005) 'The problem of how learning should be socially organized: relations between reflection and transformative action', *Reflective Practice*, 6 (4): 473–89.

Bolton, G. (2006) 'Narrative writing: reflective enquiry into professional practice', *Educational Action Research*, 14 (2): 203–18.

Craig, C.J. (2009) 'Learning about reflection through exploring narrative inquiry', *Reflective Practice*, 10 (1): 105–16.

4

ETHICS AND A NARRATIVE APPROACH

Introduction

This chapter encourages you to consider ethics and to work in an ethical way, from the first thoughts about your project right through to the dissemination of outcomes. It identifies some key ethical tenets, broadly expressed as the promotion of benefits and the reduction of harm to all involved. Balancing the benefits against the potential harm caused by the research should be at the forefront of your thinking when preparing for and justifying your approach to the research. Access to people and places is necessary when using narrative methods and you cannot ignore the challenges that access can raise. You cannot assume access, even in family and workplace contexts. There are many sensitive areas in all types of research but particularly in narrative research where participants are offering aspects of their lives for scrutiny by others. Other essential ethical qualities that emerge throughout the chapter as it develops are responsibility, respect and trust. The chapter begins with an important question and, through examples, aims to help you understand and acknowledge the influences that you bring to your project.

Identifying an Ethical Concern

The ethical questions that arise in any research process are numerous and this chapter cannot address every ethical concern that will arise in individual projects. For example, there will be specific issues arising in research with different cultures and with specific groups in any society, for which there are no straightforward prescriptions, except to urge you to develop a propensity towards understanding the needs of others involved in the research. Identifying the ethical concerns in your research is most important.

Research projects typically include some statements related to ethics such as the following, in which Peter Egg and his co-researchers (2004), with much experience in researching children's lives through participatory approaches, expressed concern about the best way to work with children during an international project in the SOS Children's Villages. They were researching the lives of children who had all experienced violence and negative influences on their lives, and were seeking to identify the children's aspirations for the future:

We knew that to ask children to respond to these questions in words alone was too abstract and too difficult and so we asked them to approach the task through images. We gave them digital cameras and asked them to photograph the most positive aspects of their lives, the things that were important to them, the things (people and places) that they loved, where they felt secure/protected and the things that were fun. (2004: 11)

The researchers thought carefully about the best way to approach the collection of data with the children involved in their research. They decided that cameras would capture the children's stories about their lives, providing an opportunity to focus on and talk about the positive rather than negative influences. Their aim was clearly to maximise the benefit of the research and to reduce the potential harmful effects of strangers entering their lives.

Using photography to elicit life stories is very useful, especially with children or other vulnerable people, but you must consider some concerns. For example, consider the risk of a child or vulnerable person walking around in potentially unsafe areas to take photographs; there are health and safety guidelines to follow. Most importantly you must consider the reactions of others, even for a child taking pictures in and around the home or local community; there are clear ethical implications in becoming a spy within the camp. Some people may object strongly to having their photograph taken. Who gives consent? Who decides the boundaries between public and private lives? Consent for children to take photographs at home or in other social situations might also include much parental control of what images are being taken of whom and when. You must also give thought to publication – how you will use the photographs and your purpose in using them. Thus, using photography to elicit life stories is not an easy option where ethics are concerned.

What Should I Ask Myself?

Various sources of information are available to help you answer this question. For example, Anne Campbell and Sue Groundwater-Smith (2007), both experienced educational researchers with a strong interest in narrative methods, edited a collection of chapters by well-known authors focusing on a range of ethical issues, including the use of participants' stories. They identify the following issues for you to address:

- acknowledging your own 'position' in the research
- access to contexts and proposed participants
- gaining informed consent
- storing data
- reporting outcomes.

On the surface this seems a straightforward list, but in reality these practical issues are very complex and fluid throughout the research process. In all research, the question of ethics is unavoidable. In the past, researchers and in particular novice researchers have mainly concerned themselves with raising awareness and acquiring permissions; that is, with ensuring that parents, children and adult participants are aware of the purpose of the research and have given their permission to be part of it. In addition, there is usually some guarantee of anonymity so that individuals and organisations are not identifiable within the research. These are important features within the framework of ethical actions, but the conceptual understanding of ethics and the subsequent actions arising from such an understanding ensure that the researcher questions any concerns related to participation much more deeply.

When we ask the question 'What does it mean to be ethical?' we find few simple answers, and some research ethics guidelines, especially in-house university guides used by ethics committees, seem to focus mainly on research that would fit into a positivist paradigm. Such guidelines are not always useful to qualitative researchers, so organisations such as the British Educational Research Association (BERA) have drafted guidelines that suit

ETHICS AND A NARRATIVE APPROACH

the social situation in educational institutions. BERA's (2004) guidelines are an excellent starting point for educational researchers seeking to ensure that they respect people, the knowledge that is gained from research, democratic values, research quality and academic freedom. My advice to new researchers is to use these in supporting the development of a research project from the outset. A particularly useful feature is the identification of responsibilities to different people: the participants, the sponsors of research and the community of educational researchers. When working with sponsors, BERA rightly advises avoiding agreement to conditions that undermine the integrity of the research, but in practice this can be very difficult since sponsors often prefer specific methods of research and want a specific type of outcome from it.

Although such guidelines are very useful, academic debate and critical reflection on the way we address ethical issues in research are also very important. In a conference presentation at BERA in 2008, John Stevenson and John Willott focused on the beneficence (promoting good, of benefit to others) of research in relation to the non-maleficence (avoidance of harm to others) in a strongly discursive paper considering the relationship between the two. They identified moral, social, political and cultural considerations in relation to ethics:

- Moral ethics around harm:
  o respect for individuals
  o duty towards others.

- Social ethics and serving the common good:
  o the development of a body of knowledge that improves social life
  o inclusive research – everyone has a right to be heard
  o the challenge of participatory research.

- Political ethics:
  o democratic values
  o academic freedom
  o government departments' refusal to publish some research results
  o manipulation of data.

- Cultural ethics:
  o respect for diversity – different cultures use language and actions in different ways
  o different codes of ethics in different cultures.

The main ethical emphasis is to seek reduction of harm to the individual and the organisation and/or production of identifiable benefits for the participants within the design and conduct of the whole research process. Building your discussion of ethics around these two principles of benefits and harm reduction is a very useful approach alongside the use of specific guidelines related to your area of interest, and any ethical checks required by your institution.

In developing a project there are six key principles of ethical research that the Economic and Social Research Council (ESRC) expects researchers to address whenever applicable:

- Research should be designed, reviewed and undertaken to ensure integrity, quality and transparency.
- Research staff and participants must normally be informed fully about the purpose, methods and intended possible uses of the research, what their participation in the research entails and what risks, if any, are involved. Some variation is allowed in very specific research contexts for which detailed guidance is provided [in the document].
- The confidentiality of information supplied by research participants and the anonymity of respondents must be respected.
- Research participants must take part voluntarily, free from any coercion.
- Harm to research participants must be avoided in all instances.
- The independence of research must be clear, and any conflicts of interest or partiality must be explicit. (ESRC, 2010: 3)

The ESRC guidelines are also a very useful guide for anyone developing a research project. The issue of transparency is an important one, but there might be times when the research involves people who are unable to fully understand the purpose of the research, for example people with a learning disability, or very young children. The ESRC explains that researchers must seek approval from the relevant people or organisations with responsibility for such people. The guidelines also discuss the justifiable necessity to use covert methods of data collection in some situations, such as observation of illegal behaviour, and they highlight the potential danger to researchers, not just to participants, in such situations. It is good that they also highlight the issue of conflicts of interest. Researchers who are researching within their own organisations often have to contend with such conflicting interests, particularly the interests of their managers and colleagues in comparison to their own. Conflicts of interest between researchers and other people in their organisations can lead to the abandonment of a research proposal, or if the research is allowed to proceed it can lead to the researcher or other individuals feeling vulnerable.

The British Psychological Society provides similar guidelines (accessible on their website www.bps.org.uk/home-page.cfm) built around the four ethical principles of respect, competence, responsibility and integrity. The guidelines describe the values associated with each principle, and the Society offers further support for researchers in applying these ethical principles. These and other professional guidelines are very detailed and generally contain the same advice about avoiding harm and aiming to use research and practice for the benefit of others.

Stevenson and Willott (2008) refer back to the 1949 Nuremberg Code, which first included the principles of avoiding harm and being of benefit to others in medical research, but they question whether it is possible to attend to both effectively at the same time since avoiding harm is not the same as being beneficial. They claim that research ethics built on harm avoidance results in researching selective groups rather than a *genuine* group representing the issues. Thus consideration of ethics has an impact on the ways in which we plan research from the outset, which can have an undesirable effect on knowledge gain. Ethical concerns might prevent important research in terms of benefits to a particular social community because the potential harm makes the project too sensitive to conduct.

The broad answers to 'What should I ask myself?' are the following:

- How will my research benefit the people and social context in which it takes place?
- How might my research harm the participants or the social context in which it takes place?

There is also another important question that every researcher ought to ask:

- How will I, and others in my research team, influence the research process?

How Do I Influence the Research Process?

As a researcher you must consider your influence on the research at all stages (Yow, 2006). You must question the motives that drive the research, your feelings about the other participants in the research and your own assumptions or self-schema about the topic under scrutiny. Although the traditional definition of objectivity cannot fit the narrative approach, it is essential that you acknowledge your subjective position and collect and analyse data with this position accounted for in discussion. First I will describe and discuss Marianne's story, the way she examined her own position in her research, as an example of how you might acknowledge and examine your influences as part of your research.

Marianne's story

Marianne, a teaching assistant and part-time second-year undergraduate student, was researching boys' reading practices and used narrative to explore her own position in the research. The narrative in the example in Figure 4.1 was part of her data analysis, effectively demonstrating her influence not only in the research but also in her professional practice.

Marianne thus established the influences on her views of reading before analysing the narrative data she collected from the children. Although she did not identify this as an ethical approach in her report, it clearly embraced the notion of acknowledging her impact on the analysis of data. She knew she was researching not with an objective stance but from a subjective experiential viewpoint. This did not lessen the impact of her analysis; indeed, it strengthened it because

Figure 4.1 Marianne's background to reading

I was brought up in a white middle-class family with two sisters. From my earliest memory my mother read to me every night. These stories would normally be fairy tales, Ladybird books and Mr Men stories. From a very young age I would memorise these stories and recite them. As I progressed to independent reading, my tastes were generally middle-class tales of adventure such as Enid Blyton. I have a strong recollection of reading Watership Down at the age of nine; no doubt much of the subtlety of this book was missed at such a tender age. I also remember the librarian at my local library being suitably impressed that I was reading James Herriot novels at the age of ten. Interestingly, although my own class and background probably determined my reading tastes, one of my favourite books as a child was Gumble's Yard, a tale set in a working-class area involving broken homes and child neglect.

My own experiences of reading were firmly rooted in a female dominated world. My father was rarely seen reading, other than a newspaper. I grew up with a love of books, which I have taken into my adult life. All these factors have moulded my own values about books and reading choices for children. It is difficult to stand back from these values as they are a part of us and what shapes us.

(Marianne, unpublished work, 2006)

she was able to compare and contrast her own feminine-oriented narrative with the narratives of the boys in her care. Her understanding of the boys' responses was deeper through recognition that they had very different values and home experiences from her own.

Developing an ethical attitude

Ruthellen Josselson (2007), a psychologist interested in human relationships and life history research, highlights the fact that narrative research engages people and places in relationships in which the researcher has the ethical duty to protect the privacy and dignity of other participants. This creates challenges in making choices, and Josselson acknowledges that there is no simple process to follow in determining what is ethical in a given situation. Instead, she promotes the idea of the researcher developing an ethical attitude towards a project, especially since some ethical choices are made *in situ* as issues emerge.

Just as narrative research is often an evolutionary process, the ethics evolve alongside the research as part of the process. The dilemmas are often caused by the dual role of the narrative researcher, that of being in a close relationship with the participants, perhaps as a colleague or as an advocate of their cause, and also of being an academic professional with a responsibility to disseminate research findings. Maxine Birch and Tina Miller (2002) suggest that an ethical researcher works with ethical values of *respect* and *responsibility*. Maxine Birch has a background in health and social care and has a strong interest in developing ethical approaches to research. Tina Miller is a sociologist interested in researching motherhood, fatherhood and identities amongst other areas. For both of these researchers, working sensitively with people in health care or social situations, consideration of ethics is paramount. Respect should guide research design and dissemination. Birch and Miller focused on the issues related to participants in the research having rights to be more fully involved in the full dissemination of the research, that is they question the levels of participation, encouraging a change from being simply a participant in a focus group to becoming a co-researcher and author of papers. Their suggestions bring further ethical challenges.

According to Josselson (2007), an explicit ethical contract with all involved should ensure a reduction of the potential harm and an increase in the potential benefits, but having a contract will not account for dilemmas arising during the research, which require ongoing consideration of ethics as an integral part of the research process. Josselson is critical of ethics committees that insist researchers point out the potential harmful effects of an interview, and that the interviewee will be offered psychotherapy if necessary. She does not believe there is a need to tell people they might be upset in a situation of trust, and suggests that such statements within consent forms disrupt the level of trust in the researcher–participant relationship. Suggesting an emotional interviewee should see a psychotherapist could be more harmful than allowing the interview to close and confirming the right of the interviewee not to have their interview, or parts of it, used as data in the research. The right of the participant to withdraw at any point from the research is a more important moral and ethical right, which gives control of the data to participants, not the researcher alone.

With appropriate examples, the next section explores participants' rights and a range of ethical concerns with a specific focus on narrative methods.

What is the Impact on Participants?

With reference to participants, we might also ask how the ethics of using narratives differs from the ethics of using any other qualitative methods. William Smythe and Maureen Murray (2000), with research interests in narrative methodologies and ethics, suggest that using narrative is an intrusive style of research. They note that the ethical challenge for researchers is to balance their perspective of a person's narrative with the person's own view. Most ethical guidelines and principles do not address this challenge.

Participatory ethics often focuses on identifying a suitable sample and considering whether participants can find the time or personal resources to engage effectively in the research. In large-scale quantitative research, the aim is to have a sample of people who are representative of different people in society so that the researchers may claim their results are indicative of a particular population. However, in smaller-scale qualitative research the number of participants will be small and often context specific, such as one department in an organisation. Some sensitive issues will lead to participants' reluctance to engage in the research, resulting in a smaller willing sample. The result of this might be a more intensive exploration of this small number of individuals who, for whatever reason, are more interested or more able to take part. Corinne Squire's (2008) research into people who are ill with human immunodeficiency virus (HIV) is an example of research where this selection by willingness of participants may occur. In such situations, there might be concerns that the narrative research process becomes more intrusive than expected, drawing on physical and emotional reserves to an extent that participants did not expect. Thus the research process might be harmful to the participants' emotional and physical well-being.

An ethical researcher will seek to balance the potential for harm against the benefits from the outcomes of the research for the participants and others they represent. Smythe and Murray (2000) place the responsibility for judging the fitness of a participant to engage in narrative research on the shoulders of the researcher. Potential participants may not be able to make the judgements themselves because they may not understand the potential for multiple understandings and interpretations of their stories. Some people may not respond well to being open to another person in the interview situation, while others may not like what they see in the final report where their story may not appear recognisable to them. Hence the importance of avoiding any form of coercion, especially among vulnerable people, family members or colleagues at work.

Another concern might be that the small number of people who wish to be part of the sample might skew the results with particular biases that can influence the conclusions drawn and the potential generalisation of the research findings. For the majority of qualitative researchers the issue of generalising findings will always be contentious since qualitative research, including narrative, focuses on deep explorations of a small number of cases in a particular context rather than the collection of numerous broadly based data. The issue of generalising is not really of concern when the aim of the research is transformation of practice in a specific context. Where the ability to generalise beyond the context is important, if you identify the participants' backgrounds, beliefs and values and you are transparent about the issues related to potential transference of findings into other situations, then you have taken an ethical approach.

Squire's (2008) HIV research provides an example of conducting illness research in an ethical way. She conducted her research in South Africa in 2001 at a time when people felt unable to talk openly about their HIV status. The ethical concerns about the broader political context together with the personal context of participants affected the nature of the materials collected. Squire focused on HIV support, treating the participants as experts, and she only used audio recording, rather than video recording, to assure anonymity. The participants thought the research was important as a way of having their voices heard. Squire did not include the topics of modes of infection, risk behaviours and HIV as a medical condition; she thus offered the participants a way of talking about their support concerns, the opportunity to seek support if they wanted it, and the right not to be viewed negatively as victims. Although ethically sound and well justified by Squire, this approach limits the research to exploring the support of victims rather than the prevention of the spread of HIV in the first instance. If a researcher wished to research risk behaviours with the purpose of promoting risk-free behaviours, for example, the ethical dilemmas would be very different; yet perhaps researchers ought to address rather than avoid them so that they can research the issue of risk behaviours if they consider it essential to do so. The overarching ethical question must be, 'Is this research necessary to improve people's lives?' And if one cannot justify the purpose for the research then it should not take place.

Informed consent is a phrase often used in ethical guidelines. In reality, many participants in narrative research will not understand the full implications of consent. Researchers are often unsure about the impact of the research since the content is unknown until a participant shares a narrative that has an impact on the process and analysis. Smythe and Murray (2000) suggest that consent is an ongoing process throughout the research. Thus anyone may withdraw their narrative at any time. One of the ongoing problems is that as a person's story unfolds and is subsequently reported, the researcher will have great difficulty in disguising who the person is, despite reporting anonymously. Anyone who knows the person and the situation they are in will be able to recognise them, especially in a small project within an organisation. Narrative researchers therefore need to seek ways to re-tell or re-present participants' stories that preserve privacy and reduce potential harm. Some use the representative narrative as a means to overcome such a difficulty. Unfortunately, some subtle influences will still exert themselves upon the participants when their narratives become public. Nobody can prevent this happening or judge what the impact might be.

An example of a situation in which participation might become an issue is when research about a child is conducted within a family setting. Although the research is in the family home and familiar to the child, the presence of the researcher might be quite unsettling. The researcher believes that the research will benefit the child, possibly leading to a false assumption that it will do little harm. Laurie Puchner and Lou Smith (2008) engaged in an e-mail discussion about the issue of informed consent in situations where the children, Lou's grandson and Laurie's son, both with attention deficit disorder (ADD), took part in some research. Both researchers are members of the Action Research Collaborative (ARC) in Missouri, and Lou has a long history of experience and publication in qualitative and narrative research. They discuss the issues around a project abandoned because of the response of the two young people with ADD.

Lou was concerned from the beginning that his closeness to his grandson would be a problem and, although his grandson was happy to take part in the research, his parents expressed reservations. Laurie thought that she might involve her son in a collaborative approach to the research, but others at ARC questioned whether she ought to involve others in the family because of the impact on them too. Eventually they abandoned the project, but in the process Lou and Laurie engaged in deeper analysis of the research ethics in involving family as research participants and identified the tensions between the personal and the professional, and the effect of the research on others within the community. They identified that, in research into their families, true informed consent was unlikely, as was the notion of true collaboration with participants and other family members. Consideration of the ethical issues caused them to agree that the project was not worth doing because of the danger of damaging personal relationships.

This section has focused your attention on the need to consider the impact of your research on any participants in it, particularly those who are young or vulnerable. It encourages you to consider the reasons for people consenting to research – perhaps to further a cause or to educate others about a condition, or even because they are your friends. Whatever the reason, you must be aware of the potential harm and discuss this with the participants. However, you cannot account for every possible scenario, and participants must also be made aware of the unknown impact arising from any aspect of the research, but most often during the wider dissemination of results, especially when other agencies such as news media become involved.

How Do My Values Influence the Research?

Jack Whitehead and Jean McNiff (2006) are both active researchers and academics in the field of action research. They actively promote and support their living theory approach to action research in the work of practitioners in education, health and other social contexts. If you are interested in how values enter the research field you will benefit from reading their texts and some of Jack Whitehead's students' theses found at the Action Research.net website (www.actionresearch.net/). Whitehead and McNiff (2006) make clear to readers of their text the values they have in relation to ontology (how we perceive ourselves in relation to our environment), epistemology (a theory of knowledge and how it becomes known), methodology (a theory of how we do things) and social purposes (what we want to achieve in the social world). People often use these words in relation to research and so Whitehead and McNiff express their values in relation to research practice. In general, they

- believe that people are capable of coming to know things in their own way
- affirm that knowledge exists in many different forms
- encourage others to develop a systematic approach and engage with the process of emergent understanding, sometimes leading to methodological inventiveness
- have a commitment to promoting equality and democratic practices through encouraging people to interrogate their assumptions.

59

These values influence the way they work with practitioners who are researching their own practice. They encourage them to think for themselves, to systematically seek knowledge in any form that is relevant to practice while at the same time questioning the normative assumptions within the workplace. They also highlight the idea that when practitioners notice something in their practice that is not working effectively it is often identifiable as the practitioners' values being denied, for example the nurse practitioner who values patient dignity but who sees that patient dignity is being compromised in practice every day on the hospital wards. Thus there are two important messages for you: that values will underpin your choice of research topic and that values will drive the methodological and ethical choices in conducting your research project. Acknowledging the potential impact of our values and if necessary challenging them and changing our viewpoint is an essential reflexive response to the research process.

Our values also affect the way we view the overall purpose of the research from the standpoint of the participants. For example, we may focus on enabling participants to advance their cause for political reasons. Bochner (2001) discusses the positivist view that emotionality distorts your judgement and reason. Using narrative to explore illness or any very personal situation could affect the researcher's ability to remain objective and present a balanced conclusion or recommendations from the research. Bochner proposes that illness narratives do not just reflect illness experience but *contribute* to the experience, thus creating a political and activist element to the research – perhaps seeking to improve the illness experience and change approaches to treatment through the research. He suggests that the empowerment of ill people through sharing their stories provides authenticity and identifies for the reader the real struggles of an ill person in society: the struggles between personal and cultural meaning. Ill persons want us to know that their suffering matters – a political goal. Their narratives require an active, reflexive reader who is willing to engage in dialogue with the writer and the story. Dialogicality is essential for the ill person's narrative to have value and meaning.

Ethically a reflexive, dialogic approach to co-construct meaning is sounder than distanced analysis from outside the situation. Writers of illness narratives hope that readers will learn from them, that is learn how to respond to illness and learn how to prepare for future personal illness. Squire (2008) found that people with HIV would not have engaged in the research if they did not think their stories would be heard and available to others for long-term use because they have invested much time and emotion into providing the stories. Bochner (2001) suggests that we should not think about facts in such narratives but consider the significance of events in a person's life. Life stories may contain facts but they are not determined by them. Narrative truth is a pragmatic truth; life stories may not convey the way things actually were but they are existential, a desire to seek meaning through the telling of the story.

60

This section's discussion focuses on the researcher valuing the participants' voices, enabling the participants to have a voice to further their cause. If you are aiming to engage in such research then your values might affect your ability to examine the data from a distanced perspective, to be reflexive and see alternative points of view and to balance the participants' responses against those of others in similar situations. However, co-constructing narratives with participants and accepting their stories as significant are probably more ethical than trying to apply a distanced, unconnected perspective.

Whose Voice is Being Heard?

As already identified, ethics permeates all aspects of the research, from initial ideas to the final reporting and wider dissemination. Attention to ethics occurs in every part of the inquiry. In using narrative in any aspect of the research process, researchers must address the ethical issues that it raises. Narrative provides a means to hear different people's voices, especially those of vulnerable people such as young children and those with special needs or illnesses. Although we can usually assure anonymity for participants when we tell their stories, this does not reduce the potential impact of harm if participants recognise elements of their own lives within the stories that make them feel vulnerable or question their capability. As highlighted in the previous section, some participants engage in the research specifically to make their voices heard and therefore they might not want the researcher to discuss critically the stories they present. It is possible to tell two research stories: that of the uncensored raw data from participants, which tells its own story, open to interpretation from others; and that of the researcher with the responsibility to present findings from a critical viewpoint.

Conflicts of interest are inevitable. This is a problem in any research involving people as participants. However, it is especially difficult when the researcher builds a relationship with the participant as confidante and then publishes the outcomes. Participants may view the research report as a critique of their practice, their lifestyle or their values. In fact, I have witnessed such a situation where one teacher researching in another's classroom reported exactly what she saw in a period of observation: a child wanted the teacher's attention and did not get it. The researching teacher made no criticism of it, but the fact that it was in the research report upset the observed teacher, even though everything was anonymous and nobody could identify her. She thought it showed her as an uncaring teacher who was ignoring a child. She suggested it was because the researcher did not understand the full situation, the events leading up to the teacher not responding immediately to the child, and the events after the observation. She objected to the event being reported in such a way that the child's experience was the only one considered. In this example the two teachers were colleagues, but the researcher was in a more senior position in

61

the school and had a very different set of values in her own teaching from those of her colleagues. Her research clearly focused on the story she wanted to tell, that of the children's experience in the classroom. The teacher participating in the research also wanted another story told, that of the teacher's experience. A stronger focus on ethics might have led to a more collaborative approach to the research and a more balanced representation of children's and teachers' intertwined lives.

William Smythe and Maureen Murray (2000) suggest that the main question is one of ownership – who owns the story and how it should be told. Both the participant and the researcher have valid claims to tell their story, so it is important to recognise the multiple interpretations, which is especially difficult when dealing with sensitive topics. Margot Ely (2007), who has a long-standing interest in human interactions and ethnographic methodologies, provides a chapter that contributes to an ongoing ethical debate about the emergence and representation of different voices. She describes and discusses a range of forms used in research writing, such as poetry, first-person stories, anecdotes and vignettes. She claims that these strengthen the readability, allowing us to hear different voices, and that researchers should pay attention to the voice that they choose to represent their research for others. Ely provides an example of a researcher using poetry to tell the participant's story, not the researcher's version of it. She raises the importance of situating the participant at the centre of the research, not the researcher.

Paul Gready (2008), whose main research interest is in human rights, expresses concern that researchers may provide the under-represented with a voice through research but that the participants often have little control over how it is represented and interpreted and to which audiences it is disseminated. The increase in globalised public communications raises questions about ownership and control; the local language, the context and the message that a narrative conveys become altered through use of different media spreading it to different cultural situations across the globe.

Through my own experience of reading research papers written about a specific culturally oriented context, I know that the authors seem to have difficulty in conveying the reality of the situational context. For example, I may read about a South African classroom but it might not give me a sense of 'being there' or of understanding the real issues for the participants in the research. I believe this is the fault of academia relying almost wholly on the written word for published academic works. However, when such works are presented in alternative media such as television broadcasts they become popularised, presented in such a way that the average British audience can watch and understand. This different medium focuses on real life and aims to provide a sense of 'being there', but in return might lose some of the academic rigour of argument and debate present in a written paper.

Some researchers (for example, Jack Whitehead) are beginning to bridge the media gap in presenting theses and papers in varied media, freely available on the internet, with the aim of providing a set of freely accessible rounded academic 'papers' that are grounded in the actual context explored. Whatever the mode of dissemination, some attention must be paid to the narrator's rights. Gready (2008) suggests that the capacity for different groups to analyse narratives from under-represented people, for example, must be retained while still acknowledging the individual narrator's right to tell their story and have it heard in a way they choose. The unpredictability of people's reactions to stories must be made clear to the storytellers; the way the story is interpreted by others in the public arena is out of the control of the researcher. Unfortunately, according to David Dunaway (2006), who researches through collecting oral histories, this can lead to narrators and the subjects of their stories taking legal action against the author of the research for misrepresentation. Dunaway has most likely gained knowledge of legalities related to ethics through his writing, including a biography of Pete Seeger, folk singer and social activist, his work on radio and his research about folk music revival. Researching celebrities brings home the importance of understanding the legalities.

One way to avoid legal action, and more importantly to ensure participants understand their involvement in the research, is to form collaborative partnerships in research where the purposes and responsibilities are shared by all involved. It seems obvious that a reflexive approach is a necessary part of the process since one ought to look at the research from a range of different perspectives and predict how others might react to it. Gready (2008) recommends a signed research contract about levels of control of materials, a range of media and writing styles, co-production of knowledge, and self-recognition for participants by naming their contributions in various research products. However, some influences do create difficulties even when the researcher takes such measures. Dunaway (2006) discusses the impact of memory on one's recollection of events. Each person involved in an event will have a different recollection of it anyway, as is often noted in eyewitness accounts. Time may exacerbate the problem, with differences between accounts becoming more obvious; or the story, having been told and shared between a set of individuals such as family members, becomes a collective account rather than a set of individual accounts. The memory often only allows recall of those events that have had a significant impact on a person, and sometimes it even gets facts wrong, even though the person has a perfect capacity for recall. This sometimes happens when someone makes a mistake in recalling the date of an event, for example a grandparent's year of birth. Even though we can retrace and correct the error, we may still retain the incorrect recalled date. The information in our memory therefore becomes flawed.

This section provides you with much to think about in developing and engaging in research with other people. You should consider how you plan to represent other people's voices at the research proposal stage, before you begin to ask people to participate and before any data are collected. Transparency in

ETHICS AND A NARRATIVE APPROACH

your approach to others is invaluable. That participants know the purpose of your research and what you intend to do with it only enhances its validity and reliability because it helps to ensure that the research story you tell is one that they would want people to know.

Roles, Relationships and Sensitivities

The previous section has highlighted the necessity to pay attention to the relationship between the researcher and the researched. This is particularly important when researching sensitive topics, as discussed by Margareta Hyden (2008). Her view is that the main sensitivity is the relationship between the researcher and the researched including consideration of cultural, contextual and personal views. Margareta's research interests are about men's violence towards women and children's vulnerability – areas in which she has much experience in using narrative and which make her aware of the different ways of perceiving sensitivities. She addresses the concepts of power and space, in particular the relational positioning of power and the influence of always focusing on the dark side of people's lives during interviewing. She makes a distinction between events that people consider sensitive or traumatic experiences, and sensitive topics that occur in discussion. Talking about a sensitive event, such as an act of violence, does not necessarily make it a sensitive topic for group discussion or research data, if the person subjected to the act of violence chooses to discuss it. This is an important distinction, which a researcher could employ within an ethical statement supporting a piece of research that some would consider unethical.

For example, I had a third-year student who was a secondary school mentor and bereavement counsellor who wanted to research children's bereavement experiences. A lecturer colleague who supervised this student's undergraduate research project did not want the student to follow her line of inquiry, asserting that it was unethical due to the potential harmful effects on the children. The lecturer's view was that bereavement in childhood was a sensitive topic that should not be researched by the student. But the student argued that having the children talk about a sensitive event, the bereavement of a close family member, was part of her usual practice, a healing process, and therefore her research into bereavement in childhood was justifiable. The student was very experienced in working with bereaved children and was following her usual practice of meeting with children to afford them opportunity to communicate about the event in any way they wished (or not). She provided a very persuasive ethical statement to justify her approach, with great consideration given to the relationship between her and the children and the potential positive outcomes that overcame the potential harm.

It is theoretically possible for any topic to become a sensitive one but we have some culturally defined norms – for example, intimate topics should not be discussed in public or with strangers but may be discussed with someone in a special relationship, such as a doctor. Hyden (2008) also highlights the importance of space and the importance of creating space for participants to talk on their own terms, which was what the student in the previous example aimed to do. Providing space is also empowering, as is the opportunity to talk about something other than the negative experiences one has had. The point being made by Hyden is that a researcher who is interviewing must be sensitive to the interviewee's response and demeanour, identify any potential harm within the content or nature of the talk, and redirect if necessary to an alternative way of seeing things, to talk about something positive and reframe one's perception of oneself. The challenge as an interviewer is to develop a range of skills for being aware and for redirecting attention, so reducing the potential harm of the interview and ensuring that it provides some good or has a healing effect.

Valerie Yow (2006) questions whether the interview process affects the researcher's reaction to the experience of hearing the interviewees' stories and perhaps not pursuing issues that might be controversial, for a variety of reasons. In 1993, Reissman noted that each researcher has his or her own perspectives, and sometimes a language specific to the situation, and therefore may modify the interviewee's story during the process of reporting. Czarniawaska (2004) also considered how the researcher may not remain impartial. A researcher listens selectively, remembers fragmentarily and recounts in a way that suits his or her purpose. However, the interviewee holds the power of knowledge that may or may not be elicited by the interview techniques. The question of researcher reactivity is important. Qualitative researchers have generally thought about reactivity in terms of the participant's reactions to the research context, not the researcher's reactions. However, within an interview situation where one is eliciting personal information, views and emotions that may or may not resonate with the researcher's personal experience there are bound to be different relationships with each interviewee.

In my own institutional research, despite keeping my interviewing techniques and broad questions to my colleagues the same, I inevitably responded differently to them. My approach was to elicit information and not to influence the response by asking controversial questions, nor to participate in creating controversy. My aim was to find out what different people understood, not to bring my own perspectives into play. This approach led to dilemmas in relation to the information shared with me, which was sometimes controversial and naturally drew me into questioning the controversy during my later analysis of materials. It also led to potential dilemmas related to the fact that this was insider research, leaving me feeling vulnerable if I delved too deeply into the controversy. Practitioner research involving colleagues has the potential to leave the researcher feeling very vulnerable, capturing data that could create difficulties between management and the workforce for example. If you plan to conduct such research in your own organisation then you must be sensitive to your own vulnerability, alongside that of your colleagues.

During a presentation to students, Anne-Marie Smith (2008), who is an experienced researcher of children's issues in international settings, discussed the ethical requirement for participants to understand the researcher role. The participants in her research – children and their families in Mexico – had little use for her as a researcher. Instead, she accepted several roles, and their associated voices, that supported the community:

- Teacher – *la maestra Ana* – the mothers asked me to formally help with school work, so that's what I did, including meetings with teachers (because of language problem of some mothers).
- Friend – developed a relationship, objectivity was not an option.
- Advocate – selling baskets (account books etc.), helping out – hospital visits.
- Foreigner – highlighted by run-in with the immigration authorities.
- Playmate – the 'unusual' adult, not married, no kids, running around with the children … a non-official adult. (Smith, 2008)

Thus to access the community it was essential to become all of these roles, pushing the role of researcher into the background but at the same time enabling the engagement in research that captured emotional, not just factual data. Relationships had to be fluid and flexible.

When you are researching in any social context, everybody should have a clear understanding of each other's roles and responsibilities. However, the previous paragraphs have demonstrated that the relationships between people are variable and can change according to context or over time. If you can adopt a sensitive approach to managing roles and relationships then you will be behaving ethically.

Data Collection

You will find that there is a description and fuller discussion of data collection methods in Chapter 6 along with some further mention of related ethical issues. For now, I would like to highlight the importance of thinking carefully about the type of questions you ask people in your research, and the ways in which you record observations.

Consider the following question aimed at eliciting people's attitudes towards different cultures, 'What would you do if a family from a different culture came to live next door?' Is the researcher assuming that the participant will respond to this question in a particular way? Is there an assumption that there is common understanding of the meaning of 'different culture'? There are many questions that you could raise about asking this particular interview question. Indeed, any interview question may be analysed to identify potential biases or influences that lead the participant into a particular way of thinking about an issue. The structure and presentation of questions require much thought to uphold the ethical tenets of respect and responsibility. Similarly, in writing down answers to questions, making observations and creating narratives about others from their data we should seek to reduce any potential harm through poor use of language and misrepresentation of observed events.

Data Storage

With reference to the collection and storage of biographical and autobiographical materials, the ethical issues arise from the harm that might occur should the materials be misappropriated or misused in some way. Some projects for collecting archive materials from the public have occurred in recent times, such as an exhibition at the Millennium Dome that invited visitors to say something about their life. Who knows what has happened to all of that information? More recently, academics are seeking to set up and maintain life story archives collected via the internet, for example The European Life Story Archive (www.valt.helsinki.fi/staff/jproos/lifestoryarchive.htm) which is not yet fully operational. In the UK, the Economical and Social Data Service (ESDS) Qualidata (www.esds.ac.uk/qualidata/) holds archives of many data sets available for open access and use. In times when people are becoming concerned about rights to privacy, the storing of personal data is subject to much scrutiny, and rightly so. What benefits might the researchers cite in support of the maintaining of a long-term collection – for the good of humankind, or for future generations – and how will they protect the participants from harm through misuse and misrepresentation? On a smaller scale, participants in small-scale projects related to their workplace, for example, ought to be aware of exactly how the information they provide will be stored, used and disseminated.

In your own research, you must follow data protection guidance and ensure that any personal information is protected from access by unauthorised persons. One specific area of concern is the way you keep any data during active research in a specific setting. For example, your research diary will hold observations and personal thoughts about other people and situations; thus you must keep your diary with you at all times and not leave it lying around. Another is how and where you store files on your computer. They need password protection if there is any likelihood of others accessing the files. If you apply some basic common sense in addition to the legal requirements, you should be able to maintain a secure system.

The Readership and Interpretive Anomalies

One of the concerns that students and their lecturers have is the potential damage caused by others close to the research reading the final reports. Researching one's workplace is challenging, especially if others are not keen to have its flaws made public. Years ago, I remember a tutor advising me to write one research account for my assessment with the full academic and practical debate about the workplace issues, and another for my workplace, tailored so that I did not upset specific people and destroy relationships. The notion of writing two different reports for the purpose of avoiding upset and maintaining good relations raises more ethical debate. However, the dilemma of reporting research outcomes to colleagues exists, and the drive to be transparent sometimes causes people to frame research questions that do not necessarily explore the exact issue they wish to explore. Alternatively, students will seek to alter their approach from one of researching 'on' to researching 'with' by engaging co-workers in a collaborative process. Thus the power relationships alter and the outcome and the written dissertation will reflect this. In any research, the issue of reinterpretation by the reader will always exist. It will be harmful if those who interpret it feel directly aggrieved, or apply their understanding of it to a similar situation with disastrous impact.

Atkinson (1990) expressed concern about the way that ethnographers weave their observations into extended accounts of social action. Ethnographers tend to provide a dual account, narrating the self-discovery of the researcher alongside or woven into the story of social action. In many accounts the researcher changes roles or positioning in relation to the research, for example from outsider to insider. As noted previously, Smith (2008) outlines the dilemmas faced by a researcher embedding herself into the social lives of others in a cultural setting different from her own, and identifies six different roles that she took on while engaging with the participants in her research. The mothers in the Mexican community asked her to help with teaching since this was an immediate need. Through working closely with the community she became their friend, helped with keeping accounts and hospital visits, played with the children. These alternative roles tended to push the role as researcher into the background, which could result in biased reporting. The ethical issues were not clear-cut and Smith questions our 'Western' academic need to work to clear protocols that will not necessarily suit the messy social situations we wish to explore. She was researching how children's rights policy translated into real practice with marginalised children – street and market working children. The research question was, 'What do children's rights mean to marginalised children in Oaxaca City?' In reality the notion of research meant little to the children and adults involved, and explaining the purpose of the research and the methods to them became redundant as part of an ethical code. Providing the participants with access to any documentation or accounts of dissemination meant very little. Thus it would be difficult to verify that such a research account was authentic in its representation. Through narrating her own experiences and asking difficult questions about research processes, Smith authenticates her own work. The dual narrative of researcher and researched can work well together.

The ethical consideration of textual representation becomes apparent when reading some ethnographic accounts. Atkinson (1990) provides an example of an account that is narrative in form, even in the presentation of data and analysis. He cites Festinger et al. (1964) who researched a cult that had predicted a cataclysmic happening on earth and presented it as a book *When Prophecy Fails* which had no theorising or commentary within it. Most ethnography embeds the observed events and participants' narratives within a framework of reference to relevant theoretical materials, while this one presented no evaluation or discussion. It did not attempt to authenticate the reported events. It seemed apparent that the researchers had entered the cult as members, undercover, in order to find out about it. The ethics of researching in such a covert way is questionable but, according to Atkinson, the way the author uses narrative to present the research is very effective.

Atkinson also cites another researcher, Krieger, the author of *Hip Capitalism* (1979), who focused on creating a transparent account through detailed chronological writing rather than on determining themes through which the data are categorised and written about without attention to the chronology. Krieger aimed to be faithful to the social world she wrote about – to create a world that the reader could recognise and become familiar with. She used an approach that paraphrased a range of different voices to create the story, rather than reporting the individuals' direct speech. It is a multivoiced approach mediated by the researcher. Atkinson notes that the focus on a chronological sequence through paraphrasing the different voices leads to some important temporal features being lost. Without an interpretive framework through themes, the reader has to develop a personal one.

Squire (2008) suggests that researchers must accept interpretive responsibility and consider whether to discuss analyses with participants. In some cases, it may seem sufficient to provide the participants with transcripts of their interviews; in others, it may be prudent to explain how the researcher interprets the transcript. The researcher might also ask the participant to comment, review the story the interview appears to be telling and rewrite it if necessary. This happens most often in long-term research where the researcher and participants revisit and review progress of a particular issue under scrutiny. Research conducted with a small number of participants over significant periods makes it more difficult for the researcher to retain complete privacy through anonymity in analysing and reporting, particularly within the small community of participants and their immediate contexts. In such situations, all participants must be responsible for the interpretations.

As a researcher, you cannot ignore the fact that everyone will interpret your work differently. What you must accept responsibility for is producing an account that does not lend itself to misinterpretation that others can mould into something they want it to say.

How Do I Write a Statement of Ethics?

Although various societies and research committees provide standard ethical statements to complete, there is a benefit to the researcher in reflecting on the ethics in a more personalised way. Mass produced ethical statements are often depersonalised tick lists that do not necessarily meet the specific needs of a project except in the broadest sense. When writing up a research report of any kind, one should attend to presenting an ethical statement that any reader may understand and that is project specific. Writing an ethical statement requires much thought about respect and responsibility towards the participants and the context of the research. Reference to relevant literature is essential to support the discussion, with a focus on respect and responsibility, potential benefits and reduction of harm.

A broad structure might be:

1 introduction: a discussion of your position in this research – the values, beliefs and assumptions you bring to it
2 the context of the research: a discussion of the potential impact to others in the context and/or the overall context itself
3 the participants: a discussion of the potential impact on participants in the research.

The ethical statement is not simply a declaration that permissions have been sought and granted but a thoughtful reflection on the real impact of the research on the lives of people and their situations. It is an integral part of your research project proposal and report.

Summary

In this chapter, I have acknowledged the existence of ethical principles and guidelines from a range of different sources. I have noted that institutions and societies expect people to complete ethical checklists alongside their research proposals, but I have also identified a need to make the consideration of ethics more strongly related to the context and nature of the research project.

Ethics is about balancing the principle of reducing harm with that of providing benefits to all involved. The process of ethical consideration relies on having respect for people and contexts alongside a sense of responsibility. Researchers must consider their role, the relationships they develop with people and how they plan to represent people's voices. These considerations are a continuous process throughout the research. A statement of ethics outlining context specific ethical decisions should be part of the proposal for the research and embedded within its final report. Ethical action should be evident in all aspects of the research process.

The application of the broad ethical tenets is relevant to each of the three core themes in this text. In autobiographical self-reflection you must seek to represent yourself in a way that is trustworthy. When using biographical data you have the responsibility to represent the participants in a way that they would wish, to their benefit. Representative constructions bring us into the realm of fiction, which some will describe as untruths and lacking trustworthiness, yet a representative construction can be a way of using data with the purpose of reducing harm to individuals while at the same time raising important issues.

As previously stated, there are no fixed rules. Ethics is a balancing act aimed at promoting benefits and reducing harm for all involved. It is your responsibility to provide the ethical justification for your research. You will base this on your knowledge of the context and people involved, and the requirements of any ethics committees or organisations that guide your work.

Suggested Reading

Birch, M. and Miller, T. (2002) 'Encouraging participation: ethics and responsibilities', in M. Mauthner, M. Birch, J. Jessop and T. Miller (eds), *Ethics in Qualitative Research*. London: Sage. pp. 91–106.

Campbell, A. and Groundwater-Smith, S. (eds) (2007) *An Ethical Approach to Practitioner Research: Dealing with Issues and Dilemmas in Action Research*. London: Routledge.

Smythe, W.E. and Murray, M.J. (2000) 'Owning the story: ethical considerations in narrative research', *Ethics & Behavior*, 10 (4): 311–36. In M. Nind, J. Rix, K. Sheehy and K. Simmons (eds) (2005), *Ethics and Research in Inclusive Education: Values into Practice*. London: RoutledgeFalmer. pp. 176–91.

5

NARRATIVE THINKING: PROVOKING AND SUSTAINING REFLECTIVE THOUGHT

CHAPTER OUTLINE

- Introduction
- Provoking reflective thinking through narrative

  - Reflective drawing, narrating and reflective conversations
  - An example from practice
  - Misha's story
  - Combining creative activities

- Sustaining reflective thinking in a reflective diary

  - Introducing the reflective diary
  - Justifying and using the reflective diary in research
  - Evaluating the diary
  - Examples of narrative data created from reflective diary entries

- Summary
- Suggested reading

Introduction

The core theme of autobiographical self-reflection is the focus of this chapter. Self-narration is an important way to extend and develop your skills of critical reflection and reflexivity as defined in Chapter 1. In Chapter 2 you read about various meanings of narrative. I describe narrative broadly to include any medium that supports the purposeful telling of a story such as poetry, photographs and drawings as narrative forms of communication. All of these creative acts or artefacts are vehicles for reflective activity, promoting reflection in, on and for action, thus forming a natural bridge between narrative and reflection. The flow can be either way: a narrative can stimulate reflective thought or reflective thinking can stimulate narrative production, a sort of symbiotic relationship. However, the connection between the two is not automatic; we cannot assume a connection, and stimulating reflective thought does not necessarily lead to critical reflection or engage people in reflexivity.

This chapter first discusses the ways in which different writers have connected narrative and reflection. It then helps you to answer two questions about using narrative:

- How does narrative provoke reflective thought?
- How may I develop reflective thinking through a reflective diary as a professional development tool and a research method, sustaining reflection and developing criticality and reflexivity?

I respond to both of these questions with reference to my own experiences with students, using narratives of my own practice and theirs.

Provoking Reflective Thinking Through Narrative

Richard Winter, Alyson Buck and Paula Sobiechowska (1999), Philip Chambers (2003) and Gillie Bolton (2006) each promote the use of narrative in reflecting in, on and for practice in slightly different ways. For example, Winter et al. describe the use of autobiography in creating a patchwork text to explore a professional role. A patchwork text begins with a story, often autobiographical, which is then used as a starting point for other pieces of writing which continue themes, explore contrasting views or open new avenues of thought. The final contribution to the patchwork will generally synthesise the key points of previous contributions to identify new theoretical insights or propose new professional practices. The purpose of the patchwork is to represent different voices, to construct the text from differing perspectives and not just to present the author's view of reality. Writing a patchwork text engages the author in a reflexive journey, challenging previously held values and beliefs.

The story-dialogue method promoted by Ron Labonte, Joan Feather and Marcia Hills (1999) also makes use of autobiography or biography, and relies on strong self-reflection and group reflection. Initially this was intended as a method of enabling professional development, but more recently Professor Jane Springett at a Northern group meeting of the Collaborative Action Research Network, a Study Day in 2008 promoted it as a means to research conceptions of 'Collaboration in action research'. The method engages a group of participants in generating and reflecting upon a story or set of stories around the same theme, with the intention to generate a new theoretical perspective and a change in practice.

The pioneers of engaging people in reflection through narratives intended their methods to support professional development. Their prime concern was one of improving practice by enabling practitioners to be more critically reflective through the creation and analysis of stories. However, over recent years people have begun to use these approaches as part of a research methodology for professional people to use. I have adopted the principal idea, that of provoking reflective thinking through narrative, and in the next section I describe and discuss some activities I have worked on with students. These include the use of drawing, narrating and reflective conversations as a means of identifying a problem within one's professional practice, or as a means of focusing a research project with examples from practice and reference to others.

I am not alone in thinking that there are connections between narrative and reflection as part of a research process. Dilma Maria de Mello (2007), who works in applied linguistics and has a research interest in art-based narrative research, agrees that the use of art in narrative inquiry is a powerful reflective stimulus. She describes art as a product of human creativity, and includes poetry, theatre, music, stories as analogy and photographs, that is a whole range of media. She explores the use of art as a stimulus to inquiry, in her own and others' research, demonstrating that the various art forms are useful for engaging people in reflective activity – a link that I too have made through working with my students. Cheryl Craig (2009) has also conducted long-term research with practitioners in a school and over time found that there is a very strong link between narrative inquiry and reflective practice. She suggests that for narrative inquiry to be effective the participants have to draw on their capacity to reflect. She discusses the capacity to reflect as being essential to the process of change in an organisation and therefore essential to action research methods. Her experience mirrors my own. Students became more able to embrace change when they had greater self-knowledge through development of critical self-reflection and reflexivity, which led to stronger understanding of the reasons for change.

Reflective drawing, narrating and reflective conversations

The importance of looking back over incidents in one's life experience is highlighted by Mason (1994) who identified that incidents can become more significant as connections are made between them, thus raising further questions to explore. Mason's thoughts about researching from the inside, which have guided my own professional development, underpin some of the work I have completed with students in using drawing and narrative to stimulate inquiry into their practice. My aim was to help them access their inner thoughts about their practices and seek to identify incidents that were significant and worthy of further research. Through such activity, one may develop an inner voice, have conversations with oneself and interrogate one's actions.

It is interesting that I am not alone in the way I try to provoke the students' reflective thinking; other academics are engaging in similar activities with their students. For example, Gwyneth Hughes focused on developing students as learners in higher education, enabling them to be self-reflective. In her paper on autobiographical writing Hughes (2009) writes about their development from what she calls self-indulgent writing to self-critical writing. In her research she used the idea of carrying a bag. Following ideas based on Schön (1984) participants explored their bags, looked at and described the contents in them, wrote a bag day story about the bag's journey, reflected on why the contents were in the bag for the journey, then underwent a second, deeper, more critical reflection on the practice of using the bag and its contents. She deliberately chose an everyday item, about which one could be creative, for exploring the process from initial description and storytelling to deeper critical reflection about the activity of using a bag. Hughes also used a shorter form of this exercise with trainee teachers to enable them to understand the process of critical reflection. The use of this exercise transferred readily into the professional setting, with students writing stories about their practice from different perspectives and teachers imagining they were students to write stories about the students' practice. Thus they moved into a phase of reflexivity, having a heightened awareness of the self and their relationships with others.

Hughes's research has some parallels with my own, both seeking to improve students' critical reflection on practice through creative activity. Her emphasis on the development of internal dialogue, in addition to dialogue with others, is an important one that not everyone readily engages with. Becoming self-reflective often takes practice, encouragement and time and belongs in a research domain where people and social contexts are the focus, not just within professional development activity. For example, Elliott (2005) notes that researchers develop reflexive ways of working when they begin to pay attention to the details in the narratives they collect and understand the role they play in shaping individual identities. The development of self-reflection about professional practice and then transferring this skill into research practice is one I used with students over a period of three academic years.

An example from practice

Following White's (2006) example, which I described briefly in Chapter 1, I introduced my students to drawing with the purpose of encouraging them to engage in the process of self-reflection before they started their research projects. One group of 34 part-time third-year undergraduate students, focusing on research projects to enhance their professional development, agreed to be part of a small research project 'Reflective drawing: identifying aspects for professional development' (Bold, 2008c). Previously these students had used the principles of reflective practice from Tony Ghaye and Kay Ghaye's (1998: 16–19) book to inform their development of critical reflective debate on e-forums (Bold, 2008a). Thus they had a reasonable grasp of the nature of reflection and critical reflection but they had not previously used drawings to support their reflective thinking.

Ghaye and Ghaye's (1998) 10 principles of reflective practice require practitioners to engage in reflective conversations that may disturb their professional identity and help them recognise and understand their existing conceptual frameworks, a reflexive engagement. They should interrogate their own and other people's experiences by asking probing questions, viewing situations problematically and exploring taken-for-granted values, beliefs and assumptions. Their social interactions will help them take a reflective turn, to create new knowledge and understandings in a new conceptual framework that informs future practice. I sought to use these principles in setting up the class activity for this research. Students engaged in the following activities.

1   *Each student completed a reflective drawing.* The following questions were kept in mind:
    - How do I view myself as a reflective practitioner?
    - How do I perceive myself in my role?
    - What challenges do I face?

    This was the initial representation. Thinking how to represent one's world to another through drawing requires much reflective thought and creativity (but not necessarily artistic skill). The act of drawing is often intuitive, thinking on one's feet, representing practice as one perceives it at that point in time, putting everything into the picture that has an impact on practice, baring emotions, possibly hiding hurtful events, championing successes. Initially the idea of drawing was scary and caused anxiety amongst some students about their ability to draw, but I overcame this by sharing some personal drawings and by emphasising that it was the process that was important rather than product. The story within the drawing was what mattered.

2   *Each student wrote the story depicted in his/her drawing (and kept this secret).* The story writing process helped students to firm up the conceptualisation of the issues, practices and potential dilemmas depicted in their pictures. It supported the identification of emotional responses, provided reasons for thoughts and actions, and enabled an acknowledgement of the self as central to the story. I viewed this activity as students engaging in reflective conversations with themselves, asking what the purpose of specific elements of the picture were about and clarifying for themselves what they intended to tell through the picture.

3   *Pairs interpreted each other's pictures to confirm and to elicit further thoughts.* Each student in turn told their partner the story they saw in their partner's picture. This act of interpretation required imagination, empathy and development of language appropriate to the context. The interpreter may have seen things that the artist did not expect, or intend to represent. Often, this stage merged into the next as the pairs began to reflect on each other's drawing.

4   *Pairs engaged in reflective conversations and identification of needs.* The pair of students engaged in a reflective conversation, central to developing the ability to reflect critically. Each of the pair questioned the values, beliefs and assumptions evident, or not, within the pictures and the practice stories they told. Through the reflective conversation, each of the pair began to identify the real dilemmas of practice and the potential areas of interest for research into practice. Thus the conversations were forward looking too. I noticed that while students engaged in reflective conversations they listened attentively and valued each other's ideas. It was clearly an appreciative approach to identifying a relevant area of inquiry into practice. In the next section, I describe and discuss one student's response to this activity.

Misha was a teaching assistant and third-year undergraduate student completing her final research project. Her drawing in Figure 5.1 illustrates the power of drawing in demonstrating her multifaceted role and the various tensions that existed within and outside it.

Figure 5.1   Misha's multifaceted role

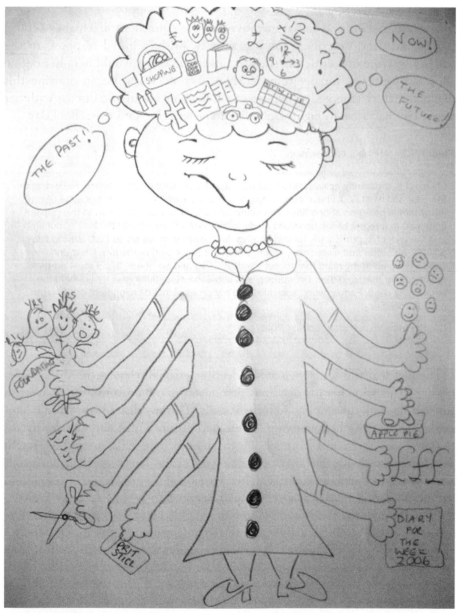

(Misha, unpublished drawing, 2006)

77

To an outsider, the drawing seems to contain too many different facets. It combines past, present and future, personal and professional. It could be difficult to make sense of it, to tell Misha's story from it. Yet its imagery is very illuminating, Misha is clearly a very busy person, with many things to do and think about. The mouth, part smile and part frown, perhaps indicates mixed feelings. The cloud in the head clearly indicates that many thoughts are held in there that relate to Misha's position now in relation to the past and the future. Do the closed eyes represent a need to focus and reflect on these things, to make some decisions?

Misha's drawing and initial narrative are the equivalent of Hughes (2009) looking into and describing the bag activity. Misha's initial response to the activity was one of scepticism; she was unsure how this would help her define an area of interest for her research. However, once she began drawing this detailed picture emerged, providing much to think about and discuss with her peers. Her narrative in Figure 5.2 tells of concerns beyond the school day.

Figure 5.2 Misha's concerns

> My mind is constantly active, thinking of the past, the present and the future. Reflecting on the past and what could have been in the present is sometimes jumbled because of the many things going on at one time. The future tends to be a worry and can at this present time lead to a regret of my decisions made in the past. I'm constantly thinking about time and the lack of it, particularly for my working day. Lessons move on so fast, leaving little time for reflection and discussion, which is then left to the end of the day. Children I support pop up in my mind throughout the day! … so-and-so needs this, I must prepare resources for that, and then I'm working with someone else, putting all thoughts to the back of my head. Family, work, social life and my professional development are always coming together.
>
> (Misha, unpublished story activity, 2006)

The fact that the activity elicited a deeply personal response in Misha, causing her to question her life decisions, demonstrates the power of the drawing in supporting and developing reflective skills. During discussion, Misha later explained that she had given up a well-paid job in which she had significant responsibility, to become a much lower paid teaching assistant and engage in part-time study, with the aim of becoming a teacher. There were many reasons why she might feel disgruntled with her decision at that point in her course and her work. The key issue at work initially seemed to be one of time management, managing the various responsibilities she had, but Misha went away and continued to develop her drawing in the spaces around it, becoming reflexive about the relationships at work. Eventually she identified a specific concern she had about the way a specific initiative in school would develop under her leadership. Thus she began with the drawing opening up all the concerns about the various demands at work, home and university, but she ended with a clearly focused project exploring a positive change in her working experience.

Like Misha, you might benefit from the experience of using drawing combined with storying and reflective conversations to develop your skills of critical reflection and reflexivity. Mello (2007) promotes the use of drawing since it offers you an opportunity to be creative and have an aesthetic experience that can unleash powerful emotions and deeper understanding of situations, as we have seen in Misha's case.

McIntosh (2008) has also explored the use of imagery and writing as part of professional development in health care education. The process he followed differs from my own research since his students wrote or used images to create a personal descriptive story first; this was followed by a period of personal analysis through creating images or in writing before the students shared the story with peers to develop a more critical analysis. McIntosh describes this as forming a *reflective reproduction* grounded in the learners' understanding of the situation. Most important is the opportunity the use of images provides to construct, through active imagination, a strong personal analysis of a situation or event. I agree with McIntosh's suggestion that images open up the dialogue and opportunity for reflexivity because of the different internal processing involved, and I agree that we need further exploration into the use of images and writing in developing self-reflection. Drawing and story writing unleash the reflective self in preparation for developing the skill of reflexivity, essential for transformational professional learning, as Sarah Deaver and Garrett McAuliffe (2009) also found when using visual journals with art therapy and counselling students. I find, as they do, that combining the drawings with narrating and reflective conversations focuses people on exploring their situations problematically, using critical reflection, rather than blindly accepting the status quo. The imagery in the drawing combined with narrative writing is the reflective reproduction that stimulates further critique of the professional scene they depict. I encourage them to question, challenge and problematise the policies that guide their work.

My strong beliefs lead me to work in these ways with students, but not everyone likes drawing, while others find it helpful to start their thought processes. Two third-year undergraduate students, Mel and Paula, give different views:

> I do not particularly find them [drawings] useful for reflection. I have always found expressive drawing difficult and find that I have to simplify my thoughts due to my inadequacies with drawing. I find it much easier to write my reflections. (Mel, unpublished feedback, 2006)

> I found it [drawing] very helpful to aid reflection about my work. At first, I did not know what to draw, but once I began to draw, many ideas came to me. Drawing is particularly helpful if the person is creative ... I was able to portray my feelings in the picture, something I normally struggle to admit to myself, as well as speak or write about. I was able to delve deep within my reflective thoughts, which allowed me to see my strengths and weaknesses. The drawing did not help me to formulate a research project, however, it did help me to start thinking about an area that I was interested in once I started to write about it. (Paula, unpublished feedback, 2006)

REFLECTIVE THOUGHT

Mel's comments are highly relevant: people who have difficulty drawing, or lack confidence in their ability to draw, might not find this approach to unleashing their reflective capacity as useful as other methods. This is why using a combination of drawing (or other creative activity) along with writing is so important. Ideally, a range of different methods and media should be available to the students so that they can choose their medium for reflective expression. Paula's view is interesting because she did find the picture useful in exploring her strengths and weaknesses, and her feelings about her work, but still had difficulty linking this to thinking about and developing a research project. Part of this might have been because she was reluctant to research actively some of the strengths and weaknesses identified in the drawing. Self-reflection can be quite unsettling and lead one to retreat to a stance that is more comfortable. In Paula's case, this stance might have been one of developing research that focused mainly on the children she worked with, rather than her own practice.

From my small project and other activities conducted at conference presentations, I believe that it is ideal to have a combination of three ways of communicating – drawing (or other creative act such as modelling or dramatising), written or spoken narration and conversing with others – to unleash the reflective thinking and develop it into more critical and reflexive ways of examining practice. Despite reluctance from some people, the act of drawing serves to 'bring memory forward' – an important feature of the reflective process highlighted by Strong-Wilson (2006), who also supports the notion of discussion as part of the reflective process. Making memory a central feature in developing reflective capacity makes sense, since students engaging in work or other practical experiences will draw on their memories of past events in order to make sense of current and future events in their daily practice.

Several people have expressed a fear of unearthing suppressed feelings during these activities, which can lead to disengagement. Many professionals probably find themselves in this position, where a student, patient or colleague has been unwilling to engage in an activity for personal and emotional reasons. Such a situation will prompt reflecting-in-action from you, and there is no single way to respond. Any activity that requires looking back at oneself in the company of others can make one feel very vulnerable, yet this is often the best way to overcome whatever fear exists.

At this point you might wish to reflect back on how you would respond to different creative activities and whether they would lead you to a more critically reflective and reflexive stance than you currently have. Developing your ability for self-reflection is a fundamental requirement for professional practice, and for academic learning and research. Becoming strongly self-reflective and developing a strong self-concept, with the ability for self-authorship as identified by Baxter Magolda (2000), enable you to examine differing points of view with a higher level of criticality, to compare other perspectives with one's own developing ideas and to make balanced judgements on the available information.

Sustaining Reflective Thinking in a Reflective Diary

In this section of the chapter, I explore the narrative use of the reflective diary as a tool for sustained self-reflection. According to Elliott (2005), narrative provides a sense of self and the development of a personal identity. Elliott suggests that autobiographical narratives do not merely represent individual identity but constitute it. Thus in writing an autobiography one is laying bare one's identity to others. The reflective diary must therefore have similar properties, and students I have worked with have often commented that using the diary makes them feel vulnerable, sharing their inner thoughts about issues and events that they dare not vocalise or publish elsewhere. This extract from a second-year undergraduate student, Brenda, towards the end of her course, illustrates the potential dilemmas:

> Today I feel like a little cog in a big machine. Sometimes the big cogs grind me down whilst at other times I'm left to spin idly on my own. There are days when I feel the machine runs smoothly, we connect and run well together. I get the chance to talk to different teachers as we go about our work supporting the children's learning. Then there are others when I feel useless, forgotten. (Brenda, student reflective diary entry, 2006)

Such openness can create ethical challenges in research, particularly when it involves relationships between people. Brenda would not necessarily want others in her workplace to see such reflections.

A research diary's capacity to support sustained self-reflection and promote critical reflection and reflexivity should justify its role as a valid research method. Few published research reports appear to use the reflective diary explicitly as research evidence, so the majority of the materials I draw upon are from second- and third-year part-time undergraduate students who work in educational settings. They are not representative of a range of disciplines or different levels of study, but the transferability of the ideas and the reasoning that sustains those ideas is evident.

Introducing the reflective diary

During our 2004–5 teaching programme, in the first module of the second year, we introduced the students to reflective diaries as a means to explore their practice in using their guidance and counselling skills with children in schools, over a period of one week. We began with a limited conception of the way students might structure the diary. The reason for this was our focus on encouraging students to distinguish between descriptive writing and reflective writing. They found the latter more challenging to achieve. At first, many of the students expressed concerns about how to use the diary, but it did become a useful tool to support their reflective skills, as I describe in Erin's story from an article written in 2006:

My diary gradually supported my reflections as I began to return to previous entries, crossing things out and writing something new on another page. I drew arrows from one point to another, wrote in the margins and corners, filling all spaces with my ideas. It began to look untidy and did not follow a logical format for the reader, but it was good that I learned about looking back at events and realising that I later had different views of the same events. (Bold, 2006b: 21)

Erin wrote an excellent diary showing progressive development in her skills to reflect critically. It contained observations and dialogue from class, additional thoughts after reflecting on the event, references to reading, and identification of counselling skills used in her practice. It was a working document, and as such became very untidy and difficult for a reader to follow, but it demonstrated her ability to reflect critically on her practice.

One of Erin's peers, Rosemary, also kept an excellent diary for this early stage in the course, presented in a much more structured and neat format, from which I reproduce one double page in Figure 5.3.

Figure 5.3 Rosemary's diary, day 2

Day 2	Reflection
John came to breakfast club looking very tired and pale this morning. He is very short tempered with his younger sister, telling her to 'leave him alone' when she wants to sit next to him at the table.	I have been thinking about how to help John. Found information about how divorce can affect boys more than girls. I discussed his worries with the class teacher and the head teacher. They, in return, have given info on family background. John's teacher promises to speak with his mum re his worries. She is unable to visit during my working hours.
When I ask if he is OK he just nods, avoiding eye contact with his peers and members of staff. I approach him in the playground at break but he says he does not want to talk.	I am worried about John's self-esteem and when I research low self-esteem John fits nearly every category. To try to counteract his negative feelings about himself I try to boost his confidence through praise. I remind him that he is capable of doing better work in class, but also that he has not got into any arguments today.
Although John does not get into any trouble he completes his class work in a hurried, uncaring manner, putting very little effort into it.	D. Plummer (2001) Helping Children to Build Self-Esteem, London: JKP
(Rosemary, reflective diary entries, 2005)	

For a part-time undergraduate student at the start of the second year, the level of self-reflection emerging here is as expected. Rosemary expresses worries and concerns based on her observations and she makes use of reading to develop her knowledge and understanding of the child's situation. The structure of having one page for observations and the opposite page for reflections was useful in some ways, the aim being to try to separate out descriptive writing from reflective writing. However, it was not always helpful: at times three pages of reflections would emerge from one page of observations. Moreover, as is seen in this extract, the reflections and their associated practical actions are developmental, building on previous observations and reflections. This cumulative effect appears in the mention of 'divorce' and 'John's worries', which were not evident in these day 2 observations but had been noted in day 1 observations. The double page structure can be too rigid and is perhaps unnecessary, but some people might find it helpful to begin with. What is clear from Rosemary's diary is the potential it offers for sustaining reflection over a period, continuing to reflect on observations from the previous day and building up over a week, culminating in Rosemary reflecting very clearly on her role as a mentor in school. She challenges the view that her role should simply be one of guide, when situations such as John's require knowledge and application of counselling skills.

This introduction to using a reflective diary was the beginning of the self-reflective journey for Erin and Rosemary. Many diaries or journals kept by practising professionals and by students on a range of different courses become logs of events rather than reflective responses to those events, which is why I prefer to use the term 'reflective diary' with the specific aim of ensuring that the text has reflection embedded in it. Its purpose is to focus you on developing a self-narrative for deeper exploration of emerging issues in your practice.

A final example, in Figure 5.4, of how you might organise a diary comes from Chris, a second-year undergraduate completing his final module. Chris organised his diary into a structure that helped him to keep track of different types of information by using different colours. For him and several other students, this was a very effective way of keeping track of their reflections and their impact on practice because of their research.

Figure 5.4   Chris explains his diary

The diary therefore will provide an opportunity for myself as an educational practitioner to think about my experiences critically in terms of what I do and why. The diary will be organised into colour-coded sections signifying a breakdown of the various elements of the direct phonics session. Black will represent the titles of each section of the direct phonics session, blue will denote events, purple will signify self-reflection and/or reflection with colleagues on events, and red will symbolise opportunities and further action for future development.

(Chris, unpublished report, 2006)

These early attempts to use diaries sought to find a way that students could manage the diary both at work, in their professional roles in schools, and at university, in their roles as students. Hence we started with a handwritten notebook that students could carry around and use almost anywhere. One of the greatest challenges for students was finding *time* to complete the diary, which was why we recommended keeping it for a short but purposeful period, such as an evaluation of practice over one week, or a small action research project. The other was that of *motivation* to complete it after a difficult session with the children or colleagues when there were other more pressing demands on time. We did not explore, at that time, the opportunities to use various different technologies for diary development, or the emerging facilities on the virtual learning systems at the university, or the internet. Initially, our aim was to keep a measure of consistency and to reduce disadvantage because, at that time, not all students had access to the full range of alternative electronic resources. Since then, successive groups of students have identified and used different ways to keep diaries, by using electronic voice recorders, video recorders, blogging, and contributions to e-forums and wikis. Some also built reflective diaries into their regular record keeping practices in school.

Our students came from different cultural backgrounds and we did not identify any differences in responses to the diary because of culture. However, we did find that students whom we had previously identified as showing a stronger level of critical reflection generally responded to using diaries more effectively in the first instance. All students showed development in their reflective thinking over a period of diary use, and over successive periods of diary use, to differing levels depending on their starting point.

Justifying and using the reflective diary in research

In generic research methods texts, a journal or diary is rarely included as a means of collecting primary data. Instead, it is sometimes suggested as something that the researcher keeps as an *aide-mémoire* to the process, to support other data rather than provide a data set of its own. In any research into our social worlds, the diary may become data. In some research it can be the most informative document, providing the backbone for all other materials gathered – primary and secondary data – from the field.

Ethnographers often keep diaries or field notes and these will record their thoughts about the situation in addition to the observations. The ethnographer's diary or field notes not only provide an account of events but support the development of their wisdom about those events through engaging reflexively with the various data (Atkinson, 1990). Ethnographers generally produce reports that involve twin narrative texts, sometimes separate and sometimes integrated. One narrative contains the observed social events and the second narrative is about developing understanding of the author; these support and strengthen the representative function of the ethnographic account. A reflective diary will be crucial to developing this twin narrative, which might also be a suitable way of reporting any narrative research. Indeed, many reflective diaries contain an unedited version of the twin narrative from the beginning, as we saw in Rosemary's diary.

Clandinin and Connelly's (2000) brief description of a teacher's research journal demonstrates the features I would expect to see in a reflective diary – detailed notes and reflections on the experience. They acknowledge that the teachers in their research sample would have considered the journal not necessarily as part of the research data but more as a place in which to record reflections that are more personal and to support the process. Reflective diaries can be time consuming, and if they are not part of the data contributing to a project, many people will be reluctant to use them. I found that students who use a reflective diary as central to their projects find them a most valuable, flexible resource that allows them to develop as practitioners and researchers.

Evaluating the diary

In 2006, I asked 56 second-year students to evaluate their use of the reflective diary against Ghaye and Ghaye's (1998) 10 principles of reflective practice to identify how the diaries had helped them sustain reflective thinking. Some connections they made are presented in Figure 5.5. These are just examples. I have no doubt that the different principles could be identified in many different ways.

The 10 principles of reflective practice were a useful way to focus the students' minds on the nature of reflection and they helped to ensure that the diaries developed in a way that promoted critical reflection and reflexivity. The examples chosen from a number of responses to the activity demonstrate that these second-year students, early in the academic year, were very thoughtful about practice. Later in the academic year, the students used the diary more as a research method than as a professional development tool. In their final research reports, they evaluated their diaries as a research method.

In the conclusion to her research report, Leanne provided a particularly useful evaluation of her methods (Figure 5.6), highlighting the diary as an essential research method for her project. Leanne clearly found that the reflective diary was essential to her research, both as a professional tool to support the changes in her work and as data to provide evidence of the processes and reflective thinking behind those changes. It allowed her emotions to emerge – her feeling of amazement at the children's response to the library and her negative feelings about working with books in school. It also demonstrated that transference of attitude towards similar experiences from one context to

Figure 5.5   The 10 principles in practice

Principles (in brief)	Examples of reflective practice evident in the diaries, identified by students
Reflective conversations that have the potential to disturb our professional identity	After meeting with the educational welfare officer about improving school attendance I asked myself, 'Do I do enough to promote a positive environment for learning?' I always thought I did but now I have doubts.
Interrogation of experiences	I questioned why lower attaining children working at Year 3 level had to endure Year 4 tests. Everyone knows they will fail to achieve and it will damage their self-esteem.
Returning to look at taken-for-granted values – a 'reflective turn'	After the teacher spent forty minutes with the children sat on the carpet (too long) followed by ten minutes to complete two activities (too short, normal practice that I had previously accepted), I questioned whether this was a constructive approach to learning.
Accounting for ourselves, describing and explaining	I decided not to run after the child along the corridor because he might think I am chasing him and run.
Viewing professional situations problematically	I considered the best way to remove a difficult child from hiding and messing in the toilets. Is it best to physically remove him, as sometimes I have had to do, or should I just wait until he responds to my polite requests to come out? If I continue to move him physically, which I can do if he is causing harm to others with his behaviour, I feel that I have failed and I might eventually have legal problems with his parents. Behaviour charts and other modification strategies are not working. I think the team needs to discuss the problem with his parents.
A process of knowledge creation	After questioning our approach to coping with the child's very difficult behaviour we realised we did not have enough understanding of the way different methods could work. We invited the local authority team to update our knowledge on behaviour management strategies. We now have an agreed range of strategies to apply and we support each other more effectively now that we understand the processes better.
Critical thinking – asking probing and challenging questions	I questioned my approach to comforting a particular child who had just been put into foster care. Could I approach this in a better way rather than relying on my 'gut' instincts?
Decoding the symbolic landscape, e.g. the 'school culture'	The expectations of staff are not always clear-cut and there have been disputes about the rise in the number of learners with different beliefs to those of the Christian ethos of the school. Some believe it is affecting learning.
Linking theory and practice creatively	The active games I read about in the behaviour management book from the library have had a positive impact on the children's behaviour. They break up the long lessons and help children concentrate.
Socially constructed ways of knowing	Meeting with outside agencies about a child's behaviour management has made me question my approach and changed my opinion on the strategies used in school.

86

Figure 5.6 Leanne's evaluation of the diary as a research method

My reflective diary showed some interesting points that I do not believe would have been identified without the use of this method of data collection. My initial entries focused around my own inhibitions as to whether the children would respond positively to any of the sessions I had planned and, if not, then how would I proceed. Having decided on my research focus I discussed this with the children and undertook a group interview in a small room used for group work. The children seemed relaxed answering the questions and freely supplied me with information about their strong dislike on books. Within my diary, I had commented that I felt the children were able to relax more and answer the questions more truthfully because they were in a small comfortable group away from children that may ridicule their ability and with just me undertaking the interview.

Reflecting on parental involvement of the identified children, I had commented on feeling great sadness at the low level of support they were receiving at home and noted that with far greater effort made from parents to support their children's reading, they may progress much faster. I had also remarked that this was a particularly poignant issue for me as it was such a contrast to my own experiences.

By reflecting on my later diary entries, I could see areas that I felt had been very successful, such as the library visit. I had identified mixed feelings on the days leading up to the visit as the children's reactions had not been very positive; however, I was pleasantly surprised by their reactions. The following extract of my diary illustrates this point:

Wow, the children's faces just lit up – this makes all the work so worthwhile. They all had their minds set on how boring the library would be and now they're actually darting from one area of the library to another, motioning for me to have a look at how many games and DVDs there are to borrow. I can't believe how much they're enjoying this and it makes part of me want to scream at their parents to make more of an effort and venture to the library with their children! The children look happier than I've ever seen them when surrounded by books. All I've done is arranging for these four children to come to the library with the teacher and myself but I feel good.

Equally, my diary was evidence of the negative feelings that I had about certain aspects of my practice such as the low motivation the children expressed towards some of the school books that I had selected for our group work. I commented that 'they didn't even look at the books but just decided they didn't want to read them without even giving them a go'. This issue was further developed within my diary following a discussion with the class teacher about her narrative. She asked me to include a comment about her reservations about the children transferring their increasing motivation into the classroom. I felt that maybe I was being unrealistic and remarked that 'perhaps I was naive in my belief that by raising the children's motivation outside of the classroom this would automatically be transferred into the classroom'. Overall, my diary proved to be a useful tool in aiding my self-reflection and provided me with much information to allow me to enhance my practice.

(Leanne, unpublished report, 2006)

another does not necessarily occur; this was an important learning point for Leanne, but is also important for educational development in general. Leanne began to become more reflexive in her approach, able to view events from another point of view, that of the children.

The benefits of reflective conversations are also evident in Leanne's diary example. Having another viewpoint from a close colleague is often very helpful when aiming to change practice. Indeed, reflective diaries do not have to be individual. A collaborative approach to keeping a reflective diary is particularly helpful in action research where a group of people are researching their practice together. Julie, another second-year undergraduate, created a collaborative diary with her teacher to help her focus on her practice. This brave step opens up reflective activity to others, who may make critical comment on your actions and behaviours. Figure 5.7 has an extract from Julie's research report, explaining how and why the collaborative diary was used in preference to a personal diary.

Figure 5.7   Julie and the teacher collaborate

The class teacher has made contributions to the diary to compare different situations and responses, interactively commenting on each other's reflections, with the main focus upon how I have implemented the sanctions and rewards strategy and looking at my educative influence upon the pupils. In a discussion before embarking on the creation of the research diary, myself and the teacher discussed the specific focus and made each other aware of the explicit instruction regarding the information needed to be included in the diary, so as not to make a tedious task of separating relevant information when analysing later on. I opted to use a collaborative diary rather than a personal reflective diary as I wanted the class teacher's support and guidance to advise me on how I could improve my practice. The collaborative research helped us to identify problems and brainstorm solutions, assess and evaluate the efficacy of the intervention and rethink until goals had been achieved.

(Julie, unpublished report, 2006)

Julie's approach ensured that her closest colleague was fully involved in systematic review of practice. There is clear consideration of the need to analyse data later, resulting in them taking a focused approach to diary use and thus avoiding an overload of materials that may not be useful for the research. The danger in being so focused is that other interesting reflections will not find their way into the diary, and there may be less likelihood of reflections related to personal feelings and attitudes related to the issue. To work collaboratively in this way requires a significant amount of trust to allow the openness required for purposeful self and mutual critique.

Teaching assistant Suzie's project in 2006 provides strong justification for the use of a reflective diary as a tool to improve practice and thus support the analysis of the research data. The extract in Figure 5.8 highlights many important features but most important is that of a vehicle for self-reflection. In this reflective diary, *engagement with* and *interpretation of* responses to professional practice were both essential for development of critical reflection. It was a place for expressing opinions, identifying emotions, making contradictory statements and posing challenging questions, and for the development of debate with one's own and other people's ideas.

Figure 5.8 Suzie justifies her reflective diary

Not only has my reflective diary been an important tool in helping me develop my research project, but also the research process itself has been important for the development of my reflective practice. Reflection is a complex business (Ghaye et al., 1996, cited in Ghaye and Ghaye, 1998) and I have tried to ensure that my diary is not just a recording of events but an important tool for reflection by including my thoughts, feelings and questions at particular dates and times. A diary is usually written under the immediate influence of an experience (Bogdan and Biklen, 1982). My diary entries included statements such as 'the noise from the instruments was loud, wonderful and uplifting!' 'Reminder to myself, write a list next time! I'm annoyed with myself for not checking the room was free, I feel so unorganised!', therefore showing how particularly effective the diary is in capturing my moods and personal thoughts at that precise time. My reflective diary provided me with important points to refer to and reflect upon throughout the research project. I was able to return to it whenever needed, add to it and make notes about the entries if needed. Having no constraints upon structure and grammar, the diary meant that my feelings, thoughts and ideas could flow smoothly. I believe, as Campbell, McNamara and Gilroy (2004) suggest, that the stage at which you write things down is when you begin to firm your ideas and ask yourself challenging questions about the methodology. My diary allowed me not only to reflect upon any weaknesses or things that had gone wrong during the project but also to identify my strengths and build upon them.

References

Bogdan, R. and Biklen, S.K. (1982) *Qualitative Research for Education: An Introduction to Theory and Methods*. Boston, MA: Allyn and Bacon.
Campbell, A., McNamara, O. and Gilroy, P. (2004) *Practitioner Research and Professional Development in Education*. London: Paul Chapman.
Ghaye, A. and Ghaye, K. (1998) *Teaching and Learning Through Critical Reflective Practice*. London: David Fulton.
Ghaye, T., Dennis, D. and Cuthbert, D. (1996) *Reflections on Learning*. Newcastle-upon-Tyne: Pentaxion Ltd.

(Suzie, unpublished report, 2006)

Examples of narrative data created from reflective diary entries

You might find the final examples particularly helpful if you are interested in the power of the narrative to illuminate issues for further reflection.

Figure 5.9 shows how another second-year student, Alison, used her diary entries to support the analysis of her work with a particular child, Timothy. The story she created from her diary entries (only part is reproduced here) reminded her of her first encounter with five-year-old Timothy. It is detailed and descriptive in nature, which demonstrates the depth of thought Alison was giving to her work with this child. She then adds another level of reflection, thinking about the possible causes of the child's behaviour and linking this to something she had read. Through writing a narrative of her first encounter with a child, Alison entered into a critique of her own and others' practice that was a starting point for practice development and further evaluative research.

REFLECTIVE THOUGHT

Figure 5.9 My initial response to Timothy

My first encounter with Timothy had been at the beginning of the school year when I was asked to work with a group of children outside the classroom. I can't remember what we were doing precisely, only that it included cutting and sticking. Timothy quite clearly did not want to engage in the activity and began to swipe worksheets, scissors and glue sticks off the table. The other children picked them off the floor, only to have them immediately knocked off the table again. Timothy slouched in his seat, refusing to do any work or pick up the things he had knocked off the table. I began by trying to reason with him, and when this had no effect I told him off and instructed the other children to leave the various items on the floor and chose to ignore his actions. Timothy was now running out of things to knock off the table as they were already on the floor or the children had a vice-like grip on the utensils they were using. He had also lost my attention as I was supporting the other children. In response, he left his chair; I naively thought this a step in the right direction as he bent down to reach one of the glue sticks. He picked it up and flung it down the corridor whilst, almost simultaneously, kicking another. Now, he had my full attention. I stood and using every inch of body language I could muster told him to go and pick up the glue sticks. Defiantly, he stood arms wrapped around his small chest and shrieked 'NO!!' As the head teacher's room is on the same corridor, it was less than a nanosecond before he was sat outside her door. The previously defiant Timothy was now a tearful subdued five-year-old child. Returning to complete the task with the rest of the now wide-eyed group of children, I began to realise why the class teacher was so insistent that I support this activity outside the classroom.

Reflections

From this first narrative, it is clear that there is no empathy shown towards the learner and it is evident that there is little knowledge of the learner's difficulties on my part as a practitioner. Timothy had no warning that he would be working outside his classroom or with another adult; he was unprepared for a change in his routine and frustrated, and giving Timothy my full attention would have been to the detriment of the other children I was working with. He displayed a lack of understanding of social conduct towards his work, his peers or myself and appeared disobedient. I had obviously formed an opinion of him and, as I was expecting him to be disruptive, this could have been the reason for his behaviour. Children gain knowledge of themselves from other people and their attitudes towards them. Learners who experience negative, hostile and rejecting behaviour will respond in a similar fashion, displaying aggression and ultimately low self esteem (Wade and Moore, 1993).

Reference

Wade, B. and Moore, M. (1993) *Experiencing Special Education: What Young People with Special Educational Needs Can Tell Us*. Buckingham: Open University Press.

(Alison, unpublished report, 2006)

Another student, Ruth, chose an alternative approach and used her reflective diary entries to create a narrative based on her own and other teaching assistants' observations and reflections. Ruth's purpose was to create a scene that is common in the teaching assistants' experience, as a baseline for changing practice. When reading Figure 5.10 you may wish to visualise yourself as a teaching assistant sitting in a classroom, waiting to fulfil an individualised support role with particular pupils but having to listen to the main lesson input from the teacher.

Figure 5.10 What the teaching assistant thought

I sat staring into space bored, smiling at anyone who would make eye contact with me. A quick sly look to the clock reveals, a painful twenty minutes had passed, oh, hell's teeth, it feels like an hour at least. I sat disappointed, the teacher's rich silky voice lamenting in the air. The classroom was nice and warm. The rain was dancing on the portable cabin roof. Rivers ran down the window panes chasing each other, competing for the window ledge. Thankfully, I was distracted now, and it was all so mesmerising. I had not long eaten my lunch so I was feeling relaxed. The lads opposite me had been playing football in the rain and so their blazers sat steaming on the radiators. Oh no! The windows are misting up I thought. No more races. Another sly look reveals that only another three minutes had managed to escape. I sat trying not to slouch in my chair. I could see him out the corner of my eye and hear his voice being carried through the now warm moist air. Oh, hold on, it was getting animated now, so I looked over and he was pointing to the PowerPoint presentation that he had 'Blue Petered' the night before. 'Oh' I thought 'is that all, for a minute there I thought it was something interesting.' I looked around, I saw a sea of blank expressions. I wanted to stand up and shout, I wanted to scream, look around you man, look at us all in this classroom, look into our eyes they are dead, for God's sake can't you see you are flogging a dead horse, cut your losses now before the badly behaved gremlin rears its ugly head. I can see him over there, and there, and yes he is sitting next to me now. Oh God, I know what's coming next.

(Ruth, unpublished report, 2006)

Ruth had identified some difficult issues faced by teaching assistants who were often in the position of observing teacher and pupil behaviour in their secondary school. The narrative highlights how undervalued the teaching assistants felt; they were just an additional part of the furniture. The narrative is a useful and evocative way to collate many similar thoughts and provide an opportunity to examine practice with a view to change. Because of this research Ruth and her co-workers were able to meet the management and explain how they thought they could support the young people in their care much more effectively. It was a creative and effective approach to researching a challenging issue, with a very useful practical outcome.

In this chapter, you have seen examples of diary entries and examples of students' justifications for their use in research. You have also seen how the diary entries may form a longer narrative illustrating and analysing some events in practice. These examples do not exhaust the possibilities, but by sharing them I hope you can see the potential to explore the use of a reflective diary in a way that suits your purpose.

Summary

Chapter 5 has focused on the role of autobiographical narrative in provoking and sustaining reflective thought. The strength of using imagery and writing to evoke self-reflection has been demonstrated using examples from practice. The techniques are useful in teaching and in research; they are dual purpose and ideally suited to action research or practitioner research in any profession or discipline that engages within a social context. The reflective diary (journal, notebook, blog etc.), which may be in either handwritten or electronic form (written, drawn or oral) to suit any cultural situation or context, may be used in a variety of ways to elicit strong self-reflective and reflexive responses. Diaries provide a combined opportunity for professional development and data collection. The examples provided illustrate the many strengths of the reflective diary but also illustrate possible weaknesses, such as the potential to be too emotional leading to a lack of criticality, as in Leanne's example. Keeping a diary can also lead to a damaging level of personal critique, thus making authors feel vulnerable. However, you might also view this as a strength, an opportunity to evaluate practice and address weaknesses.

The final example moves into the realms of reconstruction, using diary entries combined with other observation to re-create a scene for the reader to understand the baseline of the research, and to promote further critical analysis of that professional position.

Suggested Reading

Etherington, K. (2004) *Becoming a Reflexive Researcher: Using Ourselves in Research*. London: Jessica Kingsley.

Josselson, R. (2007) 'The ethical attitude in narrative research: principles and practicalities', in D.J. Clandinin (ed.), *Handbook of Narrative Inquiry: Mapping a Methodology*. London: Sage. pp. 537–66.

Winter, R., Buck, A. and Sobiechowska, P. (1999) *Professional Experience and the Investigative Imagination: the Art of Reflective Writing*. London: Routledge. Chapter 3 describes the patchwork text and provides several examples of these.

6

COLLECTING NARRATIVE DATA

Introduction

The core theme of biographical data is the focus of this chapter. Its main purpose is to provide you with examples and discussion of different approaches to narrative data collection. While it provides some discussion of how to design some elements of the data collection process, it does not intend to provide you with a comprehensive guide to the various qualitative techniques that a number of methodology texts already explain. Instead, it focuses your attention on a range of different narrative examples from the internet, from my own research activity and from researchers who are interested in understanding the meaning of the social contexts they explore.

I will consider the collection of biographical data, using some of the following range of activities and media: collecting oral narrative through interviews, written narratives, observations, drawings, photographs, video and audio.

Fitness for Purpose

A key idea in this book is to establish the use of research methods that are fit for purpose. Sometimes on reading others' research I wonder what would have been the result if they had chosen different methods. For example, Cortazzi (1993) cites research that used interviews to collect teachers' stories about awkward parents. The knowledge gained from this research was that teachers tend to pass through the same stages in dealing with awkward parents. If the purpose of the research is to find out the stages of interaction between parents and teachers, then the interviews have been fit for purpose. If the purpose is to examine and make changes in practice, then the interviews have not been fit for purpose. If I relate these findings to the teachers' practice, they will not necessarily inform teachers how to change, if change is necessary. Alternatively, a self-reflective account (autobiographical) from the teacher, a story from an observer of the teacher's practice (biographical) and a discussion with a more experienced colleague about alternative approaches might have a greater impact on practice while retaining the rigour of the research process.

Another example comes from Padam Simkhada (2008) who used in-depth life history interviews with 42 participants to find out about sexually trafficked girls in Nepal. This was the best method to obtain the details required since current information about these girls is limited in scope. For example, there are few numerical data other than estimates given by various anti-trafficking agencies in unpublished reports. Most reports focus on discussing policy issues rather than empirical research. Accessing participants is a problem because of the illegal nature of the trade, and the girls can only be identified once they have become known to health workers, the judicial system and aid organisations. The purpose of Simkhada's research was to consider how to develop anti-trafficking interventions at various levels. The in-depth interviews were the most effective way to investigate the detailed issues faced by these girls, in particular that trafficking often occurs through social networks, members of the family and friends. Another was that they were often transported by undercover means, for example by the local carpet factory. Both of these represent opportunities for intervention at the community level in preventing trafficking occurring, despite the fact that there are many social, cultural, financial and legal problems to deal with.

At all stages in the research process, you should keep the notion of fitness for purpose at the forefront of your thinking. Dougherty (2006) suggests paying attention to the mode of analysis when deciding on data collection methods. Too often people collect data without considering possible modes of analysis, leaving the researcher floundering in a sea of narratives and other materials, not knowing what to do with them. In Chapter 3 I raised the importance of developing a conceptual framework about the methodology and analysis of the research, showing that you understand the advantages and disadvantages of different data collection and analytical methods based on academic literature. Chapter 7 will provide further discussion about analytical methods with some examples from practice.

In Chapter 2 I introduced you to the characteristics of stories elicited through interviews, ethnographic accounts, conversation and dialogue as narratives. In the next sections of this chapter I will focus on some different data collection methods. I do not intend to provide comprehensive guidance that may be found in research methods texts, but will instead focus on a few specific examples to examine their potential for collecting narrative data.

Collecting Narratives Through Interviews With Individuals and Groups

In many research methods texts, interviews are described in three broad categories: structured, semi-structured and unstructured. Briefly described:

1 Structured interviews usually have a set of questions that are fixed and the interviewer will not waver from them. The responses might be in the form of short answers that are easily collated, or they might elicit longer, narrative-like answers that require retrospective qualitative analysis.
2 Semi-structured interviews usually have a set of questions that guide the interview rather than dictate its direction. Some core questions enable the interviewer to maintain focus, while allowing the flexibility to ask further questions to clarify points raised by the interviewee. Thus, some analysis and interpretation begins as the interview progresses, with the interviewer making decisions about the content and nature of the interview as it progresses. Some researchers have developed the use of semi-structured interviews into specific methods to elicit narrative data.
3 Unstructured interviews usually have no set agenda. The interviewer may set up a meeting with the intention of having an informal conversation with the interviewee. Some researchers would also include in this category the ad hoc conversations they have with people as they occur during the course of a project. These unstructured situations can lead to narrative data collection.

Some methods texts also include specific types of interviews such as the collection of life history, or interviewing with focus groups. Some will focus specifically on interviewing to elicit narrative responses. This section includes reference to several texts that you might find useful in further developing your understanding of interviews as a method for eliciting narratives.

First, I consider why you might choose to interview rather than use another research method, and I provide examples from different projects in addition to identifying various published research papers that you might find interesting and useful in establishing a methodology. In most cases the process is semi-structured in some way. The interviewer has some idea of what they will ask and perhaps a set of questions to guide the process, but also has the mind-set of allowing the interviewee(s) to tell their story, not just provide set pieces of information.

My own view of the structured interview is that it can sometimes be equivalent to an oral questionnaire. Most students who originally consider using structured interviews usually change them into semi-structured because this will suit their research purpose more effectively. However, there are occasions where a more structured interview might be desirable, when you want responses to questions on a particular theme. One second-year undergraduate student chose to use structured interviews for two reasons. First, she wanted specific answers to questions about her own teaching practice, in particular whether her support had provided the help that these children needed. The second reason was that her initial choice, a questionnaire, would not have been suitable for the children she had as participants. The structured interview was her best choice.

Asking the children 'How did you find my teaching today?' might elicit responses such as the shrug of a shoulder and 'It was OK.' The encouragement to engage in an open narrative might not work with the particular children involved. Asking a series of set questions enabled her to focus their thoughts and helped her to improve her practice. Her questions were similar to these:

1   What did you like best about today's lesson?
2   What did you find easy to do?
3   What did you find difficult?
4   How did I help you today?

Although these questions were quite focused they allowed some opportunity for open dialogue and for the children to express other thoughts; for example, asking a child what they like best in a lesson will often provoke a response about what they disliked too. The student used the answers to these questions to create short narratives about the children's responses to her change of practice. These narratives provided realistic accounts of practice that the student could use to inform her work.

Thus you can identify the need to fit not only the method but the specific details within the method (the interview questions) to the purpose of the research. The next section discusses one specific purpose for interviewing, that of eliciting a life history – especially useful when researching the impact of past lived experience on the current and future life of interviewees.

Life history and experience-centred narratives

Researchers of social contexts usually choose to interview people when they are interested in their lives: their experiences, their emotions and their thoughts about their situation. Life history research is an excellent example of using an interview for purposeful inquiry to find out the impact of past events on people's lives. Researchers can compare the life histories they collect with the political and social activity at the time. It is a way of examining the impact of political and social change on people's lives. Jack Dougherty, whose 1999 article is included in Atkinson and Delamont (2006), acknowledges that oral histories were often viewed by 'scientific' researchers as anecdotal evidence, which could change if the story was told on a different day, and therefore without much substance. However, the oral history, and indeed the process of elicitation, collection and analysis, is bound to reflect the current historical perspective at that time. Thus the oral history offers an alternative way to learn about what we think we know as the historical facts.

For example, the political processes in 1930s North America are documented in various factual reports and other accounts of the time. We can compare the documental and reported evidence with the life histories collected during that period, which aimed to represent life in all the states. You can see examples from these on the Federal Writers' Project website (http://memory.loc.gov/wpaintro/wpahome.html) such as this one for Mr Garavelli, an Italian stone-cutter. The researcher asked, 'Is the dust bad in the stonesheds?', and the question elicited this short narrative from Mr Garavelli:

> It was tough for everybody in the early days. Lots of stonecutters die from the silica. Now they've got new and better equipment; they've all got to use the suctions. It helps a lot; but it ain't perfect. Men still die. You bet your life my kid don't go to work in no stoneshed. Silica, that's what kills them. Everybody who stays in granite, it gets ... I don't get so much of it myself. Maybe I'm smart. I don't make so much money, but I don't get so much silica. In my end of the shed there ain't so much dust. I can laugh at the damn granite because it can't touch me. That's me. I ain't got no money, but I ain't got no silica either. My end of the shed don't get so much dust. It's like a knife, you know, that silica. Like a knife in your chest. (Mr Garavelli, 1930s)

Such a narrative, about a small but very important aspect of Mr Garavelli's life, tells us much about the way he thought of his experiences and their influence on his thoughts about the future, elicited from one question. A great corpus of materials such as this enables us to understand social history from a very personal point of view. Without research interviews and rigorous data collection, such stories would not exist for future generations to learn from.

Life histories can be very useful in researching social change, patients' health care, workplace relationships, and important life changes such as conversion to a particular religion. In some cultures the history of the community is passed down through stories of ancestors and their lives. Storytelling in this way is a common human trait; we might even tell a stranger we sit next to on a bus a significant part of our life history simply because we feel the need for it to be told.

Eliciting narratives is not always easy, but Jaber Gubrium and James Holstein provide some very useful ways to start interviews that will elicit life history narratives using examples from their own and others' research, including this very straightforward approach: 'Everyone has a life story. Why don't you tell me about your life?' (2009: 45). They also highlight how extended stories emerge in conversations quite naturally, sometimes because the storyteller wants someone to hear the story. Tom Wengraf (2001) devised a detailed method to follow for people who wished to elicit longer stories from their interviewees: 'the biographic-narrative interpretive method' (BNIM). This method focuses on narrative experiences and, because it asks for retrospective stories followed by a series of interviews over time that may focus on particular incidents in the interviewee's life story, it is particularly suited to longitudinal research. The focus is not the story text, but the person behind the story. For example, it could be used in researching illness by first asking the person about their life story until they became ill and the impact the illness had. The interviewer will listen to and read the story to identify points of interest within it. These will be the interviewer's choice – something that sparks their interest about the impact of illness on the interviewee. There will then be a second interview to ask the interviewee about these points if interest. Wengraf suggests that the materials may then be analysed and interpreted in several ways according to the purpose of the research project.

Life history research usually focuses on the experiences of the people involved. Life historians are usually interested in the events that have happened in people's lives and the way in which people have responded to these events within a particular context. The following paragraphs focus on Squire's (2008) *experience-centred narratives*, which she separates from *event-centred narratives* that focus solely on sets of events in the narrative and ignore the context, as in Labov and Waletzky's (1997) methods (both types were introduced with some discussion in Chapter 2). Life histories are usually experience-centred narratives. Often such narratives are elicited in oral form, but Squire (2008) also mentions experiential images and writing, which I will discuss later.

If your focus is on collecting life stories, or biographies, the sample of interviewees will usually be small. It may be opportunistic, relying on people being interested and willing participants, and the interviewing may be a lengthy process, as in life history research. If your focus is on exploring themes, the sample might be larger and interviews shorter. Most of the interviewing will be semi-structured and the amount of intervention from you will depend on what you want to gain from the activity. If you are interested in the interviewee's story as a whole, you will probably intervene little except maybe to prompt the story to continue if there is a long pause. If you are interested in a particular theme then you will develop some focused questions to ask, based on the interviewee's initial response. If you ask 'What type of question is best to elicit a story?', it is often an open-ended one.

In what may be described as experience-centred narrative research with colleagues during a study conducted in 2007–8, I asked the questions in Figure 6.1. My overall research question was: 'What are the characteristics of a teaching-led, research-informed university?' The context was my workplace, a new university at which many changes were taking place, the greatest being to build up

Figure 6.1 Semi-structured interview prompt sheet

What does 'teaching led' mean to you?
What does 'research informed' mean?
What is the relationship between research and teaching?
This may emerge through the previous questions.
What are your thoughts about the varied terminology used in different institutional documents:

- scholarship
- research
- research-informed teaching
- scholarly activity?

What happens in practice? How does this affect your department or subject area?
What do you understand by the phrase 'liberal arts inspired'?
How do these phrases inform the strategic vision of the university? (*if appropriate*)
Will the university remain a teaching-led, research-informed institution?

(Bold, 2008, unpublished research questions)

strengths in both research and teaching. The interviewees were invited and volunteered colleagues from different role levels and different departments. My main research method was that of a semi-structured interview. Interviews were limited to a maximum of 30 minutes because I did not want to take too much of my colleagues' time and because I believed that in that period I would collect the data I wanted. I was interested in what my colleagues thought were the main characteristics of a teaching-led, research-informed university, as described in the mission statement. I expected them to tell me something of their experiences as they shared their understanding of the language used in the mission statement. I used a digital recorder to maintain an accurate record of the dialogue and made occasional handwritten notes.

The first two questions prompted many of the interviewees to speak at length about their practices, especially if they were involved in teaching and research activity. The example in Figure 6.2 illustrates how these two broad questions offered an opportunity for interviewees to express their thoughts freely. The subsequent questions were often answered without me having to ask them. I wanted to hear not just the institutional rhetoric, but their real thoughts and feelings about their situation.

In the interviews my questions were often answered with very lengthy responses, as in Figure 6.2. The answer to the first question often merged naturally with the content of the second question, that is most interviewees naturally linked teaching and research. I think that this was partly because they knew the purpose of my research, and partly because the link between the two concepts of teaching and research had become part of the institutional drive at that time and therefore important to the interviewees.

Figure 6.2   Interview with a colleague

Interviewer:	And so my first question is, what does 'teaching led' mean to you?
Interviewee:	[Pause] Teaching led, it means that the most important thing that we do is we teach the students. My understanding, if I heard that out of context, about another university, and they said they were teaching led, research informed, which is I suppose what I should be answering is that the most important thing is teaching, I would be questioning why they said teaching led rather than learning led, but that's another issue, and research informed means that research is an important part of how we come to be teaching led, and an important part of what we teach, but doesn't drive it.
Interviewer:	Okay, so, in a way you've made the link there between the research-informed part, with the teaching led, I mean, do you see research informed being more than informing teaching?
Interviewee:	[Pause] The research informed is … a number of things come to mind. First of all, if you take a subject, like, take it out of the education world, and put into say computing or history; research informed naturally means that what we're teaching to most of the students, sorry, some of the students, is going to be at the cutting edge of research, so that what is currently being researched, the students will get some of that, that is going to inform it. But that's not the be-all and end-all of it; research informed means that there is research about teaching and learning in the subject area which is an important part of how we teach and the rationale for teaching, and in fact how we choose which of the bits of research at the cutting edge we actually give to students, because not all of them are going to be relevant. So, to my mind that latter bit, which is about research into how we teach and what we teach, is far more important than the research that we give to students as the content.
Interviewer:	Right, okay, so we're moving on in a sense to looking at that relationship between research and teaching, so at the moment you've said that we could use research as part of our content, and in some subjects that would be particularly important to be working at the cutting edge …
Interviewee:	But in other subjects, I'm sorry to interrupt, in other subjects, and, if I say mathematics for example, in mathematics it's horrendously difficult to get students working at the cutting edge of the discipline, I mean it's actually very difficult in a lot of areas of computing as well, not impossible, but actually very difficult.
Interviewer:	Because it's so far in advance.
Interviewee:	Absolutely, yes, I mean, you're not just talking at master's level in some cases, you really are talking several levels above that.

(Bold, 2008, unpublished research questions)

What I hope to show by this extract is that a semi-structured interview can lead to narrative-like responses, depending on the nature and purpose of the research. In addition, the semi-structured interview provides the flexibility to detour from the planned course of action and follow a line of interest, while at the same time keeping the original focus and purpose of the research in mind; it therefore allows for new insights to emerge. In the example in Figure 6.2 the interviewee provided some specific thoughts about practice that did not emerge in other responses, namely the challenge of using cutting edge research in particular subjects. At the same time this interview contained themes in common with others, for example that teaching rather than research was the most important activity for teaching staff. Both types of outcome are important in the analysis when applying it to organisational practice. The interviewee in Figure 6.2 had a desire to tell me things from experience, things that the interviewee chose to share and wanted me to hear. However, I might have encouraged a stronger narrative response if I had asked, 'Tell me about your experience of working in a teaching-led, research-informed university', and this could also have provided data to answer my research question. I chose not to use this approach because I wanted a clearer focus on the actual terminology.

Gubrium and Holstein (2009) also discuss how stories are activated by researchers through open or more subtle invitation and suggest that the researcher should pay attention to the dialogue used since it might affect the way a story is told. They have identified that storytellers and listeners create linkages between stories and experiences that support meaning making. They emphasise the need to be analytical at all stages. I noticed the impact of my responses when interviewing; finding the balance between providing a non-committal encouragement to talk and a desire to engage fully in the debate that the interviewee is encouraging is quite challenging. There is no simple answer. Whether you are new to interviewing or very experienced, each interview will present its own challenges, but I do think that greater experience helps you to be more analytical during the process, as Gubrium and Holstein suggest.

The impact of the interviewer

Interviewers might have difficulty in encouraging interviewees to give an open response to questions, perhaps because their goal is to answer a specific research question rather than to encourage a broader focus on issues that interest the interviewee about the subject in question. Novice interviewers might have some difficulty in working in such a flexible way since great skill is required to determine when an intervention will be necessary and helpful, without prejudicing the response. In the previous paragraphs is evidence that the researcher is bound to have some influence on the outcomes of the research, through the way that questions are asked or through the choices made for lines of questioning. This is inevitable and one of the reasons why you should establish your own position in the research from the beginning. You may have noticed that I entered my research with an interest in language and how people understood the language being used in the university. My questions reflect that interest and so my influence on the interview began at the point I created the questions. During analysis you may be able to account for these influences – whether they are helpful or not, whether they skew the data towards a particular perspective or whether they help to create a constructive dialogue to support understanding.

Focus group interviews are becoming more common in educational research, where researchers will work with a group of teachers to discuss practice in a collaborative project or teachers will work with a group of children instead of conducting individual interviews. One of the benefits of the group is that it provides support to those who feel overawed by an individual interview, but the group might also suppress someone's contribution. I could argue that the group is more realistic, more like practice. Children are more used to working in groups and teachers are used to collaborating about their practice. The reality is that the focus group is no more authentic than the individual interview, especially if it is an exercise purely for the research project. Individual identities become lost as the group moves towards consensus of opinion rather than dispute. Interviewing through a focus group can therefore lead to a loss of the unique case, the one that stands out as different from others.

Despite the potential weaknesses, dialogue from focus groups can create a collective narrative and this can be useful when researching some sensitive issues. However, Mike Crang and Ian Cook (2007) emphasise that the researcher's role is not straightforward. If you try to enter an established group, such as a local carers' support network, you can change the usual relationships within the group. Focus groups might be more effective when set up specifically as a new group for the purpose of professional development and/or the research project. In this way you are always part of the group and will not disturb previously established dynamics. Such groups may be most effective when they operate in a similar way to other established practices within a particular context, for example following the routines of a regular staff meeting in a workplace setting, although the nature of the meeting will be different and will require some introduction. The questions and discussions that ensue will be similar to those in any semi-structured interview except that the responses will be multivoiced.

Valerie Yow (2006), who has trained researchers in interviewing techniques, also discussed the impact of research on the researcher and looked back at how a researcher might prepare and forewarn themselves about the influences they bring to the research. She cites several writers who have focused on the need for researchers to have self-awareness and to ask questions that support this discovery: for example, asking how one's demeanour, personality and expectancies might shape the outcome. Yow provides an interesting example in which her expectations of the interview outcome affected her response to the interview process and the data collected. She had expected the interviewee to give details about her personal life and its impact on her work as an author, but the interviewee provided other information about events without any indication of the inner emotional aspects of her life. This caused Yow to put the data to one side and to take no interest in them for a period of three months before returning to their analysis.

Gender relationships, age and emotional factors all play a part in the nature of the interaction between interviewer and interviewee. Transference of feelings may occur in either direction, and they may be at an unconscious level but still have an impact on the interaction. For example, an interviewee may tell a story about an emotional event that reminds the interviewer of a similar event in his or her own experience. This could distract the interviewer, leading to personal thoughts and a loss of focus, or it could lead to a greater shared understanding of such events.

There are obvious external contextual influences such as the place in which the interview occurs and how the interviewer records it: by writing, word processing, audio or video recording. In my research I approached participants in a way that allowed them to decide where to meet: my office, theirs or an alternative space. My aim was for them to be comfortable in the surroundings, and I did not mind where I interviewed since I was used to working in other people's spaces or shared spaces for a number of years. However, I did notice that there was potential for my ideology to influence the way I reacted to the interviewees' responses and the way I followed up the discussion, although I think I was able to minimise this by trying to be impartial and not seeming to agree or disagree with their views.

Yow (2006) discusses the impact of ideology and maintains that the researcher can sometimes be too involved in the topic, too immersed in it to listen to the interviewee without their story evoking a strong emotional response. When interviewing someone with a similar ideology it is easier to empathise and be part of the same community. According to Yow, showing empathy, whether one feels it or not, will help the interview process and support the elicitation of more comprehensive responses. She suggests that we should ask ourselves a set of questions, listed in Figure 6.3, about our impact on the research process, with particular reference to the interview.

In this figure I have changed Yow's original order of questions; I considered her fourth question to be the most important from the beginning of any research project, so I placed it first. Her order emerged from reflecting back on the interview situation and her responses to the narrator, the interviewee, and so this is where she placed the emphasis. For some researchers, asking oneself about feelings towards the narrator may occur during the interview, when noticing a reaction to something the interviewee has done or said. Others might address such thoughts about the interviewee during the analysis, when it becomes clear from the transcript that certain feelings are evident. Yow's (2006) list is an excellent reminder that awareness of the

Figure 6.3 Questions to ask ourselves

---

1   Why am I doing the project in the first place?
2   How does my ideology affect this process? What group outside the process am I identifying with?

The answers to these should be in your mind from the start.

3   What am I feeling about this narrator?
4   What similarities and differences impinge on this interpersonal situation?

Awareness of these during the interview may help maintain an open mind.

5   In selecting topics and questions, what alternatives might I have taken? Why didn't I choose these?
6   What other possible interpretations are there? Why did I reject them?

These questions may come forward when analysing the data.

7   What are the effects on me as I go about this research? How are my reactions impinging on the research?

This final question might include the cumulative effects of different interviews over time.

(adapted from Yow, 2006: 228, my italics)

---

relationship between interviewer and interviewee is crucial to the research process. She is reminding us to take a reflexive stance on our research methods. I have added some comments about where we might raise the questions during the research process. Her message is clear: you must acknowledge the relationship that you develop with the person you are interviewing. The longer you interview them, the more likely you are to develop strong feelings about them and their story.

Whether interviewing or observing in social contexts, various options for the researcher to record information exist, including notes (hand or electronic), audio, video, still photography and drawing. Each has some advantages and disadvantages; these are identified in Figure 6.4, but this is indicative rather than a comprehensive list.

When choosing a medium for recording your data, consider the impact on the participants. A discreetly placed digital recorder will capture much valuable information in an interview situation with little impact on the interviewee, while physical note taking can be very distracting to both interviewer and interviewee. I have included these brief notes here to highlight the need to give clear thought to these processes, which all have an impact on the researcher and the participants involved. In many situations, a combination of methods of recording data will be most effective. Various research methodology texts will provide much more detail than here.

Figure 6.4 Comparison of methods for recording field data

Researcher's recording method	Advantages	Disadvantages
Notes (handwritten on paper or electronic tablet)	A small notebook may be carried and used discreetly at any time.	Interviewees or other participants become aware of the note taking. Impossible to note everything while actively observing and listening. Confidentiality risk if left out for others to read, or if lost.
Notes (word processed)	Word-processed records are easy to save, manage and use. Confidentiality maintained by password protection.	Unless one has speed and the ability to touch type, this method can result in missing substantial amounts of data. It usually requires a table, or at least somewhere to sit.
Audio recording	Digital recording machines are very discreet. Recordings may be kept electronically and revisited. Researcher recordings may be transcribed using a voice recognition system.	Not very useful in noisy settings. Sometimes people do not speak clearly, even in interviews. Detail of the visual context is not evident. Transcription takes hours. Possible confidentiality risk until file protected on computer.
Video recording	Ensures that some contextual information is evident. Captures gesture, facial expression, body language, and demeanour. May be watched by others for analysis and revisited by researcher at any time.	Not very useful in noisy settings where specific dialogue is important. May be distracting to participants. Transcription takes hours. Confidentiality risk.
Still photography	Useful for recording contextual information, facial expression etc. Useful as a storyboard.	Not as useful for capturing the whole story. Confidentiality risk. Possible health and safety risks in some contexts if used by participants.
Drawing	Useful if skilled in capturing relevant information in this medium. Useful as snapshots, parts of the story.	Not as useful for capturing the whole story.

Collecting Written Narratives

Although the interview is an important way to collect such data, it is not the only way, and this section considers some other approaches in designing a narrative inquiry. How the information is collected depends on the context, the purpose of the research and the proposed mode of analysis. Some choices are made not because they provide the best fit but because they are the most economic in time or cost, or because access to people and contexts is predetermined and inflexible. Many constraints on the ideal research situation exist. Each individual project design rests with the researcher(s) and seeks to make best use of all resources available within an ethical framework.

Instead of interviewing and hoping to elicit a narrative, or alternatively re-creating a narrative based on the interview, why not ask people to provide a written narrative about a situation? You can allow for a range of different ways to record narratives. For example, in Therese Riley and Penelope Hawe's (2005) research into health care promotion, the community health officers – the participants in their research – kept field diaries. They used different media: handwritten, electronic, e-mails or combinations. Riley and Hawe had to be flexible to suit the context of the field conditions at the time. Asking for written narratives is especially useful in action research projects when you would like others to contribute data relating to your practice. You might look for two different types of narrative, one the autobiographical narrative written in a diary or log and the other a biographical account. The autobiographical diary used by participants rather than yourself can provide useful insights into the impact of your work, or their own personal or professional development. For example, clients can keep a record of their interactions with you, the impact of your work with them and the way they have changed through this interaction. The biographical account might be written by a colleague who works alongside you. It could be an account of your everyday practice and their working relationship with you, or it might be a written account of an event that they observe specifically for the purpose of the research.

The extract from a discussion with Mark, an MA student, in Figure 6.5 is an example of where writing a story was the best way for a teacher colleague to provide a lesson observation. (Examples of observational narratives are given in the next section of this chapter.) Mark was able to respond very well to his colleague's reluctance to provide an observation. Many people do not like to be in the position of making judgements on their colleagues' practice and most have had little training to help them observe effectively. By suggesting that his colleague writes a descriptive story of events, Mark alleviates her concern that she might become judgemental, while still gathering relevant data that they can use later to have a professional conversation. However, there might have been other underlying concerns in her reluctance to observe that were not clear to Mark and that he is unlikely to discover. For example, she might already have formed a negative judgemental opinion of his work. Despite the potential challenges in involving colleagues in this way, the narratives they produce can be very illuminating.

Figure 6.5 Writing stories about practice

> I asked my colleague to observe a lesson and give me feedback. She hadn't observed lessons in any formal way before and didn't want to be judgemental as if it was a peer review, or Ofsted. Instead, I asked her to write a story of the lesson as she saw it. She liked this idea. She wrote a description of the events in my lesson, and we discussed practice as equals, rather than her providing me with feedback as if I was a trainee on school experience.
>
> (Mark, informal discussion, 2007)

I have always encouraged teaching assistant students to include the children they work with as active participants in their research, so that the children are fully involved in supporting the students' action research. Sometimes this can be rather scary. Some students were worried about the children over-reacting, and this occasionally did happen. But when such events occurred they were learning experiences, usually related to the way the children's involvement was set up. The other issue is whether children can actually provide the type of response we expect, and what we do with data that seem to tell us very little. Most important, if you want to involve children or other vulnerable people in this way you must follow an ethical code, and justify your methods to the children and the people who care for them.

Lucy, a second-year undergraduate, was keen to involve the children in reviewing her practice because she thought that their narratives would be crucial to her improving the way she responded to their behaviour. Providing them with an opportunity to have their voices heard was not only an essential part of the research process but a sound and inclusive professional strategy. She justified her use of pupil narratives in Figure 6.6.

Lucy's view of the children's narratives as a spontaneous response is not quite accurate, since there is a time lapse between the experience and the writing of the story, but her approach to collecting 'before' and 'after' stories is a very good attempt to capture the children's thoughts and feelings about her ways of working with them. We might question the credibility of Lucy's data. The children might write things that they think Lucy wants to see rather than their own real feelings and thoughts. However, when Lucy compared these data with other data from her own diaries and other sources, this showed that they were credible data in that they compared well with her own and other people's observations. It was a valuable insight into the children's responses to her work with them and testament to the trust that existed between them.

Figure 6.6 Justifying learners' narratives

These I found to be the most effective in terms of my own development, as it provided me with written evidence of the learners' feelings at the time, the triggers to their behaviour and their opinions on my teaching style. I felt that by taking narratives as a form of research I could receive a spontaneous dialogue from the learners. Bruner (1996) has been a long-time advocate of the use of narrative in education. He has proposed three primitive forms of 'meaning making' which involve an individual's spontaneous inclination to engage in dialogue with material, to impose some form of organisation upon it and make comparisons with an individual sense of the conventional ...

The learners wrote short narratives on their overall feelings and thoughts, focusing on a supported session with myself. The narratives took place before the beginning of my case study and then after I had developed strategies and behaviour management techniques. This was in order for me to gain knowledge as to whether the area I was developing had been improved upon and an understanding of the learner's feelings and whether they had changed since the first narrative was written.

Reference

Bruner, J. (1996) *The Culture of Education*. Cambridge, MA: Harvard University Press.

(Lucy, unpublished report, 2006)

Another second-year student, Shelley, asked her pupils to record specific responses in their learning diaries. She focused them on the information she wanted by providing headings for them to write down specific points after each lesson. Shelley was particularly concerned with one pupil's entries and she noticed from a video of the lesson (discussed later in the chapter) that she had not included the child very effectively.

The diary extract and Shelley's notes are in Figure 6.7. On first looking you might think there is no narrative in Tracey's diary because she has only written four words, but the absence of words tells a story by omission: Tracey had not been included in the lesson. Watching the video, reviewing the whole lesson and interpreting the whole situation, not just the diary entries, are all important for Shelley as the practitioner researcher. Other students have also used learning logs and diaries with the children and have found them very honest and illuminating, supporting the improvement of practice.

The idea of guiding participants to stimulate a particular style of narrative reporting was also useful in research into the work of pharmacists by Kevin Pottie and his co-researchers (2008). They collected narrative by means of reports, rather than diaries, because they sought to capture stories of team-based care and the formulation of practice innovation as pharmacists became increasingly involved in the work of family practice settings in Canada. The reporting continued over a period of one year and a narrative style of writing was actively encouraged by the researchers. Each month a narrative report was produced and, over time, the researchers altered the focus of the requirements for the report as emerging findings raised questions for the pharmacists

Figure 6.7 Tracey's learning diary

When I looked at the entry in Tracey's learning diary at the end of the lesson, she had written under the headings:

What did you learn in the lesson?

'Nothing.'

What did you find difficult?

'All of it.'

I believe she had written this because I had not involved her fully in the lesson. If I had asked her a question then perhaps I would have known that she did not understand, therefore I could have supported her learning.

(Shelley, unpublished report, 2006)

to reflect upon. Thus it was a developmental process, with the research supporting the implementation of new practice. The provision of some structure to the narrative reports was crucial to the implementation of new practice.

You might have noted that there are no set ways to collect and use written narrative data. However, in each of the examples provided the narrative was intended to engage the participants in the research, not just as respondents but as active partners in the development of practice. The next section focuses on observational narratives, which may be written but also may use various technologies to support them.

Observational Narratives

Observational narratives are one of the main ingredients of ethnographic accounts. In Philip Chambers's (2003) article we read a vivid account of a street in Mumbai where Philip has gathered data by walking and watching with the aim of creating a narrative that gives a sense of being there. He critiques his own data, acknowledging the problematical nature of trying to represent what we see and how we respond to it as reflective practice. Observation is not straightforward, yet I have heard several early years' practitioners talk about making 'objective' observations about their children. By this, they mean that they write down exactly what they see without making any judgements. My question to them is always, 'But how do you know that what you are writing is actually what happened?' The child's perspective may be very different, and adult interpretation of child behaviour seems to be human nature. As Philip Chambers demonstrates, the writer has a great influence on the way an observation is written.

There are many ways to observe and create narratives. Most often when researching social practices the researcher will become a participant observer, part of the social setting being observed. If you are researching your own practice then you will most likely be a participant observer, perhaps keeping an observational log in your diary. If you are researching another social setting then it is more difficult for you to be a participant unless you adopt alternative roles, as Ann-Marie Smith (2008) did in her research on children in Oaxaca. Most research methods texts (e.g. Wragg, 1999; Silverman, 2006) provide information about a range of observational techniques, but here I will focus on two examples that my students have found very useful when exploring their own practice in action research.

Sometimes it is useful to observe without participating, so you can concentrate on the observation and not the activity, and not be distracted by the role you have to play. Such observations are useful when you wish to learn from other people's practice, for example. Sometimes it is useful to have other people observing us, so that we can learn from their different view of our work. One second-year student, Lucy, had just gained promotion and was now teaching information and communication technology (ICT) with classes from throughout the school. She wanted to improve her practice in working with all the different classes and as part of her methodology she asked three other teaching assistants, her colleagues, to observe her lesson introductions. She believed that they were the experts with knowledge of the children in their classes and therefore could offer reliable and valid information in support of her professional development and improve her practice in working with many different children. Their observations were analysed alongside her own reflective diary and children's comments on each lesson.

Figure 6.8 contains part of one teaching assistant's observations to illustrate their potential. I find it interesting that Lucy labels these as *interpretations*. She viewed the research activity as one of collecting different interpretations of the same experience, her own (reflective diary), the children's (interviews) and the teaching assistants' (observational narratives).

The teaching assistant's observation in Figure 6.8 provides an interpretation of Lucy's practice, as she claims. It is not simply an observation but is reflective, posing questions to support Lucy's professional development. Lucy's colleague has included details that are extremely useful to Lucy, such as the impact of sitting at the back of the class, and noting her own physical and mental changes in addition to the observed behaviour of the class. It highlights one of Lucy's challenges: keeping the children's attention when she is using the laptop positioned at the side of the room. Another interesting point to note is that the observation is not judgemental but focuses on a collaborative approach to solving a problem. It is possible that writing in narrative form helps to prevent observers from being judgemental and encourages a descriptive and sometimes reflective style.

On its own, even this short piece of observation tells Lucy something about how she might develop her practice. When set alongside her reflective diary and interviews with some children, it enables her to create a reliable and valid evidence base for change.

Figure 6.8 Lesson 3, teaching assistant's interpretation

> One really significant point I found during this lesson was how my position, to sit at the back rather than the front, had a real bearing on how I felt I accessed Lucy in the lesson. By this I mean when Lucy moved from the group towards the laptop I felt myself both physically and mentally switch off and I asked myself, 'Where has she gone?' I watched as the children's body language changed too: from upright and focused on Lucy, to shoulders down and looking at friends. Perhaps this is why the children start to talk when Lucy moves away from them. I wonder if there is any way around this so that Lucy and the class can be physically closer during the whole class introduction.
>
> (Lucy, unpublished report, 2006)

Shelley, the student who provided an example from Tracey's learning diary, also video recorded two of her mathematics lessons to allow her and the class teacher to observe her practice through the same medium. It is often the case in primary schools that teachers do not have the opportunity to observe other lessons, simply because they have other responsibilities to fulfil while the teaching assistant takes the class. Video recording was an excellent way of capturing the lesson for the purpose of critical reflection on practice through observation. However, I am not suggesting that a video record captures the full essence of being in the lesson; it clearly does not, but it is useful in the context described.

Video records as data are sometimes very time consuming to use, particularly if one focuses on transcribing the dialogue and noting every contextual feature. Shelley chose to record her video observations of her own lesson in a narrative form, which meant she concentrated on those activities that were significant enough for her to notice. The teacher also wrote a narrative of the same lesson for Shelley to use in her analysis. Shortened extracts of their two narratives are in Figures 6.9 and 6.10; both narrate the same section of the lesson.

Shelley's story, when compared with the teacher's story and the entries in the children's learning diaries, helped her to identify particular aspects of practice for improvement. Shelley's observation is more detailed than the teacher's observation, suggesting that their focus is different. Shelley includes the language that she and the children use, while the teacher focuses mainly on events, on Shelley's and the children's actions. The teacher also makes a judgement about Shelley's teaching skill, while Shelley focuses on trying to write down the detail as she sees and hears it. Her account is more experience cen tred, while the teacher's is more event centred. The creation of these narratives has been influenced by the time and place that they were viewed. Shelley might have viewed the video fairly soon after the lesson, when events were also fresh in her mind as a participant. She might also have spent more time watching and rewatching the video to capture parts of the dialogue that interested her. The teacher did not participate in the lesson and might have viewed the video at a later date and so the observation for her is clearly non-participatory.

Figure 6.9 An extract from Shelley's video story

I introduce the lesson on problem solving. I ask the question, 'What do you know about problem solving?' ONLY HALF THE CLASS RAISE THEIR HANDS!!! Anne has her hand up and gives me an answer: 'You have to solve the problem.' I give praise and write down her answer on the board as a mind map. Kate has her hand up, 'You have to answer a question.' I give praise. Joanne and David also give an answer. Tracey does not say anything. John is messing with his pencil. My back is turned to the children. John is talking to Tracey. I ask John what he knows about problem solving. I have gained his attention; he is looking at the board and it takes time for him to give me an answer. Kate is talking whilst I am. I ignore her. I explain to the children that today's lesson is all about making decisions and I am going to show them strategies to help them solve a problem. I read the problem aloud as I write it down on the board: 60 children were in the school play; 36 were boys; how many were girls? My back is turned to the children. It takes time. John is talking to Tracey. I explain to the children that one way of solving a problem is to highlight the information. 'Firstly, what is it asking us to do?' Only one child puts their hand up to answer. Kate shouts out. I ignore her and highlight the question. 'What are the two facts?' Terry answers, 'The sum.' There is no sum written on the board. 'What's another fact?' John is not paying attention. I ask him. He gives me an answer. I ask the children to discuss in the group what the calculation is. They look a little confused. I hear Anne say to John, 'What's a calculation?' John has his hand up and asks me what a calculation is. I explain that the calculation is the same as a sum. The children raise their hand except Tracey and Terry. Kate gives the answer. Anne has a guess. John is unable to recognise the sum and gives the wrong calculation. He does not understand. I stop and read the problem again. David has a go, but gives the wrong answer. Kate gives an explanation to how she worked out the answer to the sum. I give praise. I write down on the board what the calculation is and the answer.

(Shelley, unpublished report, 2006)

Figure 6.10 Extract from the class teacher's video story

The session is introduced and mathematical terminology is used. John is not totally concentrating. Problems are written on the board and the word 'strategy' is used. Kate interrupts; Miss King ignores and then tells her to concentrate. Miss King encourages others to join in successfully. Kate is beginning to dominate the discussion, even when the calculation is complete she still has a tendency to dominate the discussion. John finds it hard, unable to solve the problem and unable to interpret the word calculation. Jenny and Tracey are not participating! Tracey has not spoken.

Miss King demonstrates strategy on board, good reinforcement of teaching points. She highlights key words and identifies strategies used.

(Shelley, unpublished report, 2006)

She seemed more interested in reporting events than dialogue. However, the two observations along with other data gave Shelley evidence of specific events that informed her practice, such as her failure to include Tracey fully in the lesson.

This approach to using video as a basis for observational narrative creation appeared to be an effective way of initial analysis, re-creating the scene in writing for further comparative analysis. It is not the same as using still images or video recording as part of the data set, to *speak for itself* or to *support* the narrative in the final report, which is discussed in the next section.

Artistic Forms of Narrative

Crang and Cook (2007) discuss filmic (still and moving photography) approaches, highlighting some of the problems associated with determining the *reality* of a situation. For example, they note that photographs and videos do not show an unmediated reality; the technology may create a reaction amongst participants and the outcome is interpreted in different ways. Different interpretations of the same event on video are useful as previously demonstrated in Shelley's example, but Crang and Cook do make a valid point. Even the same person watching the same video on a different day will have a different interpretation of some events. However, the reinterpretation allows for the layers of meaning in a set of events to build up, leading to deeper understanding. In action research, a video is a useful tool.

Crang and Cook also highlight the problems associated with popularising information through filmic approaches, as happened in the past when ethnographers' photographs of indigenous cultures became the subject of picture postcards, and as happens today when people present their research on television as documentary. I believe this is an ethical concern. When filmic methods depict scenes as realistically as they can do, and are included in well-structured reports that do not misinterpret the context, then they can be very effective. An example is found in Chris Jones's (2009) MA thesis 'How do I improve my practice as an inclusion officer working in a children's service?' at www. actionresearch.net/living/living.shtml. Jones considers the video clips an essential part of the reflexive process in the research; they enabled deeper professional learning and provided a way to share that learning as part of her living theory research process. She uses them in an interactive way, inviting readers to watch video clips at appropriate moments in the texts.

Despite the successes that Chris Jones and others on the ActionResearch. net website have in using video and photography as part of their living theory dissertations, Crang and Cook describe issues that other researchers have found which could prevent use of filmic approaches in some types of research and in some contexts. For example, Islamic women will not be included in any filmic activity, which can result in a skewed representation of participants in a particular piece of research. Where researchers are seeking to present multiple truths, for example city landscapes, filmic approaches can be extremely effective. ML White (2006) used digital video production as a means to enable young people to communicate in a meaningful way about their own lives and culture. The digital video emerged as a way of developing reflexivity about social situations – an enabling research methodology that she called digital ethnography. Digital Youth Project at http://digitalyouth.ischool.berkeley.edu/projects provides various examples and discussions that support White's assertions.

Any image-creating method is relevant as a record of people's reaction to their own environment, providing you give consideration to the strengths and weaknesses of the method within the context of the particular research project. We could criticise video, role-play and dramatising events in the same way we can criticise a TV documentary that presents research; it could sensationalise the event, skewing the interpretation to a particular point of view. Any narrative can do this but moving image narratives, in real life or on film, can tell very powerful stories, sometimes more powerfully than the written word. As White (2006) notes, the written word provides a much thinner description of people's experiences than using a multimedia approach which shows their complexities.

Penny, another second-year undergraduate student, embraced the idea of using photographs taken by the children of their likes and dislikes within the school playground. This is similar to the photographic research by Peter Egg et al. (2004), discussed in Chapter 4 on ethics, where children used photography to capture aspects of their lives as a means of developing a narrative. It is a form of *autophotography* as Crang and Cook describe it. They acknowledge that this is a very useful approach and advise that cheap disposable cameras are sufficient since the content and meaning, rather than the quality of the photograph, are most important. Some participants might feel unable to use a camera, for a range of different reasons, and may prefer to draw, paint, sculpt or dramatise images.

Penny chose to research an issue in her school using photographs taken by the children. She describes her approach in Figure 6.11. The photographs taken by the children were representations of their likes and dislikes about the playground, and provided a stimulus for further group discussion and data collection. They were used in Penny's report as an essential part of the story, clearly showing the children's concerns and positive actions that have taken place to improve the playground environment. The pictures alone could not tell the whole story, but the children used them to support their articulation of the issues and to promote further discussion and debate about them. They

Figure 6.11 Penny's description of using photography

> The objective is to record what they like or dislike about the playground environment before and after the implementation of the programme of structured activities with the support of a learning support assistant. The children will not be in the photographs, they will only contain scenes of the school playground … The photographs will then be analysed by pupils in small mixed gender collaborative groups and the results recorded.
>
> (Penny, unpublished report, 2006)

were an essential stimulus and means of focusing attention on issues that mattered to everyone involved.

In similar research conducted in Australia as a means of exploring the nature of inclusive education through the eyes of children aged around 11–13, Julianne Moss and her co-writers (2007) concluded that photographs taken by the young people are *visual narratives* that represent and elicit further reflection. They have no doubt that this form of evidence should have a place as data within research. Visual data can represent more effectively what young people have to say, in particular those with language or other contextual difficulties; they are an important way for disadvantaged or minority groups to communicate their innermost thoughts.

Photography, either still or moving, has some advantages over using drawing to record data, which has the same problems as using drawing to stimulate inquiry. People who are not confident with drawing will be less comfortable with this method, and indeed they will most likely feel that their drawings may not represent the context as they wish to present it; for them, this is a method that might be used alongside others. For those who are very confident and prefer drawing (or other artistic media such as painting, modelling, dramatising), it might be the main method for them to represent themselves and their environment. Artists use this technique all the time; for example, Van Gogh used drawing and painting techniques to capture the reality of working people's lives, and to some extent his own. For young children or other vulnerable people, drawing may be the most appropriate way to capture information. Whether this medium is offered to a participant will depend on the individuals involved and the purpose of the data collection.

Another second-year student, Alan, decided to use drawing when working with a particular six-year-old child, as described in Figure 6.12. Alan made a valid choice of research method that gave him additional insights into a young

Figure 6.12   Alan's reasons for using drawing

Discussions with key members of staff ... and my own personal observations have revealed that he is outstanding at drawing, from which he derives a great deal of pleasure, especially when showing it to others and explaining what is occurring in the pictures ...

Children's drawings can signify action, emotion, ideas, and experiences and relate complex stories in an imaginary or real life context, therefore, representing a form of narrative ...

Drawing is one of Sam's major strengths and one that motivates him to articulate his interests. Therefore, incorporating this medium of research will highlight those activities that he likes doing, so that expressed interests can to some extent drive such sessions. I will encourage Sam to discuss fully his pictures to ensure that there is no misunderstanding on my part as to their representation ...

Since Sam is very articulate and is exceptionally skilled at illustrations, to include the drawing is particularly appropriate.

(Alan, extracts from unpublished report, 2006)

child's mind and supported his own change of practice to accommodate more effectively the child's needs.

Ruth Leitch (2008) has identified that there is growing interest in both narrative and drawing as means to understand the child's world. She describes a research project that brought the two together, involving 1100 children aged 5–18 years in Northern Ireland. The three different methods to collect data were activities that pupils might usually complete in class:

1   After a class discussion, children were asked to draw a picture highlighting one issue they would like the Children's Commissioner to address. Each picture was accompanied by a short spoken or written narrative.
2   Groups of four or more pupils also produced posters on social issues such as crime or health, accompanied by spoken or written text.
3   Children were also asked to write stories about personal issues that were important to them.

The results of the research used the analysis of the children's priorities, as identified by the research team, together with the images which *spoke for themselves* about marginalised issues, to ensure that the children had the opportunity to influence policy making. Leitch describes three other research projects using both drawing and narrating to summarise a series of benefits of creative research methods with children, including the fact that they place the child at the centre of the research and can render emotional or difficult issues less threatening. However, she does remind us of the ethical concerns: respect, response, safety and a genuine interest in listening to the children's voices.

Researching social lives of any kind is helped by determining the interests of the participants, their preferred communication modes and their ability to perform the required tasks. For some, their preferred art form may be sculpting, model making, technical drawing, designing and making. If the process of creation and construction together with the product helps to tell their story then the effort to tailor the communication process is worthwhile. We cannot assume that the same mode would suit everyone, or that the end product can and does tell the narrative when it may only be a part. Two of my own children's very different responses to painting and model making, when they were very young (pre-school, age 3), illustrate that for my son these media provided an excellent narrative window on his young world – he told the stories as he painted and created – but for my daughter they did not. For her, the use of role-play through favourite toys was more effective in supporting the creation of narrative insights into the way she was thinking.

Use of drama or other performance, as mentioned before, should also be included as a means of generating narrative, and can in many circumstances tell the story that the participant wants to share. In particular, children and young people often prefer to express themselves through music, dancing and role-play – whatever captures their interest. There is little room in this text for exploring the use of the whole range of art-related forms of narrative, but I strongly encourage you to seek creative ways of exploring social worlds that are relevant to the issues and the people you would like to participate in your research.

Narratives from the Internet and Other Electronic Sources

The internet carries such vast amounts of information about individuals, organisations and different social issues that it is possible to complete a research project using these materials. Christine Hine (2008) provides some useful guidance for anyone seeking to use the internet in research. She warns of bias occurring because of the sample used; for example, those who are willing and able to access a computer may join in, but others will be excluded. She also focuses on using the traditional methods, such as questionnaires and interviewing, ethnographic fieldwork and documentary research, but adapted to online settings. For collecting large amounts of survey data, across different cultural contexts and over extended periods of time, an electronic survey is ideal. This type of survey is relatively easy to set up, and the technology will support the analysis of responses. Several free online versions are available to get you started, for example SurveyMonkey at www.surveymonkey.com/.

Online interviewing is not the same as face-to-face interviewing because you cannot share the same physical space, even though you might be able to see each other, and there is sometimes a short time-lapse in communication. Not many people are used to using technology in this way, and many people would prefer to use a chatroom type of environment or instant messaging, or for groups a conference-style telephone call might be more effective. The problem with interviewing without being able to see the individual or group is not being able to see facial expression and gesture, which support the understanding of meaning. The other is one of capturing the experience effectively and with groups, ensuring that everyone has the opportunity to contribute. If you have ever been in a chatroom to have an online discussion with a group you will have experienced situations where several people are trying to respond at the same time, and the resulting dialogue on screen does not flow. It all requires good management on the part of the researcher.

Through online websites such as Moodle (http://moodle.org/) you can set up your own online community, engage people in asynchronous forums (people can join in at any time), synchronous chat (all join the chatroom at the same time), wiki development, surveys and questionnaires, including short response questions for qualitative research, along with e-mail, document storage and sharing and other features. Developing wikis with a group can be very interesting because each person in the group should build on and develop the previous contribution, leading to a collaborative written contribution from the group. Setting up your own online community for researching an issue can be very useful because you can invite people to join and manage the sample. However, you might be excluding people who might not have the same access to a computer; and, if your research is about poverty and deprivation, for example, you might not be building a community that is able to respond with any significant experience of the issues. Therefore, you will need either to address the issue of access and training, or to find an alternative way to complete the research.

Developing your own online community and setting up your own surveys are proactive ways of using the internet, but what about the information that is already freely available to us? Earlier in the chapter I used one example of a narrative from a life history database available on the internet for documentary research. There are obviously clear benefits for society in maintaining records of social history, but over the last few years we have the phenomenon of a living history emerging through social networking sites such as Facebook and Twitter, which allow anyone to share information, with little real monitoring of the nature of this information. Many professional and commercial websites have open forums, some of which contain personal information about contributors, which they placed there for the purpose of the forum discussion, not for others to use in research. However, we might argue that placing personal information on such a forum is done in the knowledge that there is open access and anyone might read it.

Websites about home schooling, how to treat particular medical conditions, or how to cope with a social problem affecting your family, sometimes contain stories about experience that can usefully illustrate a social issue. However, such freely available materials still require ethical consideration of the same kind that one might afford to individuals who willingly participate in research. Another concern about such information is that the author might not be who they claim to be; this cannot always be verified easily. In times when people are becoming concerned about rights to privacy, the storing of personal data is subject to much scrutiny – and rightly so. Despite these ethical concerns, I believe that the internet is a valid way to gather information about lived experiences in specific groups of people, for example those who choose home schooling. One way of addressing the ethics is to ask the website owner if you may join the forum and distribute a question for discussion, but you are still left with not really knowing the full details of respondents, except that they are people who have a vested interest in home schooling, for example.

Another popular internet medium is the game world, many of which are free. One of my students engaged in a game world to try and research issues of disability; there were people in the game world who claimed to have various disabilities. However, there were ethical concerns that the other people in the game world were not real people; the student could not find out who they were, or if they really did have the stated disabilities. It was an interesting idea, being an online participant observer, but not necessarily one that would lead to authentic outcomes. Podcasts are also becoming popular, and are perhaps another technology to explore for using in research, particularly with young people. You might also want to examine how text messaging can create narrative, for example in researching youth culture.

These two sections on using artistic forms of narratives and the internet aim to open your mind to the alternative possibilities for gathering narrative data in addition to the traditional interview and observation techniques. You might be interested in exploring different ways of collecting narrative data, especially if the social situation you explore will benefit from such an alternative approach. Remember to choose a method that can be justified with full consideration of ethics within your project.

Summary

Narrative data collection in research communities to date has often focused on the use of the interview to elicit stories from the interviewee. Various alternative methods have been introduced through examples from students' data and references to a range of different published research projects. The chapter emphasises the range of different ways of eliciting narratives from participants and situations rather than relying on the interview and observation as core methods. Recognition must be given to the use of new technologies and the interest that many people have in these, while not excluding those who have little access to them. The internet has many resources available but, as with any source, the ethical concerns are important. Overall, research projects must be developed with *fitness for purpose* as the main tenet guiding the choice of methods. The chapter has not included in-depth descriptions of specific interview methods, for example, since these are documented in other texts. It has instead provided an overview and suggestions for further exploration in deepening understanding of techniques.

The overarching theme of biographical data is evident throughout, but you can identify the need to reflect on and analyse those data with reference to other data that you collect, for example your reflective diary with its autobiographical data or your own observational story of a particular experience.

Suggested Reading

Crang, M. and Cook, I. (2007) *Doing Ethnographies*. London: Sage. Chapter 4 'Participant observation', Chapter 5 'Interviewing', Chapter 6 'Filmic approaches'.
Hine, C. (2008) 'The internet and research methods', in N. Gilbert (ed.), *Researching Social Life*, 3rd edn. London: Sage.

7

ANALYSING NARRATIVE DATA

CHAPTER OUTLINE

- Introduction
- Analysing interview data
- Developing an analytical process
  - Structural analysis
  - Thematic analysis

- Analysing written narrative data
  - Analyses from published research
  - Analyses from second-year undergraduates

- Analysing visual data
- Summary
- Suggested reading

Introduction

You might ask 'What is analysis?' in a research context, and 'How do I know I am doing it?', or 'How will I analyse all these different bits of data?' This chapter aims to answer these questions through focusing on different ways of analysing narrative data that fit within the core theme of biographical data. Examples will come from published research papers, my own doctoral thesis and second-year undergraduate students' action research projects. My aim is to give you some different ideas, and to encourage you to develop your own analytical processes for your project, rather than adopt a method that may not suit your research. Before describing and explaining different examples I first consider the nature of analysis in research in general, and provide some discussion of the influence of interpretation on the process and outcome.

The purpose of analysis in qualitative research is to enquire deeply into the meaning of different situations and different people's understandings of the world. It often takes place with small numbers of participants, in a particular context, and for a specific purpose related to a change in practice or an improvement in social conditions. It cannot usually be generalised, yet when small research projects are shared others have similar experiences and stories to tell. Thus it is valid and reliable, in the sense that it is purposeful for the context in which it took place and it has significance for others in similar contexts and places. Sometimes larger qualitative research projects occur and large data sets are gathered, organised and archived, thus providing a record of social history. Such data sometimes *speak for themselves* with little analysis, especially if collected in narrative form. Yet these collections provide a resource for much retrospective analysis and interpretation alongside other documentary evidence of the time.

There is no single process to analyse and present narrative data as part of qualitative research. The analysis can start at any point within an iterative process: analysing, collecting data, synthesising, reanalysing and so on. Some of the examples in the chapter will demonstrate this. In action research, analysis begins when practitioners reflect on their practice to help them find a purposeful inquiry. They have to analyse their practice, the context in which it takes place and their role. Once they have analysed their situation they identify an area of development in their practice and set about collecting narrative data in a variety of ways to suit their needs. For some, the process of analysis occurs as an iterative, ongoing process, in which they review each practice-based activity and modify their practice, changing their perspective over time. For others the process of analysis begins retrospectively after all the data collection is complete, and they will review the data for recurring themes of interest and relevance to their inquiries.

In any research into social settings the researcher will most likely enter the situation with some understanding, having engaged in analysis of observed or reported events and documents, for example. In any research about social worlds the analysis may be iterative or retrospective. Most often it is a mixture of both. These different ways of working are evident in published papers and we will revisit some that were introduced in Chapter 6.

All narrative research relies heavily on interpretation (Clandinin and Connelly, 2000). The amount of data collected may be overwhelming and the meanings attached to the various data are subject to interpretation by a researcher (or research team) who has a particular position in relation to the research. Organising and collating the information from the research field takes much time, but in the process of organising it the researcher is finding answers to questions, deciding on the significance of specific pieces of data and beginning to shape the analysis. With narrative interview data, for example, Reissman (1993) suggests that the transcription process and the analysis cannot be separated because the transcript is arranged in ways to support the researcher's thinking about the meaning of the interview. How it is organised affects further analysis. Reissman shows how she retranscribed the interview dialogue and then analysed it again by reorganising it into stanzas – poetic structures which helped her to see much more clearly the meaningful statements that the interviewee was making about her experience (1993: 61–3). Analysis is therefore a complex process, not easily described as having a particular structure or following a rigid method since there will be much revisiting and reshaping before the final write-up occurs.

Bochner (2001) is critical of Atkinson and Silverman (1997) who suggested that personal narrative is only useful when subjected to cultural criticism, theorised, categorised and analysed. They stated that personal narratives are not trustworthy and that researchers should treat them with methodological scepticism. Bochner presents a different view. For him the analysis of personal narratives such as illness narratives is about acknowledging the multiple forms of representation; moving towards meanings rather than searching for facts; emphasising local stories; and moving away from categorising and abstracting. Bochner advises judging life experiences against the ethical, emotional, practical and fateful demands of life as each of us knows them. He expresses the belief that the researcher should engage in a form of dialogue with the storyteller, particularly those telling illness stories, since part of the process of developing understanding of the story is to match it with one's own lived experience and to develop empathic responses in valuing the individual insight into illness. Working with such narratives is not a search for truth but an acknowledgement of personal experiences as recounted at that moment in time. Bochner acknowledges the influence of cultural frames of reference, those of the researcher, the writer and the reader. Each interprets the narrative according to their own frame of reference, leading to multiple interpretations and thus representing the reality of social existence.

Thoughts about developing your analytical process should begin at the research proposal stage. You should identify the potential for your interpretive influence and make choices based on the context and purpose of the research. The next section presents some examples of analyses of interview data, aiming to demonstrate that the analytical process should fit the purpose of the research. It should be justified with reference to the whole context in which the research is taking place and it should help you to answer your research question, support professional development and add to knowledge and understanding of the area of inquiry.

Analysing Interview Data

In this section I will include examples from a range of different situations that can be described under the umbrella of interview, while recognising that not all situations described will be as formal as others. One of the interesting features of interview analysis is that interpretation begins in the researcher's mind during the interview. Interpretive influences become more obvious during semi-structured or unstructured interviews and focus group situations. Some researchers, over the years, have attempted to design analytical processes to suit particular types of research, sometimes to reduce the interpretive influence and achieve more credibility. These can be very effective processes, but in many small projects the research is very context laden and the purpose is often very specific, and to apply a rigid analytical process is often inappropriate.

Researching into social situations usually requires a more experience-centred approach such as that described by Squire (2008), also introduced in Chapter 2. It is an approach where the researcher is focusing on meaning rather than structure; focusing on understanding everything about the person and their situation, not just the nature of their story. Experience-centred approaches can be designed to suit the specific research project. When this occurs it is important for the researcher to explain their analytical processes and set these out clearly for others to read in their report.

The next section examines examples of two different analytical processes with the purpose of demonstrating how such processes may develop as part of the overall project.

Developing an Analytical Process

The example to be introduced shortly, made me focus on the blurred boundaries between an analytical process that aimed to present a realistic but interpretive perspective of a personal or group experience, and one using representative constructions. The fact that interpretive processes lead to reconstruction of data is one reason why some researchers are concerned about the level of subjectivity in the analysis of narrative and other qualitative data. There seems to be much reordering, interpretive analysis of the text, and resynthesising as researchers make sense of narrative data from an interview. The example demonstrates that the outcome of the interpretation is very much influenced by the researcher, despite participant feedback and a repeated cycle of creation. However, the involvement of participants in developing the final narrative does serve to demonstrate that the process has been transparent and it provides a level of trustworthiness for the data.

Hollingsworth and Dybdahl (2007: 155) provide Coralie McCormack's (2004) chart of steps that she followed when creating a story from in-depth interview conversations. McCormack used transcriptions of interviews to create *interpretive stories*, one for each participant. She called these enriched and constructed stories which she created in stages. She shared these with participants at different stages for feedback, and she reflected upon them further. She then used the interpretive stories to compose what she called the *personal experience narrative*. This appears to be a useful approach to making sense of a set of different stories; it is an analysis and then a synthesis of data, repeated in cycles to formulate the final narrative. The chart is useful for novice narrative researchers since it provides a structure that may be helpful in some inquiries: those that interview participants with the purpose of eliciting a series of stories about the same or a similar event. For example, conversational interviews with new mothers about their birthing experiences will most likely result in a set of stories about similar lived experiences. The chart may be less useful for analysing interview data where the stories are more diverse in nature. The possibility of creating a personal experience narrative about common events is less likely. As Hollingsworth and Dybdahl (2007) point out, making sense of conversational interviews is not easy and the structure of any analysis and final report will vary; there is no set way to write about them.

In developing your own analytical process you can benefit from examining and drawing on other researchers' methods, but you do not necessarily have to apply them in exactly the same way. In my doctoral thesis I gathered several hours of video-recorded narrative data to allow me to analyse the dialogue between the teacher and the children, and the dialogue between children. I conducted what I called *structured interventions* with the children involved. These entailed providing two children with the opportunity to explain the meanings of particular mathematical words to one another, in words, drawing and gesture, while being video-taped and with me as participant observer. It was not a formal interview situation but an activity designed to elicit specific information to answer my research question, 'How do children express their understanding of the meaning of specific mathematical words and phrases?'

I began my analysis by adopting Mercer's (1996) three categories of peer talk: *disputational, cumulative* and *exploratory*. Disputational talk occurs when children challenge each other's ideas, often through assertion and counter-assertion; cumulative talk builds positively on the previous utterances; and exploratory talk offers statements for joint consideration, challenge and justification. For my research it was useful to adopt these categories and others such as Mercer's *knowledge markers* usually used by teachers, for example *challenging*, questioning the wisdom of the speaker's ideas during the lesson. However, despite their usefulness, other features became much more important than these as the analysis developed. I identified that the *contextual references* children made when describing mathematic terms could affect their understanding, as could the *gestures* they used when explaining their ideas. In the extract of my analysis in Figure 7.1 the football tackle is the contextual reference.

Not only were contextual references and gestures important, but the drawings that children sometimes provided, and my involvement in the discussion, were

Figure 7.1 Extract 1 of the analysis of one structured intervention

Stuart and Tessa provided a lot of support for each other through gesture and facial expression. They sometimes negotiated turns through gesture. Their talk was an interesting mixture of *disputational* and *cumulative*. Stuart sometimes showed *exploratory* talk with himself (also noted in the pilot). Both seemed willing to take risks and present ideas. This might be because they had worked with me before and knew that I would value their ideas. Stuart began to explain 'even chance' by referring to a football tackle, a contextual reference originally introduced by another child in lesson 2 (Extract 4.16).

Extract 4.16 Football tackle

Stuart: Even chance ... mmm [looks doubtful] ... I know [hand up to stop Tessa] ... even chance ... right ... even chance means right ... say like, there's two people at football, and the ball's there, and they go into a tackle [demonstrates with fingers], and it's 50:50 [flat horizontal movement with one hand] it's an even chance like [two hands 'weighing' or balancing], they can get the ball.

The similarity between Stuart's gestures and those in the previous extract (4.15) are clear, although used alongside different words. It is interesting that two different children introduced the 'balancing' gesture, like a bucket balance, as a metaphor for 'even chance', although the teacher had not introduced it in the lesson. Gesture seemed to be an essential part of communicating meaning here.

(Bold, 2001)

essential in my attempts to find out what the children were thinking. The extract in Figure 7.2 illustrates the importance of the drawing in enabling me to clarify Stuart's thinking.

You can see that at this stage my analysis, in narrative style, consisted of some overarching judgements about the types of talk occurring, extracts of dialogue from the video-tape and discussion of the gestures and drawing, which I related back to previous observations from lessons and other structured interventions. As appropriate I referred to literature during the analytical process, but mostly it was a process of practical theory generation. At the end I summarised my overall findings into key points for improving the teaching of probability in a primary classroom before discussing my overall conclusions with fuller reference to the literature.

If you are unsure about how to develop your analytical process, the best place to look is in relevant doctoral theses and master's dissertations deposited in your academic library. The full text of my own thesis is available for open electronic access at the Open University Library, and many other libraries have similar facilities. Research articles in journals are also useful, but sometimes lack the detail that you need to understand fully all the processes involved, unless they are papers focusing specifically on analytical methods. The challenge for researchers publishing with narrative data in their research is being able to analyse their data effectively within the 6000 word limit set by most journals.

Figure 7.2 Extract 2 of analysis of one structured intervention

> Stuart supported his explanation with a drawing of two footballers at equal distances from a football (Appendix 8, Stuart).
>
> *Extract 4.17 Interpreting drawings*
>
> *Res:* Are you saying they are an equal distance from the ball?
> *Tessa:* That one's nearer to the ball.
> *Stuart:* It isn't 'cos I've got three lines … I'm not going to measure it and everything am I?
> *Res:* Right, so three lines means it's the same distance?
> *Stuart:* Yeah.
> *Res:* Yeah so what does it mean? That's an example.
> *Stuart:* 'Even chance' means like you've both like, got a 50:50 chance you know like [laugh] … mmm … like [Stuart gestures with hands flat like scales going up and down, balancing. Tessa copies gesture and smiles to Res]
>
> Tessa *challenged* the pictorial representation after I questioned to establish that Stuart thought 'even chance' in a tackle meant players at an even distance from the ball. The picture seemed to be an interpretation of the phrase 'even challenge' as introduced into lesson 2 by the teacher (Extract 4.8).
>
> (Bold, 2001)

The following sections present some examples of different analytical processes used by authors previously cited in other chapters.

Structural analysis

The analysis of personal experience narratives by Labov and Waletzky (1997; originally published 1967) was developed over a period of research into language and personal narratives from people of all ages and social backgrounds who spoke English. The model supports structural analyses of specific sets of oral personal narratives, which it treats as story texts rather than a storytelling performance or dialogic interaction with others. The story text represents past events, so the Labovian approach to analysis is event centred. It is also text centred because it takes little account of context, although Labov and Waletzky acknowledge that context is important by paying attention to the referential and evaluative features of the stories. Wendy Patterson (2008) provides a clear example of how the method works in practice, which I shall not replicate here.

The method is rigorous and detailed, splitting sentences into clauses and assigning each clause to a category. Five of the categories can be understood as questions that the narrative is answering:

1 (A) Abstract – what is the story about?
2 (O) Orientation – who, when and where?
3 (CA) Complicating action – then what happened?
4 (E) Evaluation – so what?
5 (R) Result – what finally happened?

The sixth category, coda (C), is another way of ending the narrative; it does not ask a question, but makes a statement. The category of evaluation has subcategories. The details of how these categories were used are shown in Labov and Waletzky's article. Their purposes were:

- to identify the relative effectiveness and completeness of narrative structure amongst subgroups of the population
- to analyse the more complex traditional narratives told by skilled storytellers.

If you were going to conduct research that was similar to theirs then the method might be appropriate.

Patterson (2008) identifies the advantages of this method of analysis as:

1 It enables the researcher to identify and understand event narratives.
2 It enables the researcher to compare narratives.
3 It focuses on the narrator's perspective.
4 It focuses the researcher on how narratives are elicited.

However, Patterson also identifies theoretical and methodological problems in using this method. Labov and Waletzky have defined what they call a narrative in a particular way. The method cannot be used with partial stories. Separating out the different types of clauses used as units of analysis is problematic because there are difficulties in distinguishing between clauses that report a sequence of events and those that evaluate. The approach seems to ignore the creativity of storytelling and, most important, that a story is culturally specific and often influenced by the gender of the storyteller. In different cultures, stories have different structures, and some are very context oriented rather than time oriented. The danger in having a rigid model of what constitutes a competent story is that one might consider anything that does not as less competent. Patterson (2008) notes that Labov did not make these distinctions of competence in this way, but others using such a model might do so.

The model was originally developed mainly from male storytellers and as such it ignores the subtle, intricate points in women's storytelling, often made through interrelated conversation and narration, that is collaborative storytelling. Patterson demonstrates through examples that the Labovian model is an inflexible tool for analysing anything that does not comply with a specific story structure and does not include the broader communicative events that some researchers now include as narrative such as poetry, photographic sequences and diaries. Methodologically, Patterson (2008) found that using Labovian analysis for transcripts in which people talked about their traumatic experiences was difficult because of their non-conformity to the expected narrative model. The stories did not have temporally ordered discrete events and therefore did not fit the definition of narrative as defined by the model. Another point to note is that since the model was developed, the ways that

ANALYSING NARRATIVE DATA

people use oral English have changed over the years. People do not necessarily tell stories in the same way as they did over 40 years ago.

A more contemporary approach to structural analysis is found in Heidi Hamilton's (2008) paper in which she examines the narrative structures of discourse with a person who has Alzheimer's disease. Hamilton split the dialogue into clauses and focused initially on the number of lexical items (words, phrases etc.) that contained past tense verbs. She then produced a chart to show the percentage prevalence of such lexical items and used the percentages in the chart to provide evidence to challenge claims from previous research. Hamilton then focused only on the parts of the conversations in which the person did seem to recount the past. The clauses containing past tense verbs were identified as one of two types, briefly described as:

1   narrative trace – a clause that has reference to the past but is not part of a narrative.
2   narrative clause – a clause that references the past and is part of the narrative.

Distinguishing the two is sometimes difficult, so further explanatory note is provided by Hamilton to explain what she did. She found that most of the clauses were in the form of narrative traces, and she illustrates this phenomenon with an excerpt from part of a conversation with some discussion of what might have prompted the narrative trace to appear in the dialogue 'out of the blue'.

Hamilton was interested in the narrative clauses and how these became stories, and continues her exploration by identifying specific lexical items – nouns and pronouns as nominal references – which she lists while also indicating the number of times each one was used. She identified that specific answers to the question 'Who or what was in the story world?' were found infrequently. For example, several nouns used were described as 'empty' because of their lack of specificity, such as 'people', 'group', 'thing'. She continued this way of exploring the data by asking further questions about the story world, for example 'What happened?' (verbal references), 'Where did this take place?' (spatial references) and 'When did this take place?' (temporal references). Hamilton then compared the different categories of reference – nominal, verbal, temporal and spatial – by creating a summary table. She followed this by demonstrating how the analysis applied to a short excerpt of the dialogue and discussing the difficulty that anyone reading the excerpt has in making sense of the story from the point of view of the person telling it. There are many vague references leading to a confused story world for the listener.

Hamilton describes the story elements as snapshots – parts of a story about which listeners cannot have full comprehension but which instead they have to relate to what they know about the person telling the story. Her research gives some insights into the ways that a person with Alzheimer's disease may communicate and into the possible ways for health care workers to communicate differently with people in their care. An example is to take the initiative and to focus on personal objects, which may evoke a response that conveys something of the person's identity, past and present, and not just to focus on the 'here and now' in conversations. In this respect the detailed analysis of the specific lexical items used has discovered some valuable qualities, that examining the dialogue as a whole would not have identified. What was heard by the listener as a confused oral dialogue actually had more meaning if the listener was able to link the fragments of what was said to their knowledge of the person telling the story. This is important in relation to the self-identify of the person with Alzheimer's disease.

This example demonstrates the value of using structured analysis to examine the units of language used, compared to the more thematic analysis that you will see in the next section. Searching for themes would not have been relevant for Hamilton's data. It is important for you to note that a particular 'known' model for analysing materials will often not be suitable for the purpose of your research, resulting in the need to find or create a suitable model as Hamilton (2008) has done. An effective approach to developing a model for analysis is to draw on those that other researchers have used and take from them the parts that are relevant, adapting them to your specific research project.

Thematic analysis

The term *thematic experience analysis* encompasses two ideas: that the researcher is often seeking and identifying themes (or not) within the narratives; and that experiences usually involve relationships between people and contexts. In this section I will describe and discuss some of the analytical procedures used by Padam Simkhada, previously cited in Chapter 6.

Simkhada's (2008) interviews with 42 girls who had been trafficked to India for sex work, but had since been returned to Nepal, were analysed thematically. The themes were developed to identify issues and to structure the information gathered about the girls' experiences and the processes involved in trafficking. They focused on the family background, the process of trafficking, work and conditions in the brothels, the process of return to Nepal, and survival strategies for the future. Some of the data, such as socio-demographic characteristics, are presented in tables as percentages and actual numbers. The information is useful but the use of percentages is not mathematically necessary with such small numbers involved. The main data about the trafficking trade are presented in narrative style under thematic headings and subheadings, for example:

- Theme heading: Ways of trafficking and recruitment tactics
- Subheading: False promises of jobs
- Subheading: Fraudulent marriage.

Extracts from individual interviewees' narratives are included within the analysis, serving as examples of specific experiences and practices. In addition the four main themes are also tabulated to identify clearly the relative numbers involved. For example, Simkhada identified that 23 of the 42 interviewees had gone to India because of false promises of jobs. The combination of thematic narrative analysis including specific extracts from interviews, and the tabulated numerical data, serves the purpose of providing an overall picture of the situation. The themes might have been reported without the table of data but the table provides something that a narrative style of thematic reporting cannot provide: a stronger sense of how many of the interviewees experienced the same things. Knowing that false promises of jobs are the most prevalent means of enticing girls from Nepal to India might go some way to developing measures to prevent trafficking in the future.

In the previous example the analysis was of data from interviews with individuals, but thematic analysis is also useful for focus group interviews. Focus groups also offer opportunities to examine how meaning is built within the dialogue between people, if the focus of the research is on relationships or decision-making processes, for example. The type of analysis in my thesis, focusing on the way the dialogue was built, on the meaning behind the dialogue and not just the content, is one example of a process that might be applied to analysing group dialogue. Crang and Cook (2007) emphasise the need for good audio recording and detailed transcription of data from focus groups, with the addition of notes on feelings and other impressions of the group's activity, which are essential for the analysis. They advise *coding* the data to be systematic about analysis rather than having a subjective choice of representative snippets.

Coding data is similar to the categorising that Simkhada (2008) used and Mercer's (1996) categories that I used, but Crang and Cook are using a grounded theory approach that most methods texts describe as *open coding*. This means they are not beginning with ideas about categories or themes at the start of their research, but examining the data for codes to categorise the material that emerges from the narrative data. They take the raw data, identify some interesting elements in it and give these codes – words that describe the elements. They then review the coding, search for elements that can be amalgamated, and keep working on it until they have a system by which they can explore all of their data. It is time consuming and complex, but they think it is necessary to add some rigour and system to the process. They advise the use of various electronic software packages that can help with the process, such as NUD*IST and NVivo, but my colleagues who have used these have found the process to be just as time consuming and fraught with difficulties as when not using them. I welcome the use of technology to support research but it is not the answer to everything and not appropriate for all projects. Software packages do not do the analysis; they assist with the practicalities of sorting and classifying the data.

This text is not the place to present a detailed guide on using electronic software packages, but Ann Lewins (2008) provides a very useful chapter that examines the role of software packages in qualitative research. Lewins notes that using such packages may be more time consuming than not using them, but an advantage might be the higher level of sophistication of the data management and interrogation that is possible. At the time of writing, QSR International at www.qsrinternational.com/ is a commercial website that supplies several software programs. There are useful videos advertising their products that also give some information about how such software can be helpful. Reading a textbook and looking at online information is useful, but the best way to learn more is to find someone who is using such a package and examine it in action.

A thematic approach to analysis is most effective if you have a clear focus for your research from the start and your interview questions lead the interviewees into providing the information you seek. This does not mean that you cannot be open to modifying your themes at a later date, but if you have a clear purpose at interview then the themes for analysis will naturally emerge from the data collected. Reporting thematic research means that you have to seek opportunities to illustrate specific experiences in each theme and if appropriate indicate some quantitative measure of the influence of a particular theme. An analysis based on grounded theory, with open coding, is effective when you want to allow people's narratives to provide the information they want you to hear, rather than you interviewing with specific themes in mind. For example, the research into illness narratives discussed by Bochner (2001) could use an open coded analysis, searching for the issues that emerge related to people's health care.

Analysing Written Narrative Data

This section is separated into two parts. The first focuses on two published research reports in which the authors have used different approaches to analysing the written narrative data they collected. Both were conducting research in practice-based settings, and both were using narrative as a means of professional development and as research data. The second part focuses on examples from second-year undergraduate projects.

Analyses from published research

Riley and Hawe (2005) describe and discuss their analytical method in detail in a methods discussion paper. They contrast narrative analysis with thematic analysis, describing thematic analysis in two ways: one agreeing with Crang and Cook's (2007) description of open coding, and one that begins with themes identified at the start of a project, as we saw in in Simkhada's (2008) research. Riley and Hawe suggest that many researchers in health promotion use a combination of both thematic methods, and their paper seeks to identify the benefits of using an alternative form of narrative analysis. They claim that narrative analysis is different from thematic analysis because it focuses on the dynamic interpretation of events and experiences over time, with the construction of new meanings. Narrative also begins from the point of view of the storytellers, the people involved as participants in the research, not the researcher. Narrative analysis aims to understand how people think through events over time and in context. It looks at the sense of the story, whether it is logical, whether it identifies events and their consequences, whether it evaluates, and whether there is evidence of transformation. These features cannot be identified as easily in thematic coding.

Riley and Hawe (2005) provide a table to show the steps they take in their narrative analysis of participants' diaries kept over a two-year period during a particular intervention programme. I outline their steps briefly here:

1　They examined the text of the stories and identified whether sentences and paragraphs were descriptive, consequential, evaluative or transformative.
2　They focused on why the story was told in the way it was – the types of words or phrases chosen.
3　They examined the storytelling occasion – whether it was told immediately after the event or sometime later, and whether there was a story that was not being told.
4　They questioned how the storyteller made sense of the story in relation to the broader context.
5　Finally, they identified the sequence of events and evaluations in the story, that is the point of the story.

It seems that there is opportunity in their approach for much researcher interpretation. Their conclusion is that narrative analysis in this way can be used with even short stories, but they do also comment on its time consuming nature and retrospective analysis rather than ongoing analytical action. One of the values of their narrative approach is that it highlighted the private lives of practitioners and the level of personal investment that was put into the development projects that each participant was responsible for. Within their paper they also demonstrate the use of two different thematic analyses to show how useful they could be too, and they did in fact use thematic analysis during the project to feed back data to the participants more quickly – something to consider in longer-term practice-based research projects.

Another research project over a nine-month period used narrative reports rather than diaries because the reports provided the opportunity to evaluate specific practices with the guidance of the researchers. Kevin Pottie et al. (2008) analysed the reports to monitor the progress of the integration of pharmacists into group family practices. The narratives were used as an ongoing resource to support the development of the intervention programme. The table in Figure 7.3 summarises the process. The reports were clearly part of the ongoing evaluation of a practice development. This was their primary purpose, while also providing data for the research.

Figure 7.3 A summary of the narrative report contents

Period	Report content
Months 1–4	The pharmacists wrote about their observations, their interactions with physicians, the events and people that supported them in their work and the potential innovations arising from the change.
Months 5–6	In addition to the above, participants commented on their developing roles and identities as family practice pharmacists. During this period the research team summarised their findings of the first four months and fed these back to participants for their seventh record.
Month 7	Participants provided feedback on the summary of findings.
Month 8	They commented on their developing relationship with the physicians.
Month 9	Each one commented on the tools they believed were necessary to integrate a pharmacist into their particular setting.

The research team used an iterative grounded theory approach in which they immersed themselves in the data, using open coding, which was then entered into a software package to aid the organisation of data. The team had regular monthly meetings at which they discussed emerging themes and identified questions leading to ongoing areas for exploration. Their findings are presented in narrative style, explaining the identification of a need to provide mentors for the pharmacists in their new roles, for example. To illustrate specific points they use extracts from individual narratives. Using the narratives had two benefits. The first was that the narrative reporting helped the pharmacists clarify their new roles. The second was that the narratives provided a window on the tensions and issues that existed not only in the pharmacists' work, but in the maintenance of records for the research. The researchers suggest that early feedback to participants about the ongoing evaluation would be best, to maintain interest and engagement in the process. They also suggest that the written narrative data could usefully be supplemented by follow-up individual interviews about specific themes that emerge.

These two examples demonstrate how narrative data have been analysed in professional contexts where the focus has been on the evaluation of a new initiative. The first was a retrospective analysis, looking for deeper understanding of practice through using a narrative analysis method rather than thematic analysis. This method illustrated the strong influence of professional expectations upon the personal lives of participants, who often seemed to resolve professional challenges while taking part in personal activities. A thematic analysis, especially one that had categories decided before the research, might not have allowed this information to emerge from the data. The second example was an iterative process, using open coding, while at the same time having some ideas about the area of developing practice that the participants were to report on.

ANALYSING NARRATIVE DATA

Each analytical approach was designed to serve a particular purpose in a specific project. If you design your own analytical process you may draw from features of these, but you will most likely adapt and tailor an approach to your own project's purpose.

Analyses from second-year undergraduates

The following two examples demonstrate different ways that students used their written narrative data within their analysis. The examples provide an opportunity for readers to examine and explore the students' approaches and consider how to develop them further.

For the first example, in Figure 7.4 there is an example of a child's story that second-year undergraduate Gillian included near the start of her analysis. She was trying to establish why children misbehaved so that she could change her practice and manage their behaviour more effectively.

Figure 7.4   An extract from Gillian's analysis

Children's stories about their day at school

These stories were set for homework. I asked them to write about the day they had at school.

Kasim's story

It's Wednesday, I had one of the worst days in my life. I had a supply teacher who came to my school on Monday. I was a bit silly on Monday and sometimes I got blamed for nothing. I got blamed for asking Aaron for help, I asked miss for help but she didn't come to help me. I felt angry and annoyed.

On Wednesday I thought I would be good for miss after I was silly for the past few days. When I sat down for the register I didn't get into trouble (for the first time). Then we did science and I got moved for being naughty when I wasn't, I just couldn't see the board. That made me angrier and very annoyed.

Then when we went for lunch I and some other people had to stay back for maths because miss said we didn't do enough work, so I had to do corrections. I did not get one of the questions so I asked miss but she went to help Adam. I was so annoyed after that I wanted to burst.

After lunch we went to the ICT room and I had to finish my maths there, but I still didn't get the work. So then I finally got help and I finished the work without any problems.

Kasim's story tells me that his behaviour is due to the fact that he feels he isn't always listened to and feels that he is being ignored. When he didn't understand what to do or when he couldn't see the board he behaved in a negative way, which I feel was to gain attention. This resulted in him being punished, i.e. being moved or kept in at lunchtime. When he finally received help from the teacher he was able to complete the work, without any disruptions.

(Gillian, unpublished report, 2006)

Gillian asked the children to write their stories for homework, which might not be the best place or time for the children to do this. The time lapse might affect their memory of events, and other people, such as family members, might influence the content. Gillian probably had a good reason for asking the children to write their stories at home; she was researching ways of improving her work with a group of disruptive pupils. To ask them to do it at school might have been counter-productive, resulting in further disruptive behaviour. It seemed that the children really valued the opportunity to give their individual views through homework, without fear of repercussions. Kasim's story was helpful to Gillian in supporting her recognition of him feeling ignored and not receiving the help he needed, which she might not have recognised before.

Gillian used the whole story from the child (the wholeness being important for deriving meaning from it) to begin her analysis, which at this point is simply the identification of possible reasons for the child's behaviour. Later in the analysis, Gillian begins to relate these initial ideas to other data and relevant literature about behaviour management.

Some students analysed their data in a chronological sequence, to document and analyse change in practice over time. For the second example, in Figure 7.5 we can see that Jade built her analysis around extracts from her own and the children's diaries in the first week of her research. She corrected children's spelling errors to ease readability. Diary entries are in italics, with Jade's discussion in normal font. I present a lengthy section in the figure to provide a clear representation of the data and to enable fuller understanding of Jade's developing analytical processes over the period.

Jade is clearly at the early stages of her analysis, focusing on her practice and making decisions about improvements for the next lesson, in preparation for the final summative analysis in which she provides a more critical stance and refers to further relevant literature. This form of presenting the data, lesson by lesson, proved very effective for Jade because she used the information in her diary to support practice development over the period of the series of lessons. However, we might question whether all the detail was essential in her final report, where she might instead have taken relevant extracts from her diary reflections to illustrate her discussion, leaving her more space for developing her analysis with reference to other research.

You may notice that each of the students has embraced the notion of developing their own personal analysis before focusing on the literature. I believe that this is the most effective way to develop analytical capabilities. They also adopt a narrative style in developing their analysis. The narrative approach in writing the final presentation of such research reports can be very effective and, according to Smeyers and Verhesschen (2001), the creation of a narrative involves an analytical development. The resulting narrative should not only fit the data but also bring out a sense of order and

ANALYSING NARRATIVE DATA

Figure 7.5   Jade's analysis

Date: 10/01/06

Lesson: history introductory lesson

Number of children: 16

Initial reflections:

I do not feel that the children were engaged. Paul and Sam in particular were very disruptive initially and not on task during the discussion which was a negative start to the lesson. Most of the class appeared to be interested and enthusiastic to share their previous knowledge of the Egyptians, although on reflection, I failed to encourage Sarah and Faye to contribute and I am sure they knew a lot, as they are both bright pupils. The main activity was to create a title page in the children's history books, as this was our first lesson. I gave each table a selection of reference books to help with ideas. The children seemed eager to use the books and Claire found information we had been discussing earlier. Paul, Sam and Callum settled down well to this activity and even worked well when choosing words from the brainstorm to develop into sentences. Paul required some support to remain on task.

This week the data gathered have highlighted for me the importance of planning thoroughly before each lesson. After reflecting on all the evidence, I have found a common theme appears to be the lack of engagement of a number of pupils. My initial reaction to the lesson was that it was unsuccessful, as I did not have the 'feelgood' factor. However, after deeper reflection I now can see that for the children who learn best from visual or auditory input, the lesson was enjoyable, the children were on task and retained information, which has been recorded in their diaries.

13/01/06 Further reflections:

After reflecting more deeply about my first lesson I can now see that not all of the children were engaged throughout the whole lesson, and this leads me to question whether I adequately catered for children such as Paul and Sam at the start of the lesson when Paul in particular was becoming fidgety and disruptive during the discussion. MacRae (2004) suggests that if on reflection you are finding children wiggling in their seats, becoming disengaged or not participating in discussions, then perhaps information is not being provided according to their sensory preference. As Paul, Sam and Callum in my opinion prefer to learn through moving and doing (kinaesthetic learning style), I do not believe that I catered for their learning style for a large proportion of the lesson. Next week I will have to plan more thoroughly to ensure that I improve this so that there is less disruption and better learning opportunities for all of the children.

As this was the first lesson, it was necessary to spend a large proportion of the lesson discussing what the children already knew about the Egyptians and identifying what they would like to find out. For children such as Sam, Paul and Callum, if I had been better prepared I could have made this activity a more kinaesthetic learning experience. According to Campbell, Campbell and Dickinson (2004), a characteristic of a kinaesthetic learner is 'someone who learns best by direct involvement and participation and remembers more clearly what was done, rather than what was said or observed' (p. 66). Involving these learners in the discussion by allowing them to get up and move, for example acting as scribe for me, may have resulted in them remaining on task. In addition, I could have incorporated regular brain breaks, which would allow all the children to rest and refocus on the task. My knowledge of Brain Gym exercises and the importance of using brain breaks such as Brain Gym for accelerated learning could have been put to good use during this lesson.

significance within their meaning. In action research, about change in practice, the narrative report should also indicate the changes needed along with their justification through use of data.

The focus in this section has been on written analysis and the underlying development of analytical skills through a focus on personal analysis before developing a more critical stance with reference to other literature. I believe that the analytical process should begin from your perspective. What are you looking for that helps you answer the question or solve your practical problem? You should first write your own draft analysis based on your knowledge and understanding of the events. In my experience, this approach leads to greater depth of thought and the development of analytical strategies. Once a personal analysis is complete then further analysis and comparison with relevant research literature support even deeper analysis.

Of course, one cannot make simple rules about how a specific analysis will progress, but the key elements are those of deep reflection, problematising apparently simple events, and the critique of relevant literature. I believe, from my own experiences and observation of students, that the development of an autobiographical understanding – an understanding of one's position and thinking in relation to the research – is essential to the interpretive analytical process. Freeman (2007) describes autobiographical understanding as a tool for ethical and moral recollection, revisiting the experience and making sense of it from a distance. I agree.

Analysing Visual Data

In earlier chapters I have introduced some examples of visual data. Visual data, more readily than written or oral data, have the capacity to capture the audience, possibly creating an emotional response and offering the opportunity to open the mind to new ideas. These features can cause visual data to be ignored because of their subjectivity and their potential for multiple interpretations. In the modern world we cannot ignore such data; we are surrounded and sustained by the visual narratives that invade our lives through television, advertising, game machines and satellite navigation tools. Visual data are important for capturing the detail of social worlds and lived experiences, as demonstrated by Chris Jones (2009) and others on the ActionResearch. net website. However, they are not without their challenges in analysis, and the following examples serve to provide some ideas and further reading to help you identify the potential advantages and disadvantages of moving into a multimedia world in research.

Silverman (2006) writes about three different kinds of analysis of visual materials: content analysis, semiotics and workplace studies. Content analysis seems straightforward; it comprises a retrospective focus on the content of visual materials and the identification of content categories that are of interest, for example watching television adverts for sexist images of women. Focusing on the content alone means that the context in which the image was created and the way it is received are ignored, and in some studies these elements will be very important. Semiotics is usually applied in linguistics, but Silverman gives examples of how images such as cartoons may be seen to represent words in different ways, that is the conveyed meaning of the visual image depends on how the materials are presented to give a particular message. This too is a retrospective analysis of existing materials using a system that was intended for analysing language. Silverman's third category is workplace studies, and he cites examples where gesture, facial expression and body movements are studied in video data of patient–doctor interactions with the conclusion that the bodily conduct is part of the story. This is similar to the findings in my thesis where gesture was identified as important to developing an understanding of mathematics language. Without the analysis of video records I might not have noticed the gestures in the detailed way that I did.

The focus of the workplace research cited by Silverman is clearly about identifying how workplace practice might change, or identifying the complexities of work or machines that cannot always be represented in handbooks and guidance manuals. The analyses seem mainly narrative in nature, describing and explaining the events, identifying the complexities and the conflicts between systems. This is not the same as action research where a practitioner might use visual methods of data collection to explore personal professional practice. In Chapter 6 I gave an example of a teaching assistant, Shelley, using a video recording from which she and the teacher created narratives. These two narratives formed the data for Shelley's analysis of her practice along with other data gathered from the children she taught. Using the video in this way allowed for two interpretations of the scene, which along with the children's narratives of the lesson allowed Shelley to identify key issues in the way she worked with the children. The narrative analysis of the video was more useful than a thematic analysis would have been in this piece of research. However, if Shelley had decided to video several lessons she could have viewed them to identify themes across the set of videos, which might have resulted in an even deeper understanding of her practice.

Crang and Cook also provide a brief but useful critique of different approaches to analysing visual data (2007: 123–6). Some focus on turning the visual image into text to prepare it for analysis, which does not allow the visual image to tell its own story, or even to support the story. Instead, this type of analysis focusing on content or themes in the transcript generally serves to tell the story that the researcher interprets from the image, unless there is some means of verifying the intended meaning with participants, or a collaborative approach combining and comparing different interpretations by different people. Another analytical approach described by Crang and Cook uses sets of questions to explore patterns and regularities within sets of images in order to identify their purpose, what they were about and how they were made. This is an analysis of the images, the whole story, from production to presentation. It could be a useful approach to analysing how different sets of people are represented in images, such as family photographs from different cultures or spanning a historical period. The questions the researcher will devise and ask about a set of images will depend on the purpose of the inquiry.

Much visual research has developed with the purpose of involving children or vulnerable groups of people who perhaps have difficulty expressing themselves in words, but can use visual methods such as photography, film, artworks etc to explain themselves and their thoughts. This is a way of collecting data, but some researchers have then involved the participants in analysing the information. In Chapter 4 I introduced the research by Peter Egg and his co-workers using photography in an ethically developed project with children as co-researchers. They researched in several countries.

Egg et al. (2004) used photographs to conduct research in an SOS Children's Village in Thailand. It was an interpretive study in which the outcome was presented as case studies written in narrative style. A key feature of their approach to analysis was that the children and the adults in the villages made the choices about which photographs represented what they all wanted to say. Peter Egg focused on children taking photos, and families sharing photos that showed the absence of violence. It was a purposeful activity for the children to imagine they were creating something for other children who had been brought up with violence, to show them there were other things in life. Once the photos were collected the children and adults in the village chose photos that most represented what they wanted to show and put them into categories. The children voted for the topics that were symbolised by various photos. Their choices reflected peaceful, profound and unspectacular photos rather than an emphasis on action. The second part of the case study presents some of the photos with researcher or child comments about them. For example, 'freedom' was represented by a photo of a girl sitting on a jetty with her toes just touching the water. The scene of tranquillity symbolised the absence of violence.

Egg et al.'s (2004) case study is intended to engage the reader in making interpretations of their own by presenting some information about the life of the village, and being part of that as a participant researcher in addition to the photographic data interpreted and categorised by the children. The analysis was appropriate for child participation in research intended to alter their perspective and encourage them to think about alternatives to violence. The photographs were interpreted in a way that was relevant to the project, which is why the children were involved. If taken out of context and interpreted by others the photos might be given a different meaning.

Similar research was conducted by Julianne Moss et al. (2007) with middle school children in Australia. In pairs, children took photographs and made notes to depict scenes of spaces around school that were: inclusive and exclusive; best and worst; comfortable and uncomfortable; and welcome and unwelcome. The children decided on the order of importance of their photographs and their dialogue was audio-taped. The researchers then coded the data to create themes and, after themes were compared, 10 images were chosen to represent the common themes of the context. These were then displayed and used to discuss issues of inclusion and exclusion around the school. The process of taking photographs, making notes and identifying specific areas of school was the children's analysis of their situation in relation to the concepts of inclusion and exclusion. The researchers supported the analysis by coding and collating results from different pairs of children. The pictures and the associated children's comments tell their own story.

An interesting three-year project about identity and inclusion by Pat Thomson and Christine Hall (2008) focused on analysing children's self-portraits. Their focus was to ask what opportunity the self-portraits afforded the children to represent their identities. Their analysis was one of making meaning, discussing with the children what their self-portraits were about. They found that before talking to the children they had misread the meanings of many of the self-portraits; sometimes very different meanings were reported by the children. They also found, through discussion with one child, that multiple meanings could readily exist in the mind of the child. In their chapter they present excerpts of the discussions to illustrate these examples. The interpretations given by the children in interview discussion were retrospective, and could have been different from the original meaning of the picture when it was created.

In this section you will note very different approaches to analysing visual data. Some try to emulate the analysis of a written text, seeking themes and open coding. Others focus on the content, relying not on interpretation but on what they actually see, although avoidance of interpretation is difficult. For some the visual images tell their own story, and for others the visual images become part of a larger story told by others, not just the researchers. Clearly the challenges of analysing and interpreting visual data sometimes seem greater than those of analysing textual materials. Despite this the advantages of visual data in working with children and vulnerable people are evident, as are the benefits of visual data in enhancing the understanding of communication processes using gesture, body language and facial expression.

Summary

Chapter 7 has focused on different analytical processes using a range of data from interviews, written narrative and visual images, fitting the core theme of biographical data. The structural approach focuses on examining the linguistic structure of a narrative. A structural analysis is most useful when seeking common elements in a set of stories. It is not useful for developing understanding of the meanings behind the stories, the reasons for actions or justification of choices. A thematic analysis focuses on the content of the narratives, the events that occur, the experiences that people have and the meanings that emerge through finding a set of themes within the data. The themes may be decided upon before the research begins or may be determined by a method of open coding, identifying the themes that emerge from the data in a grounded theory approach to analysis. Some methods of analysing visual data draw on the structural and thematic processes of analysis, but others are more broadly interpretive and include the participants in supporting the development of categories and meaning within the images.

It is evident from all the examples provided that the analysis of data is a process that is designed to suit a particular project. Researchers draw on previously used processes and adapt them to suit their own context. The analysis may be iterative, ongoing throughout the data collection process, or it may be retrospective, analysing the data after they have all been collected. Sometimes there will be a mixture of these two processes. The aim of any analysis is to produce credible and trustworthy evidence to support the researcher's initial questions, identified issues or proposed hypotheses.

Suggested Reading

Cortazzi, M. (1993) *Narrative Analysis*. London: Falmer.

Patterson, W. (2008) 'Narratives of events: Labovian narrative analysis and its limitations', in M. Andrews, C. Squire and M. Tamboukou (eds), *Doing Narrative Research*. London: Sage. pp. 22–40.

Reissman, C.K. (2008) *Narrative Methods for the Human Sciences*. London: Sage.

The journal *Narrative Inquiry* published by John Benjamins is a peer-reviewed journal that provides a forum for theoretical, empirical and methodological work on narrative. It tends to focus on the work of psychologists and linguists but various articles provide a meaningful discourse about analysis in any subject discipline or profession in which there is an interest in narrative.

USING NARRATIVE IN RESEARCH

8

REPRESENTATIVE CONSTRUCTIONS
IN NARRATIVE ANALYSIS

CHAPTER OUTLINE

- Introduction
  - Narrative truth?
  - From fiction to representative construction
- Taking a brave step into the land of fiction
  - Using fictional narrative to analyse questionnaire data
  - Same data – different analytical process
  - Layered stories
- Further examples of using representative constructions
  - Sue writes letters
  - Isabel's analysis
- Summary
- Suggested reading

Introduction

This chapter will explore the challenge of using representative constructions in the analysis of narrative and other data. Using representative constructions is one of the core themes of this text because they require serious consideration as an analytical process. One of the concerns expressed by those with a positivist perspective on research is that representations or fictional narratives are too subjective, too likely to allow skewing of the analysis to suit the researcher. The traditional ethnographic methodology also suffers from this problem since it attempts to re-create the reality of the situation, but ethnographers acknowledge that their own position in the research will have an impact on the way they interpret it. Crang and Cook (2007) provide a discussion of the issues related to subjectivity in ethnographic data and conclude that *all* research, even that which claims objectivity, is subject to the influence of the researcher. I agree with them.

The postmodern approach to research accepts that interpretation is inevitable in *all* research, but particularly in research involving people and their interactions with each other and the environment. The postmodern approach to professional research accepts that professionals enter their research with significant knowledge and understanding about practice, identifying and addressing the need for change through systematic evaluation. Professional or social research therefore lends itself to narrative approaches of all kinds, since the stories of practice and relationships exist already and form the networks within organisations and communities enabling them to operate effectively.

As noted previously, all research involves interpretation. The conclusion of a positivist report is also an interpretation of the findings (Czarniawaska, 2004) and therefore the claim that only positivist approaches to research can provide a truthful conclusion has little truth itself. Different scholars might provide different interpretations of the same research findings. Just as there is no set way to interpret narrative, there is no set way to deconstruct data in order to reconstruct a meaningful narrative from them. According to Czarniawaska, narrative analysers ask not only 'What does a text say?' but 'How does a text say it?', that is, they show a clear interest in establishing the meaning of the text. Others might ask 'Why do they tell the story in this way?', that is, they have an interest in a phenomenon, not the text itself. As with other chapters, this chapter emphasises the notion of 'fitness for purpose' and researchers providing clear justification for their chosen approach. The chapter questions whether an account can ever be factual and at the same time challenges the notion of fiction as being entirely constructed from imagination (as many people perceive it).

Narrative truth?

Badley's (2003) review of *Narratives and Fictions in Educational Research* by Peter Clough (2002) raises questions about the truth of stories and acknowledges that a single 'truth' may not exist. Even in presenting a factual account, a writer provides an interpretation of the facts. On reading a factual account, the reader interprets the facts in a different way. Clough (2002) used what he describes as 'storying methodology' to research people's social lives. His stories are constructed from interviews and other data gathered, in and beyond various educational settings. His aim was to examine real events and present the story of these events as he sees them, allowing his personal, moral and ethical response to provide an appearance of reality, an experiential truth (his words). His stories are based on facts, yet are fictions because of the way they are presented, and he claims they have a biographical truth that cannot be judged by the usual tests of positivist research data – reliability, validity and replicability. Instead he would prefer them to be judged by their aesthetic standard, their emotive force, their verisimilitude, and criteria of authenticity or integrity to the people they portray.

Even though we can question the existence of truth in any story and therefore cannot judge narratives by their 'truthfulness', I am not convinced that we should completely abandon the concepts of validity, reliability and replicability. When judging the usefulness of fictional or representative accounts in research, perhaps we should reconceptualise validity, reliability and replicability within a narrative framework. Peter Clough's stories are convincing; their validity lies in the relevance of the lives explored, and their replicability is not in the ability to repeat the research and find the same conclusions, but in the comparisons that readers make with the lived stories that they know. The stories have already been replicated a thousand times over in a range of contexts and experiences within the readers' minds. Thus they are reliable – telling stories that are common in many ways to others.

From fiction to representative construction

Initially I, like others, used the word 'fiction' to describe the stories I began to create in my research, but now I prefer to name them 'representative constructions'. First, the various meanings of the word 'fiction' lead to different understandings. Two in particular are not helpful in relation to claiming credibility in research that makes use of fictions:

- fiction as that which does not exist
- fiction as that which is not true.

Second, the representative constructions are based on information that is about real events. The information is reconstructed or represented in a form different from the original information while aiming to maintain the reality. Critics of the use of 'fiction' within research analysis tend to focus on the non-existence of truth claims. However, researchers using such representative constructions do not generally aim to claim the absolute truth (e.g. Clough, 2002) and they view the representation as a form of analysis and reporting of the research data. In addition, even if reconstruction did not occur and participants' stories were told in their entirety, we can never be sure that the stories from the field are the truth. Unfortunately, as Clough discusses in his rejoinder to Badley (2003), people reading research accounts often search for the truth in them, provided by the writer, rather than accept that there can be several versions of the truth of a situation and find their own truths in what they read. Participants' stories are their interpretations and are most likely reconstructions of actual events that will change each time they are told.

Using the words 'representative' and 'construction' together in *representative construction* suggests that the story is constructed to represent a particular type of person or set of events. It is not simply a re-presentation of the same materials in a different format, a rhetorical device to evoke discussion; nor is it simply a reconstruction of data without any attention paid to the meaning for the reader. Ely (2007), in writing about the use of narrative in research reporting, suggests that writers focus on two important ideas – readability and wider communication – while always aiming to represent the people and events in the research fairly. I believe that the use of representative constructions is justified in situations where the researcher seeks to make sense of diverse realistic data through analysing the parts and then synthesising them into a realistic framework – a narrative that is readable and meaningful – in preparation for further analysis. Ely (2007) provides several examples of data presented in different ways, for example layered stories. This is a technique in which the researcher places himself/herself in the shoes of other people to tell their stories; I have used this approach with some modifications, as discussed later in this chapter (Bold, 2005; 2006b; 2008b). Using various examples, Ely discusses the different ways that one may re-present data in a report. Czarniawaska (2004) cites others who use different words to justify narrative methods and validate claims in analysis. For example, when reading a research report one may ask the following questions:

- Is the analysis in the research report *trustworthy*?
- Are the findings *applicable* in similar contexts?
- Are the findings *consistent* with other findings and my own understanding?
- Have they been reported and analysed from a *neutral stance* or from a *particular philosophic position*?
- Do they seem *authentic*? And *plausible*?
- Have the data been analysed from a *critical standpoint*?

According to Czarniawaska, legitimacy emerges from the response of the reader rather than by demonstrating a set of attributes. Trustworthiness, plausibility and criticality are judged by the reader in relation to the reader's own knowledge and experience. A reader might ask, is this a credible account in my experience? The next section contains examples of my explorations into this type of analysis and they should demonstrate some of the features discussed by Czarniawaska. I tell the story of my own professional development in using narratives to support the analysis of data. At the start I called these fictional narratives, so this is also the story of how I moved towards reconceptualising the fictional narrative as a representative construction.

Taking a Brave Step into the Land of Fiction

In my own research (Bold, 2005; 2006b; 2008b) I explored ways of using fictional narratives of data gathered in order to (1) help me make sense of a diverse set of information and (2) help the audience better understand the 'story' it is telling about real people's lives. Czarniawaska (2004) supports the notion that there are many good reasons for making a consistent narrative out of a set of incomplete or fragmented ones. This was how I viewed my data:

fragmented and incomplete, yet potentially rich if organised into something that made sense. For me it was a brave step, taking me out of my comfort zone, testing out a creative approach to analysing information.

One of the greatest challenges in creating a fictional narrative is rendering others' stories with respect for the participants' voices. Respect for the participants in research requires the researcher to retell the stories so that participants' voices are heard in a way that best represents their situation. In using narrative in this way, researchers have to acknowledge their influence on the construction and in addition may pay attention to participant validation. As in any research, these issues emerge and require open discussion. Mello (2007) would call this an arts-informed approach to analysis, transforming the field data into a research text that is a way of informing meaning. In the arts-informed approach, the researcher has an aesthetic experience, allowing reflection on the field data to draw together and make sense of parts by synthesising them into something new. Mello cites others who have used letters, poems and drawings as part of their sense-making process.

Using fictional narrative to analyse questionnaire data

At a British Educational Research Association study day, I reported a small action research project 'Reflective diaries as professional development tools' (2005). I surveyed second-year undergraduates' thoughts about the use of a reflective diary as a professional development tool and the impact of using it as a university assessment, administering the questionnaire with open-ended questions in Figure 8.1. The purpose of the small piece of research was to review whether to keep the diary as part of the assessment, and to identify ways in which the team might introduce the students to the notion of using a reflective diary more effectively.

From a cohort of 80 students, 34 provided responses with full permission for their use. The data were very varied and difficult to categorise. I decided to analyse responses to each question by allocating them to two categories. On the response sheets I highlighted, using different colours, phrases (sometimes whole sentences)

Figure 8.1 Reflective diary questionnaire

1 How useful was the reflective diary in supporting your development as a reflective thinker about your workplace practice?
2 How successful were you in using the suggested format of using two pages, one for observations and comments and the opposite page for reflections and further reflections? (You should relate this answer to your mark awarded in addition to your own comments on the process.)
3 What is the difference between reflecting in action in your workplace and reflecting in writing for an assessment?
4 If you used a research diary again, how would you organise it to support your reflective processes?

147

that were *positive* in nature and phrases that were *negative* in nature. A positive phrase might be one about how the diary supported professional development, while a negative phrase might be one about a difficulty of using the diary in practice. I used my professional judgement about the nature of the phrases, and some were difficult to categorise as either positive or negative. Most students' responses showed that they thought the diaries had a mixture of positive and negative attributes, which is what I would expect to find as the normative response.

I collated the phrases into two documents with the purpose of using the words from the students' comments to create narratives written by two fictional teaching assistants. One (Una) found using the diary a positive experience and one (Duet) found it mainly a negative experience. My purpose in exploring this approach to collating and representing the data was to (1) make use of the students' words and (2) provide a clear overview of each end of the experiential continuum so that we might learn how to improve the experience for the students.

You might ask why I chose to make the lists into stories instead of searching for further subthemes, for example. Immediate comparison of these lists showed clearly that there were more positive (124) than negative comments (82) about using the diary. Some comments might have fitted into a set of subthemes, but most were very different and there seemed little benefit in using subthemes which would not necessarily help the sense-making process. In list format it was difficult to imagine the reality of being a student experiencing either of these two ends of the continuum: hence the development of two fictional narratives, which I will now refer to as representative constructions. For the two narratives I focused my attention on the responses to the first question, where 55 were positive and 25 negative. This was because the narratives would be lengthy, and at the time my aim was to explore whether the idea would work in practice, whether it would be useful and produce a credible result. Looking back at the data now, there is much more that could be included in these two stories, but this does not prevent them from representing much of the student experience.

So that you can see the process of narrative creation, in Figure 8.2 I have listed some of the positive attributes out of the whole list, and following this I present a section of Una's narrative that has been constructed using these phrases. The numbers represent their position in my list, showing that I did not construct the narrative simply by taking each positive attribute as listed. Their relative positions have no significance except that they were in the order of the questionnaires as analysed. The narrative therefore required some creative thinking, fitting phrases together that I thought made an interesting and reliable construction.

As you read the constructed paragraph you will identify the phrases from the list. It is almost entirely constructed from the students' words, but arranged by me. My arrangement was rather intuitive; I didn't sit for a long time thinking about what to put, I just picked out items as they seemed to fit and made the narrative flow. You can see that it is not purely fiction, as in something that does not exist or is not true. It represents what the students were saying as a collective group.

Figure 8.2 Constructing Una's story

Phrases from the questionnaires identifying positive attributes

1	kick-started my reflective thinking
4	supported development as a reflective thinker – could jot notes and snippets
5	think much more
9	made me aware of situations that I might have ignored previously
12	systematic and organised approach
16	most effective tool, positive tool
19	the diary as a 'working document' was most refreshing
21	intense insight into a situation that might have passed unnoticed
52	events in a chronological order
53	all information in one place
54	more natural than structured writing
55	useful to compare situations

Una's story (first paragraph)

The diary, a 'working document', was most refreshing and it 'kick-started' my reflective thinking. It provided a different medium to support understanding of practice and was a most effective, positive tool. I could jot notes and snippets and think much more about them in a systematic, organised and focused approach. It made me aware of situations that I might have ignored previously, providing intense insight into a situation that might have passed unnoticed. I found it extremely useful to watch, monitor and reflect on children's behaviour patterns and it helped me to recognise and adapt to different learning styles. Writing in the diary was more natural than more structured writing and provided information in chronological order in one place. Because of this, I found it useful for comparing situations.

(Bold, 2005)

Una's narrative was an opportunity to analyse the data within a representation of reality for an imaginary student who had a wholly positive experience. One criticism might be that finding such a student is unlikely and a more realistic approach would be to construct narratives to represent the normative experience. As a team, we knew that many students had a mixed experience. This was obvious in practice and from the students' questionnaire responses. Our purpose in focusing on the extreme cases was to identify very clearly the positive and negative attributes of using the reflective diary before modifying the way we introduced and developed students' use of it. Students who read Una's story could identify the positive attributes in relation to their own experience. Most interesting was that students' identified positive attributes that they had not put on their responses to the questionnaires, through reading Una's story. It added to their reflections on their experience.

Similarly, Duet's negative story, part reproduced in Figure 8.3, prompted identification of potential problems that some students had not previously identified. These included the need to practise and maintain a diary for some time before feeling confident and competent, and the idea that the diary might become a fiction itself, with things being made up just to fill it!

149

Figure 8.3 Constructing Duet's story

Phrases from the questionnaires identifying negative attributes

10 risk of being self-critical and instil poor self-confidence in the ability to deal with issues
11 the reflective diary can only be honest if it is solely used by the individual or a known audience
12 I was continually looking for things to reflect on, even if the objective had been completed successfully
18 might make up or exaggerate situations to include in the diary
21 lack of security if it was left lying around
22 confidentiality
23 may not be enlightening enough to share with colleagues

Duet's story (final paragraph)

The reflective diary can only be honest if the individual or a known audience uses it. I thought there was a risk of being too self-critical and it could instil poor self-confidence in my ability to deal with issues. I was continually looking for things to reflect on, even if my objective had been completed successfully. I might even make up or exaggerate situations to include in the diary. I felt that the contents might not be enlightening enough to share with colleagues. I also had concerns about confidentiality since there was a lack of security if it was left lying around.

(Bold, 2005)

The discussions we had with students about the positive and negative attributes, based on these two narratives, helped the team make changes to the way that we introduced students to the use of reflective diaries. For example, both Una and Duet kept records at work. One viewed the diary as a positive extension of this process, while the other considered it an unnecessary addition. We explored this issue with the students and considered why these two different perspectives might exist. We thought of ways to alleviate any issues arising and to support students in making effective use of different media to enhance their reflective thinking. The two narratives had helped to organise the bland lists of information from the questionnaires into a 'living experience' format to which students related, rather than a set of coded, thematic items taken out of context. Thus the narratives fulfilled their purpose in being an analytical tool that led to further analysis and change in the professional context. Since this was an exploratory process, introducing students and the teaching team to the use of narrative in research, it served another purpose in providing academic development related to researching our practice.

Same data – different analytical process

Because the previous narratives only drew upon the answers to the first question on my questionnaire, I sought another way to compare and contrast student

---

experiences using all the data collected, including the students' reflective diaries. In this second exploration of the data, I chose three students who had presented very different diaries as part of their assessment. In Chapter 5 I have already provided a part example of Erin's story and an example of Rosemary's diary. Their diaries were analysed alongside their questionnaires, their assessment feedback, classroom observation and knowledge of the students, and their module engagement with tutors in class and on e-forums. An internal university journal published the report 'One assessment – three experiences' (Bold, 2006b).

I used representative constructions, one anonymised narrative for each student, allowing comparison of the three students' experiences. In these narratives I altered the content and context of their reflective diaries so that the identification of the participants was minimised. The three students read the narratives and only one recognised the narrative that represented her own experience. This was because it was in a unique setting in comparison to the other students and therefore more difficult to disguise. None of them recognised the other students involved. After some clarification, discussion and a minor change, each agreed that the narratives represented their particular position. Using participant validation in this way highlighted the ethical issue of potential harm. The students might have felt threatened by reading representative constructions of their experience, albeit in anonymised narrative format. Fortunately the three students said that they had not felt threatened by it at all on this occasion.

Figure 8.4 provides Rosemary's responses to the questionnaire. They were very brief, but alongside her diary, assessment feedback and classroom discussion, her story was re-created to include these, as an interpretation of their meaning, not as a reproduction of the actual text. On looking back at my interpretation I can see that I might have missed including some elements she mentions, for example the need for a conclusion. But this is covered broadly in the final sentence where she states that she could have shown this reflection in an essay. Rosemary's story, also a representative

Figure 8.4 Rosemary's questionnaire responses

---

1 I found the diary helped me focus at a later date on events that had taken place. It is easy to forget what exactly has happened during an event if it is not recorded.

2 Fairly successful. However it was difficult to keep the information to one page. Some days there was a lot to record, others very little.

3 Reflecting in action is a passing thing which does not always get acted upon. Reflecting in writing allows you to analyse an event more deeply.

4 I would use a similar format but perhaps add an overall conclusion at the end.

(Rosemary, unpublished questionnaire responses, 2005)

REPRESENTATIVE CONSTRUCTIONS

construction, relied more on holistic interpretation to draw different pieces of data together, rather than using the actual language in Rosemary's questionnaire responses.

Rosemary's responses to the questionnaire suggest that she found the diary a mainly positive experience, but her contributions to class discussions suggested otherwise. The response to question 3 clearly shows her understanding of the different levels of reflection that can occur in practice and in writing. In question 4 she does not really engage with the challenge that she had of fitting materials into the suggested diary format, and her suggestion of adding an overall conclusion within the diary is perhaps an indication of her preference to analyse and summarise the cumulative events within the diary rather than in a separate essay.

In Figure 8.5 I have reproduced Rosemary's story. The emphasis is on the suggested diary structure and the fact that it limited Rosemary's approach. If you look back at Figure 5.3, Rosemary's diary, you will be able to recognise links to the story, where it refers to the structure. However, the theme within the story is also influenced by dialogue during classroom activity and Rosemary's oral feedback.

As you examine my analytical process in Rosemary's story, you might want to compare it to those I produced for Una and Duet, two fictional characters, and consider which approach seems more credible.

Figure 8.5 Rosemary's story

Although I was a little unsure about whether the diary would be useful to me in the format suggested, I was willing to try it and focus my attention on using one page for observations and a second page for reflective thoughts. I understood the reasoning behind the structure – to encourage us to be reflective rather than descriptive. I knew that we could use it for immediate reflections and further reflections about my responses to changes in learner behaviour related to relevant reading, but I doubted that I would be able to fit all the reflections in one place. I wrote my diary in 'rough' to begin with. One of the tutors had recommended this but the other tutor said there was no need. It was meant to be a working document and presentation was not important even though it was for assessment. I still preferred to write it in rough so that I could present a neat copy at the end. This approach was successful and I achieved high grade even though I had used three pages for reflection on one page of observations on occasions. I suppose I overstepped the boundaries but in doing this, I showed that I could think in some depth about my approaches to using guidance and counselling skills in my role at work. My main failing was not to integrate my reading with my reflective comments. I just listed books. However, if I had done this my reflective pages would have taken even more space. The diary was useful in helping me show my reflections but, since I do reflect on my practice a lot anyway, I am not sure it was useful as an assessment. I could have shown these reflections in an essay.

(Bold, 2006b: 22)

The previous example, constructing three stories from different participants of the same event, is a way of providing layered stories. Each one presents a different meaning of the event, providing a broader understanding. Ely (2007) writes about layered stories that stem from the idea that one event can have different meanings for the different participants in it. Using different representative constructions for individuals experiencing the same events can help others recognise that there can be different interpretations and that it is not always possible to draw data together and create common themes that have any real meaning. The different representations do not claim to be representative of all people who have experienced the same event, but act more as examples of experiences from different perspectives.

I put this idea to good use in another research project resulting in a published paper, 'Peer support groups: fostering a deeper approach to learning through critical reflection on practice' (Bold, 2008b). The use of representative constructions was the most effective way to draw together data from an action research project focusing on developing students' ability to reflect in organised peer group discussion sessions. Different strands of data – the tutor-researcher's diary, tutor observations and students' reflective records – provided a triangulation of sources resulting in three narratives offering different perspectives of the same event. The participants agreed that the final narratives represented the reality of the learning situation, thus suggesting that the content is reliable and trustworthy analytical information. Engaging in the development of these narratives prompted a realisation of the need to be careful about language used, for example when attempting to show the strength of a trend in broad terms. I used words such as *most* to present a situation in which most students seemed to agree a common view. However, words such as *most* are vague and might have little meaning when writing about a small group of 20 students. This is a simple illustration of a dilemma faced by narrative researchers in attempting to provide a credible story.

Further Examples of Using Representative Constructions

In this section I have included two examples of different practices in using representative constructions to provide you with further ideas. I will present most of it with little discussion, with the intention that you will draw your own conclusions and develop your own perspectives on the use of representative reconstruction as an analytical process. One of the challenges of writing a chapter about analytical processes is to provide examples that give a realistic sense of what you should actually do and perhaps provide some ideas about what to avoid. In the first example I take a small part of the analysis to show how the system of analysing information proceeded, but it is not complete. The second example is presented in its entirety. It is impossible to provide a real sense of how the representative constructions are part of the analytical process without leaving it whole.

First I include examples from Sue Warren's (2001) doctoral thesis in which she uses letters as representative constructions as part of an iterative research process in her work with school mentors.

Sue writes letters

Sue Warren's (2001) doctoral thesis demonstrates a thoughtful iterative approach to analysis. Her analysis of an action research project in developing school mentor roles went through several stages. First, she collected an evaluation from the mentors and collated their responses. This was her first-order analysis. Figure 8.6 shows the responses to one question about the mentor–student relationship.

Figure 8.6   Mentor responses about the mentor–student relationship

Mentor–student relationship is delicate.
Student must not become dependent on the mentor.
Don't become too 'friendly' or 'familiar'.
Be aware other staff need to be 'won over'.

She then identified statements that demonstrated their use of experience to inform planning and other statements related to the advice they would give new mentors. Figure 8.7 shows how the responses in Figure 8.6 become one of four points of advice to new mentors.

Figure 8.7   Regrouping responses into advice to new mentors

Mentor–student relationship is delicate, don't allow students to become too dependent, ensure they read and produce the goods.

She shared this analysis with the mentors, as participant validation. The medium she chose was a letter, part reproduced in Figure 8.8, which she created and shared with the mentors whose voice she had interpreted, noting their reactions and comments. The letter was written as though it was from the experienced mentors (the participants in the research) to the new mentors. In her thesis Sue uses the mentors' own words as part of the letter and identifies them in blue print while her own voice is in black. Her own voice is derived from her field notes and observations.

Figure 8.8   Part of Sue's letter from the experienced mentors to the new mentors

The first year I had students I tried really hard to set them at ease, to be a friend and confidante. As time passed though I came to think that I'd set myself up as the shoulder to be leant on – especially when deadlines came round and that terrible course leader wanted work handing in or the students wanted me to intervene and sort things out for their benefit. I wanted to be kind and help the students to sort out their problems so I telephoned Leeds for them. I realise now what I'd bitten off!! Why didn't I tell them they were adult graduates who should be able to be responsible for themselves and sort out their own problems? Surely they ought to have been able to telephone Leeds themselves – isn't hindsight a wonderful thing? I certainly won't do that again! They've got to learn to stand on their own two feet.

(Warren, 2001)

The links between the responses to the questionnaire and the letter are evident in the sense that both convey the message that students need to learn to be independent and to take responsibility for their own actions. The content of the letter was verified by sharing it at the mentor group meeting to observe their responses and to discuss the content of the letter. Not only was it verified, but it provided a learning experience for the mentors as they found new information and ideas not previously shared within the group.

This first action cycle, along with other activity, led to setting new targets for development and moving into a second cycle. The letter construction is an important part of the analysis because it brought together many different responses from the mentor questionnaire and provided a realistic representation of these to share with the mentor group before moving into the second phase of the research. Later in the process Sue created a letter in which the new mentors responded to the first letter, thus continuing the communicative flow through an accessible medium. The letters therefore served two purposes: one as a means to draw data together as part of the analytical process, and the second as a means to promote professional development and a second stage of data collection.

Isabel's analysis

A second-year undergraduate, Isabel, a learning mentor in a secondary school, explored her practice in supporting children who had transferred from another school. She focused on a group of six children's experiences, but in her analysis she collated their responses and those of their parents and teachers into one story to represent each group. She created a fictional child, Simon; a fictional parent, Simon's mother; and a fictional teacher, representing the three teachers involved. Using interview data she compiled lists of key information, and from these she created narratives that helped her analyse in more depth. In creating the narratives she identified a problem, but she persisted with the process because she thought it was the best way to start the analysis. During her discussion she outlines the dilemma she faced in making choices for inclusion into the fictional child's narrative that left it not representing all the children in the group. However, in her analysis Isabel discussed the absence of some individual responses which did not reflect the majority experience and in this way included them in the analytical process. For example, only one child had complained of difficulties in making friends during an interview but later observations of all the children showed that they were all experiencing some difficulties in getting to know their peers. Her experience also warns against over-reliance on data from interviews without corroborating evidence from observations, since she found later that the children tended to claim they had many friends, when her subsequent observations showed they seemed isolated in the playground.

I present her whole analysis to demonstrate the role of her representative constructions in aiding deeper analysis of situations involving people and organisations. I invite readers to explore Figure 8.9 to identify features of the analysis of practice, to raise questions and to promote discussion.

Isabel has analysed in different ways. First, she has identified key issues and ideas within her data from each participant. Second, she has used the key issues and ideas to create representative constructions. Third, she has analysed the narrative content from a personal and professional perspective, with some analysis through reference to other relevant readings. One of the thorny issues in assessing analyses is making judgements about the level of *criticality* evident in the final report. I have previously asserted that I believe that skills of critical reflection and critical analysis begin with personal constructs about situations before seeking comparison with other literature about the subject. Isabel's analysis demonstrates her developing ability to critically analyse the situation and inform her practice. She develops the use of literature more strongly in formulating her conclusions.

You will note in all the examples provided that the analytical process has started with the researchers' interpretations of the data. This is something I have encouraged throughout because I believe in developing analytical skills based on professional judgement and personal experience before comparative, critical analysis with the literature. You might prefer to incorporate more reference to other literature throughout the analysis if it is appropriate to do so. Either approach is acceptable providing it is rigorous and leads to credible outcome. You cannot really separate the analysis from other sections of a research report; it usually sits somewhere between the literature review and the conclusion and links closely to them both.

Figure 8.9 Isabel's analysis

The following lists represent an overview of data extracted from the responses made by the children, parents and teachers approached for this research. These responses were woven together to create fictional narratives used for analysis. The creation of the narratives did not represent all the responses of the targeted groups and I had to use professional judgement when collating the evidence to produce stories representative of a common perspective. This did, however, result in some individual responses which did not reflect the common experience being excluded from the stories for analysis, and I saw this as a potential problem, as explained in the analysis of the story of Simon's mum. The characters created are Simon, who recently transferred schools, his mum and Mrs Smith, Simon's teacher.

Parents' responses

- Transferred because of problems at old school.
- Transferred because we moved house.
- We did not know about or understand anything about the work of the learning mentors.
- I would have liked to know more about the new school, but didn't like to ask.
- Teachers are 100% supportive.
- I didn't want to take up the teacher's time discussing problems at the old school, I thought they would already know anyway.
- There were problems transferring information from the old school.
- My child has fitted in well at the new school because they were unhappy at the old school.
- My child felt very isolated because we changed schools and moved house at the same time.
- I was worried whether I had made the right choice to change my child's school.

Children's responses

- I didn't know anything about the new school, I was worried about this.
- I was bullied at my old school.
- My mum told me not to make a fuss at the new school.
- I didn't make new friends easily, I was called names, and I had lots of friends at my old school.
- I have no idea who the learning mentors are and what they do.
- I felt awkward asking for help because I didn't know the helpers.
- I made friends easily, I hated my old school.

Teachers' responses

- Information never arrives before the children.
- Children have often been taught using different methods.
- You never know what to expect, we never get pastoral information.
- New children can have a negative effect on an established class, both socially and academically.
- New parents can be a problem; they can be overprotective and unsupportive of staff.
- Children always settle eventually.
- There should be a programme of integration that all new children participate in led by learning mentors.
- There should be integration and support for parents so they understand new procedures, policies and teaching methods.

(Continued)

(Continued)

Simon's story

Last October I had to change schools. At my old school I had been bullied by some boys in my class for a long time, this upset me a lot, it got so bad I didn't want to go to school anymore. My mum said it would be best if I changed schools to get away from the bullies because no one seemed able to solve the problems there. I was worried at first about moving because I didn't know anyone at the new school. My mum and me went to look round before I started, the head teacher introduced me to my new teacher who seemed very nice, but I didn't get a chance to talk to any of the children there. The night before I changed schools I couldn't sleep because I was worried about fitting in, I didn't know anything really about the new place, it all looked so different from my other school. Mum said it wouldn't take long before I fitted in. She said not to say about the trouble at the other school in case the new people thought we were trouble makers, she told me teachers don't like to hear you complain about other teachers.

When I started at the new school, it was so much better because no one picked on me there. Some of the boys in my class let me join in with their football games, so I made lots of new friends. The work is different from my other school and I don't always understand it but it is sometimes difficult to ask for help from the adults because although I know my new teacher Mrs Smith I don't know who the other helpers are and what they do in school. When I'm struggling I just start messing around with Billy, he always gets a laugh and all the attention. I don't want to tell mum that I am struggling with my schoolwork because she was very upset when I was at the other place. All the routines are different too and I don't like to keep asking about school clubs and things because it doesn't look 'cool' in front of my new mates.

Simon was clearly concerned about having to change schools, it wasn't his idea, even though he had encountered problems with bullying. The fact that he knew very little about the new place and had only been allowed a short visit worried him before he transferred. He explains it is difficult to ask for help because he doesn't understand the roles of adults in school with the exception of his teacher. Simon's comments surrounding this would suggest a lack of communication within the school on support available. It highlights the difficulties faced when relationships with significant adults within the school community have not been created. It would appear that Simon desperately wants to fit in with his new classmates and as a result is frightened of looking silly if he keeps asking for help. His comments about making lots of new friends are interesting since the evidence from other participants is conflicting. Simon's mum tells this story.

Simon's mum

Last year we had big problems with Simon at school. He was being bullied by a group of boys. We told the teacher but no one seemed to sort the problem out adequately. After talking to some of the neighbours, I decided to find Simon a new school, even though he wasn't keen to change. I telephoned the other school nearest to us and the head teacher arranged for us to have a look round. It seemed very nice, although we only had a short visit, and the head teacher agreed to take Simon. I had some reservations about the transfer because, apart from the bullying issues, Simon would be leaving behind some friends. I worried whether he would fit in at the new school and make new friends but Simon tells me he has made lots of friends now, although he rarely invites any of them home, like he used to at the old school.

The whole transfer process was very quick, it only took a couple of weeks, but Simon's records were not transferred at the same time as him and this meant his new teacher knew very little about him. I don't like to keep calling into school to make a fuss about anything, I know all the teachers are very busy, but I would like to know more about the school and what is on offer there, not just for the children, but adults too.

Simon's mum was obviously worried about her decision to remove him from his old school. Her main concern was that he would find it difficult to settle and make new friends; she voices her concerns by commenting on the lack of school friends visiting the home, unlike before. However, if Simon's comments are read in isolation without comparison to the perspectives of both his mum and teacher it would appear that he had made lots of new friends and fitted in well with established peer groups. The inconsistencies in Simon's perspective prompted me to observe the behaviour of the transferring children during their free time in school over a two-week period. This was done to assess whether they were actually being included in established peer groups and playing cooperatively as stated by the majority. Only one child in the group had originally reported difficulties in making new friends during the investigation, and because this was said in isolation, I chose not to include it in the narrative. My subsequent observations revealed that in reality the new children were not freely included in peer groups; all six children were observed to be alone during free time, talking to adults or involved in games instigated by the adult play leaders. The following entry from my reflective diary was representative of many.

I watched Simon today in the yard, all the boys were playing football, and he just shuffled around the perimeter. When Mrs Smith came out on duty, he made a beeline for her and started chatting. This worried me as I have noticed he stands alone on most days.

This inconsistency in view intrigued me and caused me to reflect upon the reasons for this and undertake wider reading on the subject. Peer acceptance in school is important for all children but can be vitally important for transferring children in order to maintain high levels of self-esteem and motivation towards work. Robson (2003) suggests peer rejection can occur simply because a child is perceived as being different in some way. Difference can be due to ethnicity, disability, physical characteristics or simply because the child is a newcomer to the class group. Coie (1990) describes the years of middle childhood (key stage 2) as being vitally important for peer relationships. At this age, there is a shift of reliance for friendships and social interaction, from parents and teachers to peers. Children rejected by peer groups tend to stay rejected and disturbingly it is rare for them to move fully out of this category into full acceptance. Rejected children are more likely than others to display conduct disorders, even as far as adulthood (Robson, 2003). One could speculate that Simon's denial that he had struggled to make friends at his new school could be because he was so unhappy at the old school and just glad to get away to make a new start. He did however admit he was bullied at his old school and Robson (2003: 3) makes links between victims of bullying, low self-esteem and peer rejection, resulting in long-term problems associated with forming relationships with others. This aspect of inclusion of new children in established peer groups is one aspect for further exploration to improve my work as a mentor.

Simon's mum also wanted to know more about the new school and what it had to offer but didn't like 'bothering' the teacher. From this comment, it would appear that opportunity to build good home/school liaison is being lost. This highlights a problem in communication between the school and home for new families, with the school failing to acknowledge the importance of background information on children provided by parents. The need for improvement in communication and liaison between the stakeholders, if both children and parents are to participate fully in the school community, could be addressed through the mentor scheme. My experience of transition work between primary and secondary school and being a common point of contact in this situation, in addition to my involvement in induction meetings for Reception parents, could easily be utilised to provide induction for transferring families. I have noticed that parents who have been involved with the mentor scheme are often happy to seek information and discuss issues with me because they perceive me to have more free time to deal with pastoral issues than teaching staff. Simon's teacher also has concerns about both children and parents transferring schools. This is Mrs Smith's story.

(Continued)

REPRESENTATIVE CONSTRUCTIONS

Simon's teacher, Mrs Smith

There is always a feeling of unease when new children enter a class that has been established. Last year I had three new children joining my class, the last one of these was Simon. The things that tend to go through your mind when new children join mid-term are: what effect will these children have on the class in terms of behaviour, attitude and achievement? Quite often, especially with older children, they move schools because of behaviour problems, and the major concern for you as a class teacher is, will these problems continue and what effect if any will they have on the existing children. Recently, Simon has had a major negative impact on my class in terms of both behaviour and achievement, leading to the situation where at least 65% of this class are now underachieving and have regressed in terms of value added progression. If he doesn't understand the work, he starts to distract others and is attention seeking. As a class teacher, I need to ensure that the introduction of new children is undertaken as smoothly as possible, not only for them but for existing children. Appointing a peer mentor often helps to smooth the way. I asked Andrew to look after Simon, but because I knew very little about Simon, I'm not sure if they have much in common.

New children often find new routines and adults intimidating. They will react negatively to this, which can lead to false first impressions of newcomers. Teachers need to work hard to overcome this and allow newcomers time to settle and find their feet. Sometimes it can take half a term or more for a class teacher to gain a true insight into a new child. If a teacher shows any negativity towards a new child, this can also affect the way they are regarded by their peers, so a cautious approach is necessary. I find it very difficult to find the time in my heavy workload to support a transferring child fully. New children can impact dramatically on existing peer relationships within the class. If a new child makes friends with certain members of a friendship group but not others, the impact can be devastating for the child or children involved. This once again leads to pastoral issues for the class teacher to deal with and at this point parents will often become involved because all they can see is their child's unhappiness. Simon is more concerned with being accepted than learning at the moment and I think he doesn't want to draw attention to himself by asking for help when it is needed. He often starts messing around with Billy, who is the class clown – always after attention and acting the fool when he is struggling with his work. I've had problems with Simon's mum too because she tells him to do his work in a different way than I have shown him, because that was how he learned at the other school; if what he says is true, she tells him not to listen to me and do his work the way he knows how to.

Pastoral information is rarely forthcoming from other schools. Whilst this should be sent automatically, often the receiving school has to chase up the required information and it rarely arrives in school in time for the receiving school to use the information to make transition smoother. In Simon's case, I had to wait four weeks before the information was received. I feel that particularly in terms of behaviour issues, other schools may be reluctant to divulge information in case it is perceived that they may have failed with a particular child. Simon's previous school, we have noticed due to the number of children transferring from there, appears to have a problem with bullying issues. Head teachers of receiving schools can also provide a barrier to gaining pastoral information to class teachers receiving new children. This has happened to me at least twice, when the head teachers involved felt that by divulging information on social and welfare background, I would make inappropriate assumptions about the child, which would then affect the way I dealt with them. This is unjustified. As a professional, I need to be aware of all issues surrounding any children in my charge in order that I can effectively support their needs.

Mrs Smith's story conveys the problems associated from an experienced teacher's perspective. She obviously has concerns from both a pastoral and an academic point of view, every time a new child is allocated to her class. Alongside Mrs Smith's responsibilities for the academic achievement of the children, she finds integration of new pupils an additional burden, which she has very little time to address. In addition to these problems, the major barrier highlighted by her story is a lack of communication between staff, children and parents. This appears to be a common pattern throughout all three stories. There are obvious ethical issues related to the transfer of sensitive information without parental permission. Mrs Smith thought it undermined her 'professional standing' by not being included in the transfer of certain information, and I would agree with her comment, to some extent. However, in my experience, some kinds of information, particularly community gossip, can be used unprofessionally by some members of staff to make inappropriate judgements of a pupil and their family. If these judgments are fair and correct, appropriate support can be given, but the opposite may happen if personal experience is allowed to affect professional support. Not allowing children a fresh start when joining a new group may result in them being singled out from their classmates. If children have been labelled with poor behaviour from their old school, it may become a self-fulfilling prophesy that they cannot change if hasty judgements are made by the new staff before incidents happen in the new setting because of transferred information. We saw in Simon's story that mum wasn't keen for him to share information with his new teachers about the bullying issues encountered before, perhaps because she thought he would be labelled a problem child. It is clearly important to consider whether all members of staff should have access to information about transferring children.

After comparing the stories produced, to gain insight into how the transfer of information could be improved ethically, I invited one of the new parents into school for an informal discussion on how their child was settling in. This was done during school hours at a convenient time for the parent. The room used was the staff room, but I ensured there would be no interruptions by placing a 'do not disturb' notice on the door. I also made sure there were refreshments available to make the atmosphere informal. At the outset I explained my role in school and how I supported children and their parents transferring to high school; also how I was involved in behaviour management and emotional and social support for children and families. The parent was very willing to attend the meeting and was very open about her child's feelings on the new setting. She explained it was sometimes difficult to talk to the teacher because she didn't like to take up too much time, but having someone like a mentor whose job it was, made her feel so much happier. The parent was not aware that pastoral information had not been transferred and thought the previous school would have thought it important to pass on information that her child had previously been the subject of bullying. She was happy to talk freely, without prompt, about problems encountered at the previous school and behaviour problems displayed by her own child both at home and in relation to school. To comply with good ethical practice I asked the parent's permission to share the information divulged.

References

Coie, J.D. (1990) 'Toward a theory of peer rejection', in S.R. Asher and J.D. Coie (eds), *Peer Rejection in Childhood*. Cambridge: Cambridge University Press.
Robson, K. (2003) 'Peer alienation: predictors in childhood and outcomes in adulthood', Working Papers of The Institute for Social and Economic Research, WP2003–21. Colchester: University of Essex. www.iser.essex.ac.uk/publications/search#papers.

(Isabel, unpublished report, 2006)

Summary

The main focus of Chapter 8 has been on the use of representative constructions, one of the core themes of the book, as part of the analytical process. The stories constructed by researchers represent a person or set of events and experiences and enable further depth of analysis through making often diverse and bitty pieces of data into a coherent, readable and understandable whole. Representative constructions cannot be judged by positivist frameworks but should instead be judged by qualities such as their trustworthiness, plausibility and applicability and the critical standpoint of the researcher. Readers must judge these qualities for themselves. Examples provided from my own and students' explorations into the use of narrative aim to demonstrate the potential uses and open up opportunities for debate. The examples speak for themselves in showing the potential for developing the researcher's analytical competence from a personal and professional standpoint. Such competence is a prerequisite for developing deeper critical analyses in comparing personal and professional constructs with those of other writers and researchers.

Suggested Reading

Badley, G. (2003) 'The truth of stories: Graham Badley reviews *Narratives and Fictions in Educational Research* by Peter Clough, with a rejoinder by the author', *Research in Post-Compulsory Education*, 8 (3): 441–9.

Bold, C. (2008b) 'Peer support groups: fostering a deeper approach to learning through critical reflection on practice', *Reflective Practice*, 9 (3): 257–67.

Clough, P. (2002) *Narratives and Fictions in Educational Research*. Buckingham: Open University Press.

Douglas, K. and Carless, D. (2009) 'Exploring taboo issues in professional sport through a fictional approach', *Reflective Practice*, 10 (3): 311–23.

Ely, M. (2007) 'In-forming re-presentations', in D.J. Clandinin (ed.), *Handbook of Narrative Inquiry: Mapping a Methodology*. London: Sage. pp. 567–98.

9

REPORTING NARRATIVE RESEARCH

CHAPTER OUTLINE

- Introduction
- What is the purpose of academic writing?
- Typical broad expectations in reporting

  o Guidance for structuring your dissertation

- How might narrative reports differ?
- Examples of report writing

  o Abstracts
  o Engaging beginnings
  o What, no research question?
  o The apologetic ethnographer
  o Sticking to tradition
  o Starting with narrative

- Some guiding principles
- Summary
- Suggested reading

Introduction

This final chapter aims to bring together elements from previous chapters that contribute to the finale of the narrative research project – its reports. Reporting any research is fraught with difficulties. Some difficulties arise because of the nature of the research, the ethical principles involved and the audience for whom the research is intended. Other difficulties arise because of externally imposed constraints such as word limits and section headings. Narrative research, in particular, has difficulties with some of these constraints because its nature requires sufficient word length in a written report to allow for sufficient use of data in the form necessary to demonstrate quality analysis. Many narrative research projects do not fit neatly into the structured headings of a typical dissertation, thesis, commissioned report or published paper, yet they will require the same features and characteristics presented more flexibly to suit the project.

Research findings, from narrative or otherwise, may find themselves reported in any of the following: postgraduate or undergraduate assessments, professional journals, research journals, conferences, books, in-service training events or the popular press. Reporting may be in oral, visual or written formats. It may use various technologies such as the internet to disseminate it widely. Thus the audience may range from one or two tutors who mark and second mark an assessment to a worldwide international audience of different cultures. In considering how to present narrative research, one must consider the audience and the purpose of the report in addition to its potential to be shared amongst a wider audience than originally intended. One piece of research may be reported in different ways to different people, albeit communicating the same message.

People in professional roles who study for masters' or doctorates will often find themselves having to produce different reports for different purposes. Typically they will research practice within their organisations, so the organisation may want a formal report to the board of governors, and a presentation to the staff. They will often have to prepare a formal thesis structured according to university guidelines, and in addition they may decide to publish their research in a journal which will have editorial guidelines. Each report will be different, meeting the needs of the different audiences and the requirements of different organisations. This chapter will not address all of the potential ways that the research may be reported, but will focus on two core activities: the dissertation or thesis, and the published academic paper.

The focus of many students is on completing their report in the style required by their tutor. They do not necessarily consider the writing process to be part of their academic development; it is often a means to an end. Sadly, academic writing for peer-reviewed journals can sometimes fall prey to the same attitude. Some academics write because they are expected to in order to keep their position at their institution and to gain promotion. For others, writing is a process of self-development; through writing they formulate their understanding of the phenomena around them. The next section focuses on discussing the purpose of academic writing.

What is the Purpose of Academic Writing?

'What is writing really about for scholarly practitioners?', ask Pete Mann and Davina Clarke (2007) as they explore the relationship between being able to think for oneself, sticking to our own ideas, while producing writing to be scrutinised by others. Mann and Clarke discuss the idea of researching practice through action learning with an emphasis on the purpose of the writing in research. They explore the relationship between *writing down* experiences and other data, *writing out* ideas to inform thinking about what they are writing down as data, and finally *writing up* the significance of their explorations and learning. They emphasise the importance of formative thinking (and perhaps what I call development of personal analysis competencies) and the issue of people who step in and prevent the personal development by deferring to the higher knowledge of others already published in the field. Their concern is how to achieve the right balance between being a researching professional wishing to find one's voice to demonstrate learning, and having to write up inquiries with much reference to expert opinion and in a context where emergent learning is not necessarily valued.

The use of narrative fits well with action learning approaches to developing practice and supports the development of critical thinking about practice, starting from the development of personal critique and followed by a critique of other research in the same field. Mann and Clarke (2007) appear to be critical of the expectations of many enablers (supervisors) in supporting a practitioner-researcher when writing about practice-based research. There is a sense that practitioners (of any kind) may be guided (driven?) towards a focus on other people's *knowledge* rather than creating and developing their own.

Writing as a process can be viewed as action research, according to Richard Winter and Graham Badley (2007). They present an interesting paper that raises the question of academic writing as something that enriches our practice rather than something that we produce to pass an assessment or to fulfil a professional academic role. Winter asserts that for academic writing to be an opportunity for growth it should be not just a critique of knowledge but a critique of the organisations in which knowledge is applied. Winter, like others, is placing importance on the application of the research or other academic ideas within organisational contexts. Narrative research writing often falls into the category of critique of action and application in specific social contexts, and therefore ought to have frameworks for writing and reporting that enable this critique of action to emerge rather than frameworks that constrain.

Typical Broad Expectations in Reporting

The typical headings for organising the writing of most dissertations and theses are: abstract, title, introduction, focus, literature review, methodology, analysis of findings, and conclusion. Such a rigid structure may not appear to allow a researcher to present their research in the best way to suit the narrative methods used, but it is possible to report narrative research within such a structure providing the writer can be flexible about the word count of each section. Within these sections the researcher should present the following information in the best way possible, so that any reader can understand the whole project.

The following is an example of the information I gave to MA students to support the structuring of their dissertations. Some will use reflective diaries, observations and interviews that provide narrative data. The guidance is tailored to suit the academic requirements of the institution and to ensure that students successfully address the learning outcomes of their dissertation module. Note that it includes broad word counts for each section as a guide, and students do not have to stick rigidly to the structure if they have good reason for presenting their dissertation in other ways. Some, for example, may include video data as part of their analysis.

Guidance for structuring your dissertation

Introduction (around 1000–2000 words)

The introduction should describe and explain the context of the research and the people involved without naming institutions or people. The context will include information about the setting in which the research will take place and some of the broader social context, such as socio-economic area. You should explain your role and your reasons for this research and how it will inform your practice. Explain the values, beliefs and assumptions behind the research and clarify what you are aiming to achieve. Indicate the nature of the participants, their roles in the setting and whether they will be collaborative partners in your research. In developing this section you might also refer to relevant documents, policies, popular press or theoretical ideas that have influenced your thoughts in formulating your project.

Research question or area of inquiry (around 500 words)

In this section you will focus on the phenomenon being researched. You should make very clear to the reader your area of inquiry and the specific question(s) you propose to answer, the problem you aim to resolve or the practice you aim to evaluate through systematic inquiry. One or two main research questions are sufficient.

Literature review (around 5000–6000 words)

The literature review is a critique of a relevant literature base in relation to the phenomenon. It should have strong links with the research question. In the literature review you may use any relevant source materials: news articles, policy documents, videos, TV programmes, academic texts about the subject, and published research papers. Be judicious in your choice of materials, especially from the internet. The balance of literature should be towards the academic and research materials in order to enable a level of critique suitable for master's. The literature review should be written in a critical discursive style, not merely describing what others say but critiquing it, considering whether it agrees with your experience and with what others say. This section should be completed before beginning the collection of data, although you will go back to it to review, modify and add to it.

Methodology (around 2000–3000 words)

The methodology section is most important and also relates back to the research question(s). Most such sections will be an action research methodology, exploring your own practice and performance with a view to changing it; or a practitioner research methodology, where you are exploring an issue within your setting or evaluating a programme of work, for example, but not necessarily focusing on your own practice. Reference to action research texts and/ or practitioner research texts is essential. Either methodology will draw on any type of research method suitable for the project. You must choose methods that are most suitable to answer the question or area of exploration. Each method must be justified by explaining why it is best and why it has been chosen in preference to others. To justify your choices, reference to relevant research methods texts is essential.

You should also include:

- Illustrations of interview questions, or questionnaires, or other documents used.
- A full discussion of the ethical issues with reference to relevant texts and ethical guidelines, such as the British Educational Research Association guidelines. Ethics is not just about access and permissions but about weighing up the potential benefits of the research against the potential harm for each participant and the organisation as a whole.
- Consideration of how the methods, or the way a method is used with different people, may triangulate to help you formulate a clearer understanding of the situation.
- A clear indication of timescale.

Sometimes a diagram of the research process can be very helpful in presenting all this to others in a succinct form. You may wish to consider including one.

Analysis (about 4000–6000 words)

At the start of the analysis section, you should explain the analytical process: what you have done with the data collected and how you will present them. The analysis brings together the findings from the data with the literature from the literature review. It is a way of critiquing the evidence you have in order to answer your research question (or evaluate practice, or explore a phenomenon of interest). The evidence you present will be chosen from the data you have collected and if necessary collated in some way. The choices you make about what to present in the analysis must be justified; for example, you might choose to include a small piece of your research diary to provide an example of a particular child's response to an event and your reflections upon it. There has to be a reason for it and a reason for not using other parts of your diary. Not all raw data will be included in the written analysis, especially diary entries, detailed observations and interview transcripts that you intend to use. However, you must discuss fully all the selected data with reference to the literature and your own experience. Some of you might find the use of narrative, in the form of representative constructions, a useful way to draw together a mass of information from different sources. Please ask for guidance about the analytical style adopted. Diagrams that help to show the relationship between elements of the evidence can also be useful in this section.

Conclusion (about 2000–3000 words)
You should provide a clearly justified conclusion including the following two sections:

1 *Evaluation of process.* With reference to relevant literature (from the methods section), review any issues arising from the methods used to collect information and your analytical process.
2 *Evaluation of outcomes.* With reference to relevant literature (from the literature review), consider what you have learned from the analysis of your evidence and outline your ideas for developing future practice/developments in your setting.

Finally, state your overall conclusion for the project.

Reference list
Note that you are asked not to provide a bibliography but to limit this section to an alphabetical list of those materials actually cited within your dissertation. Please use the Harvard style in a consistent manner. Guidance to Harvard is available in the booklet provided.

As stated before, this is one example of the typical requirements that students and tutors often have to adhere to because of university regulations, learning outcomes and external examiner feedback. The advantage of having such a structure is that it does ensure that all the relevant elements are included in the report. However, it does not necessarily lead to better quality of reporting since some people have difficulty in creating the links between the sections and fail to maintain the flow of the whole research process. Many students seem to have difficulty writing the analysis, usually because they are overwhelmed with data and their proposed analytical processes are not designed to make them into a succinct account and keep it to the required word count. If you are in the position of writing to guidelines and are unsure, you should ask the people who set them to clarify their requirements.

How Might Narrative Reports Differ?

The analysis of narrative, or analysis using representative constructions, will require more words than some other types of data to allow the incorporation of narrative data along with critical discussion. When constrained by word limits, some students resort to putting their narrative data in an appendix where it will probably fail to have the impact intended through its use. How the writer presents narrative data depends on the nature of the project, the actual data and the constraints of word length. In most dissertations or theses, the writer will have to make judicious choice of relevant extracts or vignettes of narratives to illustrate points in the analysis rather than presenting the whole narrative. Although I have discussed fitting in with the generally required structures of academia, I believe that research reporting can be and should be much more flexible and creative, opening up opportunities for different ways of thinking. Later in the chapter, I refer to various published papers that provide examples of different ways to present research, or that discuss different ways of conceptualising what we are doing when we write about research. I can only provide brief details, and the best way to explore academic writing of various kinds is to read research papers and theses, and to search for a style of writing that suits both your personal and your professional preferences.

Ely (2007) provides a set of tenets to follow when embracing narrative research writing. They are a very useful guide for the novice writer of narrative research and for those tutors who have little familiarity with narrative and seek to force scientific notions and structures onto students' assessed work. The traditional and often rigid structure for research journal articles also pervades the academic system, serving to reduce opportunity for publication in some journals. However, the resistance to change is slowly being eroded as more professional master's and doctoral programmes focus on qualitative inquiry methods including narrative, and journals have emerged that support and encourage diversity in academic writing. Academics in different disciplines are beginning to acknowledge each other's research strategies and are sharing their expertise in a cross-discipline pooling of experience and critique. The tenets supplied by Ely (2007), cited from an earlier publication by Ely et al. (1997), are discipline free:

1 There are many ways of coming to know something, and even then such knowing is partial.
2 There are numerous ways for us to report.
3 All our messages have agendas – personal, political, gendered, racial, ethnic.
4 Our language creates reality.
5 As researchers, we are deeply interrelated with what and who is being studied. Research is context and culture bound. So is writing.
6 Affect and cognition are inextricably united.
7 What we understand and report as social reality is multifaceted, sometimes clashing and often in flux.
8 We cannot say that narrative reflects 'the' reality. We can say that with the help of the reader, narrative creates a version of reality.

These tenets are very useful in considering the structure and development of reports of narrative research.

Ely's tenets clearly show a move away from positivist frameworks for judging the quality of research reports, encouraging diversity and acknowledging that we cannot separate affect and cognition. She is clearly engaging with some ethical issues – those of the agendas our writing contains because of our interrelationship with the situations we study. Most important she acknowledges the limits of our notion of reality and that narrative provides a version of that reality rather than trying to reflect it. This idea supports discussion earlier in the book that identifies issues with the concept of truth in research. Ely is therefore indicating that we should accept narrative in research for what it is, rather than trying to attribute characteristics to it that it does not have.

Examples of Report Writing

This section will describe, rather than discuss, some examples of writing different elements of reports in different ways, with reference to published papers and student reports. The examples aim to show how narrative in research writing can emerge in different places and for different reasons. I recommend that you seek out some of the published papers if you are interested in exploring these ideas.

Abstracts

Abstracts are often required at the beginning of dissertations and theses, and always for a published paper or an outline of a conference presentation. The abstract summarises what the paper is about so that readers of the paper may use it to decide whether the paper has any relevance to their own research. Unfortunately, not all abstracts make the content of the paper as explicit as we might like it to be, but the word limit usually constrains the writer. Most people write the abstract after completing their report to try and ensure that everything is represented. Figure 9.1 provides an example of typical guidance for writing an abstract for an MA level dissertation.

Figure 9.1 Guidance for writing an abstract

An abstract not exceeding 500 words should appear before the beginning of the dissertation. It should not extend beyond a single A4 side and, to facilitate this, single spaced typing is permitted for the abstract only. The author and title of the dissertation should be included in the form of a heading. The abstract shall provide a synopsis of the dissertation and shall state clearly the nature and scope of the research undertaken and of the contribution made to the knowledge of the subject treated. There should be a brief statement of the method of investigation, where appropriate, an outline of the major divisions or principal arguments of the work and a summary of any conclusions reached.

Organisers of conferences, editorial teams for journals and most higher education institutions provide such guidance. Not all abstracts will focus on a research project; some might be an abstract of a conceptual paper or an alternative way of writing about research. Rita Wilder Craig (2007) provides the abstract in Figure 9.2, which has a narrative style to it. This suits the style of the paper, which is about presenting the role of social workers through personal narrative. It also includes a citation to a literature source, another feature found in some abstracts. If you read Wilder Craig's paper, you will be able to judge whether the abstract represents the paper's content.

Figure 9.2 An example of a journal abstract

Social workers have always used narratives in the service of their clients. Many of us spend half our days listening to stories and the other half repeating them in one form or another, whether in assessments, in advocating for services or for a more accurate understanding of a client's circumstances. While we excel at this kind of storytelling, we have been held back from using the narrative genre in telling our own story. That story is one that describes the intricacies and variety of social work practice as well as the uniqueness that distinguishes us from other helping professions. For hospital social workers, who have experienced profound change in recent years, it is especially important that we find innovative and interesting ways to convey a richer and deeper understanding and appreciation of our role. The genre of personal narrative allows us to do this in a voice suitable for the task. When narratives are used in this way they can be seen as a tool of advocacy for both ourselves and our clients (Chambon, 2004).

Reference

Chambon, A. (2004) 'What can narrative approaches do for social work?', *News-magazine, the Journal of the Ontario Association of Social Workers*, 31(1): 1–6.

(Wilder Craig, 2007: 431)

Engaging beginnings

Consider the introduction of a research report, which usually sets the scene for the reader, establishing knowledge and understanding of the purpose and context of the research and the researcher's position in it. As Ely (2007) discusses with clear examples, narrative is an interesting way to begin, using poetry, stories, conversations and anecdotes. This writing strategy fits well with the idea of using writing to stimulate inquiry, discussed in Chapter 3. Any visual and written reflections in the identification of a research interest can become part of or even the whole introduction.

The example in Figure 9.3 is part of an introductory section to a research project report from Leyla, a third-year undergraduate who was a teaching assistant in a school that was merging with another. Leyla's introduction helps the reader gain a realistic perspective of a school that provides an oasis of learning in a deprived area. It captures the essence of the purpose in the school, that of stimulating and motivating children to know about and aspire to a different way of life. In presenting the introduction like this, rather than as a set of 'factual' sentences based on the school's latest Ofsted (Office for Standards in Education) report, she lays bare some of her emotional attachment to the situation which is bound up with her conceptual knowledge and understanding of her professional practice. Thus it provides the essential information about her setting in a form that is interesting to read and has the capacity to enter both the heart and the mind of the reader.

Figure 9.3 Leyla's introductory narrative

> It is a small primary school, which teaches approximately three hundred children. Several generations of the local community have been taught here. After this academic year, no more children will walk through its corridors, learn in its classrooms, or play on its playground, as it is due for demolition in the summer to make way for a new school, which will bring us together with another local primary school. It is now a small, single storey building, grey (apart from the bright bold lettering that names the school) with paint peeling from the walls. However, it is only when you remove an example of the children's work that this peeling paint is revealed. As you walk through the corridors, more work and colourful displays burst from the walls, three-dimensional clay dragons, *Charlotte's Web* or *George's Marvellous Medicine* are among the many.
>
> (Leyla, unpublished report, 2007)

Gill, another third-year undergraduate, used a small vignette from her diary to raise the questions she was interested in for her research. The vignette in Figure 9.4 follows the issues in her practice that she raised during a drawing and storytelling activity in class. She writes about the day when she has to provide preparation, planning and assessment (PPA) cover for teachers, which many teaching assistants began to do with little experience of managing whole classes.

It is good that Gill raises questions in her diary. Writing down these questions allows retrospective thought about them. The danger in the questions is that they suggest a potential for self-destruction, accentuating the negative comparison of the children's responses to her compared with the teacher. It would have been useful for her to problematise the issue further, considering some specific events of challenging behaviour, noting exactly when they happen and identifying positive ways to try to avoid them happening.

Gill blames herself for everything that she perceives to be going wrong in the Year 6 classroom, and the vignette provides the reader with evidence of her desperation, her fear of the 2.00 p.m. lesson and identification of the problem – her approach to managing behaviour in the Year 6 class.

Figure 9.4 Using the diary to raise questions

> It's Wednesday, PPA cover day. The time usually goes quite quickly until 2 p.m. and then it's time for the dreaded Year 6 class, the only class in the school I find difficult to work with. It's their behaviour; as soon as the teacher leaves the room the little angels change into little devils. Why? Why am I so different to their teacher? What am I doing wrong?
>
> (Gill, unpublished report, 2007)

The research project focused on the student's strategies for managing behaviour and ways for improving the learning situation.

The two examples show how even a small piece of narrative can engage the reader in understanding the context or the purpose of the research, early in the research report.

What, no research question?

Another consideration is whether every piece of research requires a research question. It is certainly a requirement of many dissertations and theses, often causing much angst in its formulation, but is it essential? Consider autoethnography, a piece of research about one's lived experience through personal narrative, an autobiographical approach that does not necessarily seek to answer a question but explores a critically reflective journey over time. Emilia Afonso and Peter Taylor (2009) present such a paper in which the stimulus for the inquiry was a thought-provoking question from a student, 'What is Mozambican chemistry?' The inquiry was an autoethnographic exploration into Afonso's professional practice as part of Mozambican culture. The paper provides historical and contemporary narratives woven into a meaningful paper with critical review of meanings and understandings. It includes two voices, Afonso's and Taylor's, one disrupting the other, creating an opportunity for clarification of research processes and understandings of what it means to use narrative in research. The paper is clearly a conceptual investigation into practice, a critically reflective look at history informing the current situation. It didn't need a research question because it developed a momentum of its own, seeking a sense of agency, an understanding of the self, rather than an answer to a question. In fact, it resulted in Afonso generating further questions about the student's intention behind the original question, and Afonso asserts that her appreciation of the underlying paradox in the question asked by the student was more sophisticated than previously.

The apologetic ethnographer?

Atkinson (1990) explains the different approaches to ethnographical accounts of research and notes that the ethnographer often positions him/herself as someone blundering through the situation in explaining the methodological approach and the need to change to suit the circumstances. He provides examples from different research accounts and some phrases indicating that the researchers tended to acknowledge their weak position – one stating that he had little confidence in the situation and another describing himself as functionally an infant. Since Atkinson presented these ideas there have been changes in the ways that ethnographers work. They now seem to be confident in their approach and less apologetic towards the dominant positivist culture that still pervades some academic publishing and research quality assessment procedures. Some ethnographers embrace the fictional approach, especially since the fictional approach allows them to raise and discuss controversial issues. An example provided by Kitrina Douglas and David Carless (2009) uses a fictional narrative created from data they collected to explore the taboo issue of rape and its impact on self-identity, which is often silenced because the issues are considered too dangerous to explore. Following the story, Douglas and Carless present a set of reflections about writing the story and thinking about the impact it had on them, plus sharing it with students and the emotions it stirred within them. Researchers such as Douglas and Carless are challenging the boundaries of acceptability and encouraging appreciative debate about different methodologies. Their approach certainly did not follow the conventional expectations of many academic journals, yet the use of fiction allowed them to raise real issues based on a real-life experience, while maintaining the confidentiality of the person involved. The fiction allowed them to discuss critically and it promoted sustained reflection in those who engaged in their research process.

Sticking to tradition

A slightly more traditional approach to writing up narrative research was adopted by Tansy Jessop and Anne Williams (2007) when writing about research into the experiences of black and minority students at a small university in England. They set the context, explain and justify the methodology, but then present their findings with reference to relevant literature in four sections related to the four themes they explored. In each section, they present short extracts of stories told by the students and use literature to help them explain and analyse the experiences. Thus they avoided a section that focused solely on the literature (traditionally called the literature review) on the topic before presenting their findings and analysis. Most interesting is an acknowledgement that there is no conclusive evidence to support massive discontent amongst black and minority students. Their narratives were contradictory. Instead, the research highlighted potential tensions and issues in relation to ensuring the curriculum reflects diversity and which racist discourses identified and contested. It is a good example of how much qualitative research does not claim to provide definitive truths but instead raises further areas of concern to explore and change in practice.

Starting with narrative

Some narrative research reports begin with a narrative of what happened, as in an action research report by Emrys Jenkins and others (2005). The authors are nurse practitioners and their lecturers who are engaged in learning on two action research modules as part of an undergraduate degree programme. They tell the story of engaging with the programme and all the contentious issues it raised, such as the pervading feeling that theory mattered more than practice. The story tells of a reflective journey, of developing new practical and academic skills in tandem, of the development of confidence and trust between the students and the lecturers. The second part of the report focuses on the changes that students perceived in themselves, and here their reflections and links between their thinking are illustrated with extracts of diary notes as evidence of enduring change in their thinking and in their practice. One key to the changes in their thinking was the act of writing. One purpose for writing things down was to assist in the understanding of issues – a good reason for attending to the way the final research report is written.

Some Guiding Principles

Action research, or practitioner research, appears quite often in the examples I am using, perhaps because action researchers are disposed towards alternative approaches to researching and writing about research. Many qualitative researchers write in a range of different styles, as evidenced in the journals that focus on qualitative inquiry. There has been much debate in recent years about the quality of action research writing in particular. Because research quality processes still veer towards more traditional ways of conceptualising research practice and writing up research reports, anything that strays from the formalised, theoretically driven, academic approach is viewed as less worthy of inclusion in some institutional portfolios. The debate will no doubt continue for years to come, but there are people who seek to find ways of validating what we write about in action research, especially when using narrative. For example, Hannu Heikkinen, Rauno Huttunen and Leena Syrjälä (2007) propose five principles for validation of action research as narrative. They are seeking ways to demonstrate how others may judge action research against those principles, each of which relates very strongly to the characteristics of narrative research. The five principles in brief are:

1   The principle of historical continuity: action research is part of a historical evolution and recognises the previous events leading to a current position.
2   The principle of reflexivity: the researcher is aware of how reality is being represented within the narrative texts produced.
3   The principle of dialectics: truth is constructed through interaction, the credibility of the research, how well others' voices are represented.
4   The principle of workability: the action research gives rise to change within the researchers and their processes or within the context and other participants.
5   The principle of evocativeness: the research demonstrates the ability to awake and provoke new thinking.

REPORTING NARRATIVE RESEARCH

These five principles echo many of the ideas presented in previous chapters with reference to narrative research. It is useful for novice researchers to structure their writing around these tenets because it will help them present an interesting, thought-provoking report that represents other people's voices and sets the research into a temporally related context.

Pat Sikes and Ken Gale (2006) emphasise the idea that all research processes result in a construction of the researcher's interpretation of data. To evaluate narrative reporting of research they suggest the following criteria:

- Substantive contribution: how does the narrative contribute to knowledge and understanding of social life?
- Aesthetic merit: how does the narrative invite interpretive responses?
- Reflexive and participatory ethics: does the narrative represent participants fairly and acknowledge the contextual conditions in which the data were gathered?
- Impact: what is the impact on the audience?
- Experience near: does the narrative appear real, and present a fair and reasonable account of the contexts it claims to represent?

These are useful too, since they include criteria that should be applied to any research evaluation – contribution, impact and experience near – while applying evaluative criteria that are more specific to practice-based or social research, namely reflexive and participatory ethics and aesthetic merit. If we apply these evaluative criteria to narrative research then surely they will demonstrate the strength of such research to generate deep thinking about social issues and the encouragement of a questioning attitude towards the *outcomes* of research. Such open encouragement to re-interpret and question is often missing from scientifically orientated research.

When planning the chapter I felt it necessary to acknowledge that students and other academic writers are often in the position of having to adhere to a set structure (I have had this experience too). Thus in sharing some relevant readings that move away from the expected structures I hope that I have encouraged people to think outside the box that they find themselves in, and to persuade their supervisors or students that alternative ways of organising and writing are just as valid in the academic world.

Etherington (2004) noted that reflexive texts are complex and multilayered, and therefore difficult to manage: the line between text and context is blurred. As indicated in the previous chapters, such texts might include a wide range of data, including interviews, field notes, conversations, photographs, drawings, dreams, poems and diaries. They may even include performance. If we are able and willing to know and relate to the data differently, we might open ourselves up to creative and transformative opportunities for personal growth and new learning. Novice narrative researchers can take up the challenge, as demonstrated by the undergraduate examples presented throughout.

Summary

In writing this chapter I gave some thought to the nature of the normative expectations in dissertations and theses but then broke away from the constraints to explore alternative ways to present narrative research. The examples described from recent academic journals demonstrate a range of approaches that have the rigour and quality expected in peer-reviewed papers but make the issues come alive and provoke thought in the readership.

Suggested Reading

Heikkinen, H.L., Huttenen, R. and Syrjälä, L. (2007) 'Action research as narrative: five principles for validation', *Educational Action Research*, 15 (1): 5–19.

Winter, R. and Badley, G. (2007) 'Action research and academic writing: a conversation', *Educational Action Research*, 15 (2): 253–70.

REFERENCES

Afonso, E.Z. and Taylor, P.C. (2009) 'Critical autoethnographic inquiry for culture-sensitive professional development', *Reflective Practice*, 10 (2): 273–83.

Ahmed, R. (2011) 'The challenges in teaching culturally and linguistically diverse learners', in C. Bold (ed.), *Supporting Learning and Teaching*, 2nd edn (in preparation). London: Routledge.

Andrews, M., Squire, C. and Tamboukou, M. (2008) 'What is narrative research?', in M. Andrews, C. Squire and M. Tamboukou (eds), *Doing Narrative Research*. London: Sage. pp. 1–21.

Askew, M., Brown, M., Rhodes, V., Wiliam, D. and Johnson, D. (1997) *Effective Teachers of Numeracy*. London: King's College London, for the Teacher Training Agency.

Atkinson, P. (1990) *The Ethnographic Imagination: Textual Constructions of Reality*. London: Routledge.

Atkinson, P. and Silverman, D. (1997) 'Kundera's *Immortality*: The interview society and the invention of the self', *Qualitative Inquiry*, 3: 304–25.

Atkinson, P. and Delamont, S. (2006) 'Editors' introduction: narratives, lives, performances', in P. Atkinson and S. Delamont (eds), *Narrative Methods*, vol. 1. London: Sage. pp. xix–lii.

Bach, H. (2007) 'Composing a visual narrative inquiry', in D. Clandinin (ed.), *Handbook of Narrative Inquiry: Mapping a Methodology*. London: Sage. pp. 280–307.

Badley, G. (2003) 'The truth of stories: Graham Badley reviews *Narratives and Fiction in Educational Research* by Peter Clough, with a rejoinder by the author', *Research in Post-Compulsory Education*, 8 (3): 441–9.

Baxter Magolda, M.B. (2000) *Creating Contexts for Learning and Self-Authorship: Constructive Developmental Pedagogy*. Nashville, TN: Vanderbilt University Press.

Beach, D. (2005) 'The problem of how learning should be socially organized: relations between reflection and transformative action', *Reflective Practice*, 6 (4): 473–89.

BERA (2004) *Revised Ethical Guidelines for Educational Research*. Macclesfield: British Educational Research Association.

Birch, M. and Miller, T. (2002) 'Encouraging participation: ethics and responsibilities', in M. Mauthner, M. Birch, J. Jessop and T. Miller (eds), *Ethics in Qualitative Research*. London: Sage. pp. 91–106.

Bleakley, A. (2004) 'Education research in the postmodern'. www.edu.plymouth.ac.uk/RESINED/postmodernism/pmhome.htm, accessed 28 August 2009.

Bochner, A.P. (2001) 'Narrative's virtues', *Qualitative Inquiry*, 7 (2): 131–57.

Bold, C. (2001) 'Making sense of mathematical language in a primary classroom'. DEd thesis, Open University.

Bold, C. (2005) 'Reflective diaries as professional development tools', conference presentation, British Educational Research Association Practitioner Group Study Day, Liverpool.

Bold, C. (2006) 'One assessment – three experiences', *Practitioner Research Journal*, no. 2: 19–25.

Bold, C. (2008a) 'Cross-campus collaboration to improve critical reflection through asynchronous on-line discussion', *The Journal of the Further Education Alliance*, 1 (2): 123–46.

Bold, C. (2008b) 'Peer support groups: fostering a deeper approach to learning through critical reflection on practice', *Reflective Practice*, 9 (3): 257–67.

Bold, C. (2008c) 'Reflective drawing: identifying aspects for professional development', conference presentation, European Teacher Education Network, Reflective Practice Thematic Interest Group, Liverpool.

Bold, C. and Chambers, P. (2009) 'Reflecting meaningfully, reflecting differently', *Reflective Practice*, 10 (1): 13–26.

Bolton, G. (2001) *Reflective Practice – Writing and Professional Development*, London: Paul Chapman Publishing.

Bolton, G. (2006) 'Narrative writing: reflective enquiry into professional practice', *Educational Action Research*, 14 (2): 203–18.

British Psychological Society (2009) *Code of Ethics and Conduct*. Ethics Committee of The British Psychological Society. www.bps.org.uk/document-download-area/document-download$.cfm?restart=true&file_uuid=E6917759-9799-434A-F313-9C35698E1864, accessed 8 February 2010.

Campbell, A. and Groundwater-Smith, S. (eds) (2007) *An Ethical Approach to Practitioner Research: Dealing with Issues and Dilemmas in Action Research*. London: Routledge.

Chambers, P. (2003) 'Narrative and reflective practice: recording and understanding experience', *Educational Action Research*, 11 (3): 403–14.

Clandinin, D. and Connelly, M. (2000) *Narrative Inquiry: Experience and Story in Qualitative Research*. San Francisco: Jossey-Bass.

Clough, P. (2002) *Narratives and Fictions in Educational Research*. Buckingham: Open University Press.

Cortazzi, M. (1993) *Narrative Analysis*. London: Falmer.

Craig, C.J. (2009) 'Learning about reflection through exploring narrative inquiry', *Reflective Practice*, 10 (1): 105–16.

Crang, M. and Cook, I. (2007) *Doing Ethnographies*. London: Sage.

Czarniawaska, B. (2004) *Narratives in Social Science Research*. London: Sage.

Deaver, S.P. and McAuliffe, G. (2009) 'Reflective visual journaling during art therapy and counselling internships: a qualitative study', *Reflective Practice*, 10 (5): 615–32.

Digital Youth Project (2008) *Digital Youth Research: Kids Informal Learning with Digital Media*. http://digitalyouth.ischool.berkeley.edu/, accessed 22 February 2010.

Dougherty, J. (2006) 'From anecdote to analysis: oral interviews and new scholarship in educational history' (1999), in P. Atkinson and S. Delamont (eds), *Narrative Methods*, vol. 1. London: Sage. pp. 197–210.

Douglas, K. and Carless, D. (2009) 'Exploring taboo issues in professional sport through a fictional approach', *Reflective Practice*, 10 (3): 311–23.

Dunaway, D.K. (2006) 'Method and theory in the oral biography', in P. Atkinson and S. Delamont (eds), *Narrative Methods*, vol. 1. London: Sage. pp. 235–46.

Egg, P., Schratz-Hadwich, B., Trübswasser, G. and Walker, R. (2004) 'Seeing beyond violence: children as researchers', SOS Children's Villages. www.sos-childrensvillages.org/Publications/Reports-studies/Pages/default.aspx, accessed 12 May 2007.

Elliot, J. (2005) *Using Narrative in Social Research: Qualitative and Quantitative Approaches*. London: Sage.

Ely, M. (2007) 'In-forming re-presentations', in D.J. Clandinin (ed.), *Handbook of Narrative Inquiry: Mapping a Methodology*. London: Sage. pp. 567–98.

Ely, M., Vinz, R., Downing, M. and Anzul, M. (1997) *On Writing Qualitative Research: Living by Words*. London: Falmer.

ESRC (2010) *Framework for Research Ethics 2010*. Economic and Social Research Council. www.esrcsocietytoday.ac.uk/ESRCINFOCENTRE/OPPORTUNITIES/research_ethics_framework/, accessed 8 February 2010.

Etherington, K. (2004) *Becoming a Reflexive Researcher: Using Ourselves in Research*. London: Jessica Kingsley.

Federal Writers' Project (1930s) *Voices from the Thirties: Life Histories from the Federal Writers' Project*. http://memory.loc.gov/ammem/wpaintro/garavel.html.

Finlay, L. and Gough, B (eds) (2003) *Reflexivity: a Practical Guide for Researchers in Health and Social Sciences*. London: Blackwell.

Fivush, R. (2008) 'Remembering and reminiscing: how individual lives are constructed in family narratives', *Memory Studies*, 1 (1): 49–58.

Freeman, M. (2007) 'Autobiographical understanding and narrative inquiry', in D.J. Clandinin (ed.), *Handbook of Narrative Inquiry: Mapping a Methodology*. London: Sage. pp. 120–45.

Gephart, R. (1999) 'Paradigms and research methods', *Research Methods Forum*, 4. http://division.aomonline.org/rm/1999_RMD_Forum_Paradigms_and_Research_Methods.htm, accessed 20 July 2009.

Gergen, K. and Gergen, M. (1991) 'Toward reflexive methodologies', in F. Steier (ed.), *Reflexivity and Research*. London: Sage Publications. pp. 76–95.

Ghaye, A. and Ghaye, K. (1998) *Teaching and Learning through Critical Reflective Practice*. London: Fulton.

Gready, P. (2008) 'The public life of narratives: ethics, politics, methods', in M. Andrews, C. Squire and M. Tamboukou (eds), *Doing Narrative Research*. London: Sage. pp. 137–50.

Gubrium, J.F. and Holstein, J.A. (2009) *Analyzing Narrative Reality*. London: Sage.

Hamdan, A.K. (2009) 'Narrative inquiry as a decolonising methodology', *InterActions: UCLA Journal of Education and Information Studies*, 5 (2): Article 5. http://repositories.cdlib.org/gseis/interactions/vol5/iss2/art5

Hamilton, H.E. (2008) 'Narrative as snapshot: glimpses into the past in Alzheimer discourse', *Narrative Inquiry*, 18 (1): 53–82.

Heikkinen, H.L., Huttenen, R. and Syrjälä, L. (2007) 'Action research as narrative: five principles for validation', *Educational Action Research*, 15 (1): 5–19.

Hine, C. (2008) 'The internet and research methods', in N. Gilbert (ed.), *Researching Social Life*, 3rd edn. London: Sage. pp. 304–20.

Hollingsworth, S. and Dybdahl, M. (2007) 'Talking to learn: the critical role of conversation in narrative inquiry', in D.J. Clandinin (ed.), *Handbook of Narrative Inquiry: Mapping a Methodology*. London: Sage. pp. 146–76.

Holt, J. (1964) *How Children Fail*. New York: Pitman.

Hughes, G. (2009) 'Talking to oneself: using autobiographical internal dialogue to critique everyday and professional practice', *Reflective Practice*, (10) 4: 451–63.

Hyden, M. (2008) 'Narrating sensitive topics', in M. Andrews, C. Squire and M. Tamboukou (eds), *Doing Narrative Research*. London: Sage. pp. 121–36.

Jenkins, E., Jones, J., Keen, D., Kinsella, F., Owen, T., Pritchard, D. and Rees, S. (2005) 'Our story about making a difference in nursing practice through action research', *Educational Action Research*, 13 (2): 259–73.

Jessop, T. and Williams, A. (2007) 'Minority ethnic student narratives about racism, identity and difference: implications for teaching and learning', conference presentation, Pedagogical Research in Maximising Education (PRIME), Proceedings of the 1st Pedagogical Research in Higher Education (PHRE) Conference, vol. 2, no. 2, pp. 39–48.

Jones, C. (2009) 'How do I improve my practice as an inclusion officer working in a children's service?' MA dissertation, Bath Spa University. www.actionresearch.net/living/living.shtml

Josselson, R. (2007) 'The ethical attitude in narrative research: principles and practicalities', in D.J. Clandinin (ed.), *Handbook of Narrative Inquiry: Mapping a Methodology*. London: Sage. pp. 537–66.

Labonte, R., Feather, J. and Hills, M. (1999) 'A story dialogue method for health promotion knowledge development' *Health Education Research*, 14(1): 39–50.

Labov, W. and Waletzky, J. (1997) 'Narrative analysis: oral versions of personal experience', in P. Atkinson and S. Delamont (eds) (2006), *Narrative Methods*, vol. 1. London: Sage. pp. 1–40.

Leitch, R. (2008) 'Creatively researching children's narratives through images and drawings', in P. Thomson (ed.), *Doing Visual Research with Children and Young People*. Oxon: Routledge. pp. 37–58.

Lewins, A. (2008) 'Computer assisted qualitative data analysis (CAQDAS)', in N. Gilbert (ed.), *Researching Social Life*, 3rd edn. London: Sage. pp. 394–419.

Mann, P. and Clarke, D.M. (2007) 'Writing it down – writing it out – writing it up: researching our practice through action learning', *Action Learning: Research and Practice*, 4 (2): 153–71.

Mason, J. (1994) 'Researching from the inside in mathematical education: locating an I-you relationship'. Centre for Mathematics Education. Milton Keynes: Open University.

McCormack, Coralie (2004) 'Storying stories: a narrative approach to in-depth interview conversations', *International Journal of Social Research Methodology*, 7 (3): 219–36.

McIntosh, P. (2008) 'Reflective reproduction: a figurative approach to reflecting in, on and about action', *Educational Action Research*, 16 (1): 125–43.

Mead, M. (1928) *Coming of Age in Samoa*. New York: Morrow.

Mello, D.M. de (2007) 'The language of arts in a narrative inquiry landscape', in D.J. Clandinin (ed.), *Handbook of Narrative Inquiry: Mapping a Methodology*. London: Sage. pp. 203–23.

Mercer, N. (1996) 'The quality of talk in children's collaborative activity in the classroom', *Learning and Instruction*, 6 (4): 359–77.

Moss, J., Deppler, J., Astley, J. and Pattison, K. (2007) 'Student researchers in the middle: using visual images to make sense of inclusive education', *Journal of Research in Special Educational Needs*, 7 (1): 46–54.

Patterson, W. (2008) 'Narratives of events: Labovian narrative analysis and its limitations', in M. Andrews, C. Squire and M. Tamboukou (eds), *Doing Narrative Research*. London: Sage. pp. 22–40.

Polkinghorne, D.E. (1988) *Narrative Knowing and the Human Sciences*. Albany, NY: State University of New York Press.

Pottie, K., Haydt, S., Farrell, B., Dolovich, L., Sellors, C. and Hogg, W. (2008) 'Narrative report to monitor and evaluate the integration of pharmacists into family practice settings', *Annals of Family Medicine*, 6 (2): 161–5. www.annfammed.org.

Puchner, L.D. and Smith, L.M. (2008) 'The ethics of researching those who are close to you: the case of the abandoned ADD project', *Educational Action Research*, 16 (3): 421–8.

Reissman, C.K. (1993) *Narrative Analysis*. London: Sage.

Reissman, C.K. (2008) *Narrative Methods for the Human Sciences*. London: Sage.

Riley, T. and Hawe, P. (2005) 'Researching practice: the methodological case for narrative inquiry', *Health Education Research*, 20 (2): 226–36.

Schön, D. (1984) *Educating the Reflective Practitioner*. San Francisco: Jossey-Bass.

Sikes, P. and Gale, K. (2006) 'Narrative approaches to educational research'. www.edu.plymouth.ac.uk/RESINED/narrative/narrativehome.htm, accessed 30 May 2009.

181

Silverman, D. (2006) *Interpreting Qualitative Data*, 3rd edn. London: Sage.

Simkhada, P. (2008) 'Sex trafficking: life histories and survival strategies among trafficked girls in Nepal', *Children and Society*, 22: 235–48.

Smeyers, P. and Verhesschen, P. (2001) 'Narrative analysis as philosophical research: bridging the gap between the empirical and the conceptual', *Qualitative Studies in Education*, 14 (1): 71–84.

Smith, A. (2008) 'Research in Oaxaca City: engaging with "real world messiness"'. Undergraduate research project lecture, Liverpool Hope University.

Smythe, W.E. and Murray, M.J. (2000) 'Owning the story: ethical considerations in narrative research', *Ethics & Behavior*, 10 (4): 311–36. In M. Nind, J. Rix, K. Sheehy and K. Simmons (eds) (2005), *Ethics and Research in Inclusive Education: Values into Practice*. London: RoutledgeFalmer. pp. 176–91.

Springett, J. (2008) 'Collaboration in action research'. Northern group – Collaborative Action Research Network (CARN) study day workshop. Ambleside.

Squire, C. (2008) 'Experience-centred and culturally-oriented approaches to narrative', in M. Andrews, C. Squire and M. Tamboukou (eds), *Doing Narrative Research*. London: Sage. pp. 41–63.

Stevenson, J. and Willott, J. (2008) 'Balancing ethical principles: the implications for educational research when the principle of non-maleficence outweighs that of beneficence', conference presentation, BERA 2008, Heriot-Watt University.

Strong-Wilson, T. (2006) 'Bringing memory forward: a method for engaging teachers in reflective practice on narrative and memory', *Reflective Practice*, 7 (1): 101–13.

Thomson, P. and Hall, C. (2008) 'Dialogues with artists: analysing children's self-portraits', in P. Thomson (ed.), *Doing Visual Research with Children and Young People*. London: Routledge. pp. 146–63.

Valentine, C. (2008) *Bereavement Narratives: Continuing Bonds in the 21st Century*. London: Routledge.

Van der Waal, K. (2009) 'Getting going: organizing ethnographic fieldwork', in S. Ybema, D. Yumon, H. Wels and F.H. Kamsteeg (eds), *Organizational Ethnography*. London: Sage. pp. 23–39.

Warren, S.E. (2001) 'The mentor's role: an action research investigation into professional development of primary teacher mentors'. PhD thesis, Leeds Metropolitan University.

Washington, B.T. (1901) *Up from Slavery: an Autobiography* (2009 e-book). Online at www.bartleby.com/1004/

Webster, L. and Mertova, P. (2007) *Using Narrative Inquiry as a Research Method: an Introduction to Critical Event Narrative Analysis on Learning and Teaching*. London: Routledge.

Wengraf, T. (2001) *Qualitative Research Interviewing: Biographic Narrative and Semi-Structured Methods*. Thousand Oaks, CA: Sage.

White, J. (2006) 'Reflective practice: the use of other vantage points', *Local Research, Global Community: Action Research in a New Century, Collaborative Action Research Network (CARN) Bulletin*, 11A: 24–7.

White, ML (2006) 'Filming ourselves: an ethnographic study investigating the processes and pleasures of digital video production in informal education', conference presentation, British Educational Research Association, Warwick.

Whitehead, J. and McNiff, J. (2006) *Action Research, Living Theory*. London: Sage.

Wilder Craig, R. (2007) 'A day in the life of a hospital social worker – presenting our role through the personal narrative', *Qualitative Social Work*, 6: 431–46.

Winter, R. (2002) 'Truth or fiction: problems of validity and authenticity in narratives of action research', *Educational Action Research*, 10 (1): 143–54.

Winter, R. and Badley, G. (2007) 'Action research and academic writing: a conversation', *Educational Action Research*, 15 (2): 253–70.

Winter, R., Buck, A. and Sobiechowska, P. (1999) *Professional Experience and the Investigative Imagination: the Art of Reflective Writing*. London: Routledge.

Wolfson, N. (1976) 'Speech events and natural speech: some implications for sociolinguistic methodology', *Language in Society*, 5: 189–209.

Wragg, T. (1999) *An Introduction to Classroom Observation*, 2nd edn. London: Routledge.

Yow, V. (2006) '"Do I like them too much?": effects of the oral history interview on the interviewer and vice-versa', in P. Atkinson and S. Delamont (eds), *Narrative Methods*, vol. 1. London: Sage. pp. 211–34.

REFERENCES

INDEX

USING NARRATIVE IN RESEARCH